AEPS®

Assessment, Evaluation,
and Programming System
for Infants and Children

SECOND EDITION

VOLUME 1 Administration Guide

Other volumes in the *AEPS* Series
edited by Diane Bricker, Ph.D.

**AEPS Test for
Birth to Three Years and
Three to Six Years**
by Diane Bricker, Ph.D., Betty Capt, Ph.D., OTR,
and Kristie Pretti-Frontczak, Ph.D.,
with JoAnn (JJ) Johnson, Ph.D., Kristine Slentz, Ph.D.,
Elizabeth Straka, Ph.D., and Misti Waddell, M.S.

**AEPS Curriculum for
Birth to Three Years**
by Diane Bricker, Ph.D. and Misti Waddell, M.S.,
with Betty Capt, Ph.D., OTR, JoAnn (JJ) Johnson, Ph.D.,
Kristie Pretti-Frontczak, Ph.D., Kristine Slentz, Ph.D.,
and Elizabeth Straka, Ph.D.

**AEPS Curriculum for
Three to Six Years**
by Diane Bricker, Ph.D. and Misti Waddell, M.S.,
with Betty Capt, Ph.D., OTR, JoAnn (JJ) Johnson, Ph.D.,
Kristie Pretti-Frontczak, Ph.D., Kristine Slentz, Ph.D.,
and Elizabeth Straka, Ph.D.

AEPS®
Assessment, Evaluation,
and Programming System
for Infants and Children
SECOND EDITION

VOLUME 1 Administration Guide

by

Diane Bricker, Ph.D.
Center on Human Development
University of Oregon, Eugene

Kristie Pretti-Frontczak, Ph.D.
Kent State University
Kent, Ohio

JoAnn (JJ) Johnson, Ph.D.
Research and
Education Planning Center
Nevada University
Center for Excellence
University of Nevada–Reno

Elizabeth Straka, Ph.D.
New England Early Intervention
Counsulting in Developmental
Disabilities
Wells, Maine

with

Betty Capt, Ph.D., OTR, Kristine Slentz, Ph.D., and Misti Waddell, M.S.

·P A U L·H·
BROOKES
PUBLISHING CO®

Baltimore • London • Sydney

Paul H. Brookes Publishing Co.
Post Office Box 10624
Baltimore, Maryland 21285-0624

www.brookespublishing.com

"Paul H. Brookes Publishing Co." is a registered trademark of
Paul H. Brookes Publishing Co., Inc.
"AEPS" is a trademark of Paul H. Brookes Publishing Co., Inc.

Typeset by Barton Matheson Willse & Worthington, Baltimore, Maryland.
Manufactured in the United States of America by
The Maple Press Company, York, Pennsylvania.

The following AEPS forms, found in Appendixes C, D, and E, can be purchased separately in packs:
Child Observation Data Recording Form I: Birth to Three Years, and II: Three to Six Years
Family Report I: Birth to Three Years, and II: Three to Six Years
Child Progress Record I: Birth to Three Years, and II: Three to Six Years

A CD-ROM of printable masters of the AEPS forms is also available, and also includes a Child
Observation Data Recording Form with Criteria for Birth to Three Years and Three to Six Years not
found in any of the volumes. To order, contact Paul H. Brookes Publishing Co.

Please see page ii for a listing of the other volumes in the AEPS series. All AEPS materials are available from Paul H. Brookes Publishing Co., Post Office Box 10624, Baltimore, Maryland 21285-0624
(800-638-3775 or 410-337-9580). Find out more about AEPS on www.brookespublishing.com/aeps.

Library of Congress Cataloging-in-Publication Data

Assessment, evaluation, and programming system for infants and children
    edited by Diane Bricker . . . (et al.)—2nd ed.
      p.   cm.
    Includes bibliographical references and index.
      ISBN 1-55766-562-1 (v. 1) — ISBN 1-55766-563-X (v. 2) — ISBN 1-55766-564-8 (v. 3) —
ISBN 1-55766-565-6 (v. 4)
      1. Assessment, Evaluation, and Programming System.   2. Child development—Testing.
    3. Child development deviations—Diagnosis.
      RJ51.D48 A87 2002
      618.92'0075—dc21

                                                          2002071124

British Library Cataloguing in Publication data are available from the British Library.

CONTENTS

ABOUT THE AUTHORS

Diane Bricker, Ph.D., Professor, College of Education, and Director, Early Intervention Program, University of Oregon, 5253 University of Oregon, Eugene, Oregon 97403

Diane Bricker is Professor and Associate Dean for Academic Programs, College of Education, at the University of Oregon and a highly respected, well-known authority in the field of early intervention. She has directed a number of national demonstration projects and research efforts focused on examining the efficacy of early intervention; the development of a linked assessment, intervention, and evaluation system; and the study of a comprehensive, parent-focused screening tool. Dr. Bricker directs the Early Intervention Program, Center on Human Development, at the University of Oregon.

Kristie Pretti-Frontczak, Ph.D., Assistant Professor, Department of Educational Foundations and Special Services, Kent State University, 405 White Hall, Kent, Ohio 44242

Kristie Pretti-Frontczak is Assistant Professor in the Department of Educational Foundations and Special Services at Kent State University. She received her doctorate in early intervention from the University of Oregon and has extensive experience in preparing preservice and in-service personnel to use an activity-based approach to working with young children and their families. Dr. Pretti-Frontczak also directs the Early Childhood Intervention Specialist Program at Kent State University where she is responsible for preparing preservice teachers to work with children from birth to age 8. She frequently provides training and technical assistance to programs across the United States of America interested in the *Assessment, Evaluation, and Programming System for Infants and Children* (AEPS) and activity-based intervention (ABI). Her line of research also centers on the treatment validity of the AEPS and efficacy of ABI.

JoAnn (JJ) Johnson, Ph.D., Director, Research and Educational Planning Center and Nevada University Center for Excellence in Developmental Disabilities, University of Nevada–Reno, Reno, Nevada 89557

JoAnn (JJ) Johnson is Director of the Research and Educational Planning Center and Nevada University Center for Excellence in Developmental Disabilities. She also has an adjunct faculty appointment in Curriculum and Instruction and teaches courses in early intervention and program evaluation. Her professional experience includes hospital-, home-, and center-based early intervention and developmental services; developmental assessment and evaluation; supervision and program coordination; and university and outreach training and instruction. Since 1998, Dr. Johnson has provided workshops and training throughout the United States of America on the use of the AEPS for families and professionals working in applied settings.

Elizabeth Straka, Ph.D., CCC-SLP, Consultant, New England Early Intervention Consulting, 58 Turtle Cove Lane, Wells, Maine 04090

Elizabeth Straka provides training and technical assistance to agencies that provide services to young children with disabilities and their families. She provides training seminars nationally in regard to recommended practice in assessment and intervention with young children and their families, with an emphasis on team collaboration. Dr. Straka continues to practice as a therapist, focusing on the assessment and treatment of developmental disorders in young children.

Betty Capt, Ph.D., OTR, Research Associate, Early Intervention Program, University of Oregon, 5253 University of Oregon, Eugene, Oregon 97403

Kristine Slentz, Ph.D., Professor and Chair, Special Education Department, Western Washington University, Miller Hall 318b, Mail Stop 9090, Bellingham, Washington 98226

Misti Waddell, M.S., Senior Research Assistant/Project Coordinator, Early Intervention Program, University of Oregon, 5253 University of Oregon, Eugene, Oregon 97403

ACKNOWLEDGMENTS

The *Assessment, Evaluation, and Programming System for Infants and Children* (AEPS) is the culmination of years of work by an array of thinkers, developers, users, and evaluators. One strength of this curriculum-based measure has been the multiple theories, perspectives, frameworks, and needs that have shaped its continuing evolution since its inception in 1974. Trying to organize this multiplicity of perspectives into a conceptually cohesive approach and manageable test and curriculum has been a significant challenge that has admittedly resulted in uneven success. From the beginning, the actualization of the ideals that underlie the AEPS (i.e., the development of a reliable and valid measure that yields results directly applicable to the development of functional and appropriate goals and intervention content and that can monitor child progress) has outstripped our collective abilities to reach these ideals. However, a comparison between where we began in 1974 and where we are today with this second edition of the AEPS offers solid proof of important progress toward reaching those ideals. The thousands of hours that have been spent in the refinements of the AEPS Test and associated curricular materials have produced important modifications, expansions, and changes in the second edition of the AEPS. The "perfect" test and teaching materials still beckon far beyond our collective reach; however, we believe that the second edition of the AEPS moves us closer to actualizing those original ideals. We believe that using the second edition of the AEPS will yield accurate, valid, and reliable test outcomes; will produce appropriate, timely, functional, generalizable and measurable goals; will support effective intervention efforts; and will enable the efficient monitoring of child progress.

The various changes incorporated into the second edition of the AEPS are the result of a collective effort of the seven authors who brought their own experience and knowledge to the discussions, as well as feedback they received from hundreds of other professionals and caregivers who have used the first edition of the AEPS. Users' suggestions and noted deficiencies served as powerful instigators of the changes made in the second edition, and we are grateful to the many individuals who have provided their perspectives, feedback, and thoughtful ideas about improving the AEPS. We are particularly indebted to our colleagues Jane Squires, David Allen, Jantina Clifford, Alise Carter, Naomi Rahn, and Natalya McComas for providing insightful observations, helping with material development, and generally keeping us centered on the task.

The size, complexity, and interrelated nature of the AEPS Test and curricular materials have required iterative reviews, readings, and editing. Dave Allen, James Jacobson, Kate Ray, Renata Smith, and Erika Hinds helped with these tasks. This multilevel and nested project has been like assembling a jigsaw puzzle. Karen Lawrence has been extraordinary in checking the content of each piece and getting the pieces assembled and sequenced in the right order. Her attention to detail has been enormously helpful. We are grateful to her for her ongoing assistance in completing this truly challenging work. In addition, the staff of Paul H. Brookes Publishing Co. has been of great assistance by their commitment to this large and complex project, their openness to change, their responsiveness to requests, and their positive and supportive feedback. The AEPS began as a collective effort, continues as a collective effort, and likely will continue to evolve as a collective effort.

AEPS®

Assessment, Evaluation, and Programming System for Infants and Children

SECOND EDITION

VOLUME 1 — Administration Guide

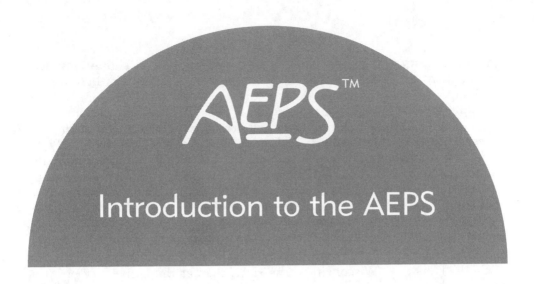

Introduction to the AEPS

The importance of early experience to young children's development has long been recognized and has served as the foundation for early intervention programs designed for young children who have or are at risk for disabilities. Beginning with unclear expectations and a narrow focus, early intervention programs have evolved into comprehensive approaches that produce positive changes in the lives of participating children and their families. In large measure, the increasingly positive outcomes engendered by early intervention programs have occurred because of the growing sophistication of personnel, curricular materials, and assessment/evaluation tools. The assessment, goal development, intervention, and evaluation system described in this set of volumes is an example of this growing sophistication, which will, in turn, enhance future intervention efforts with young children in need of services.

This introduction sets the stage for the second edition of the *Assessment, Evaluation, and Programming System for Infants and Children (AEPS)*™ four-volume series and provides the reader with a historical context. Specifically, the material in this introduction addresses three areas: 1) history of the AEPS's development, 2) description of the first edition of the AEPS, and 3) description of the second edition of the AEPS.

HISTORY OF THE AEPS'S DEVELOPMENT

At the October, 1974, organizational meeting of the American Association for the Education of the Severely and Profoundly Handicapped (now called TASH), a group of frustrated people convened. The meeting was not planned but occurred spontaneously in a dining room over breakfast. The topic of conversation was the need for a functional and accurate measurement tool for young children with severe disabilities. The conversation was a magnet that drew people from adjoining tables as well as passers-by. It seemed that everyone within earshot who worked with young children was feeling a strong and urgent need for some alternative to using standardized norm-referenced tests or

1

homemade tests with questionable validity and reliability. The interest was intense then and has remained so for many of us into the new millennium.

From 1974 to 1976, conversations continued periodically among a group of people who were highly motivated to address this pressing measurement need. In the spring of 1976, professionals from six universities met in New Orleans to discuss the possibility of developing a tool that was specifically designed for children who ranged from birth to 2 years of age (developmentally) and that would yield educationally relevant outcomes. In addition, the group discussed the possibility of developing this tool through a consortium effort. Personnel from five of the six universities agreed to work toward a collaborative effort to fill this measurement gap. The initial participants included Diane Bricker, then at the University of Miami; Dale Gentry, Owen White, and Robin Beck, then at the University of Washington; Lizbeth Vincent, then at the University of Wisconsin; Verna Hart, then at the University of Pittsburgh; and Evelyn Lynch, then at Indiana University.

A second official meeting was held in Madison, Wisconsin, in June, 1976, when the group, whose constellation had changed slightly, formalized responsibilities and adopted the name of Consortium on Adaptive Performance Evaluation. Two other meetings were held in 1976, one in Kansas City in October and one in Pittsburgh in November. During these meetings, plans were formulated to write an application to be submitted to the Research Branch of the Division of Innovation and Development, Bureau of Education for the Handicapped, now the Office of Special Education Programs. The grant application, written primarily by Dale Gentry and Owen White, was submitted in December, 1976, with the American Association for the Education of the Severely and Profoundly Handicapped as the sponsoring agency.

The application was approved and funded, permitting formal continuation of the work begun by the consortium members. During the 3-year period of the grant, a number of individuals from the five participating universities shared in the development of the instrument. The major players during this period were Dale Gentry, Diane Bricker, Owen White, Lizbeth Vincent, Evelyn Lynch, and Verna Hart.

During this period, conceptual as well as empirical work was undertaken. The principles underlying the tool were refined, and the first data collection on the preliminary instrument was conducted. It was perhaps at this time that members of the consortium began to realize the magnitude of their task. Owen White argued that one area be developed, tested, and modified before tackling the other test areas. Although outvoted, hindsight suggests he was probably correct, and development might have proceeded more rapidly had the group followed his suggestion. The size of the task was particularly intimidating because other commitments prevented those involved from allotting sufficient time to the project. In addition, although the consortium participants could agree on the need for a tool, compromise between developmentalists and behavior analysts was time consuming and exhausting and often led to contentious meetings; however, much of the strength of the ensuing instrument was the result of these divergent views.

In 1980, under the leadership of Dale Gentry and with the assistance of Katie McCarton, a supplemental award to the Handicapped Children's Early Education Project grant of the University of Idaho provided support for the project. (By this time, Gentry had moved to the University of Idaho and Bricker to the University of Oregon.) During this period, the first complete and usable assessment/evaluation tool became available for comprehensive field testing. The tool was called the Adaptive Performance Instrument (API). The data and informal feedback on the API were extremely interesting but troublesome. The tool had more than 600 items for the developmental range of birth to 2 years. This depth of coverage provided detailed and useful descriptions of children's behavioral repertoires but also took 8–10 hours to administer. Thus, the tool's strength—generation of detailed behavioral profiles—was also its weakness— excessive administration time.

After completion of the federal supplemental grant, consortium members considered seeking a commercial publisher to disseminate the API. Several consortium members believed, however, that adequate psychometric data had not been collected on the test and, thus, continued study was in order. Also, there was a nagging problem of administration time. A complete copy of the API was sent to the Bureau of Education for the Handicapped as part of the final project report. In addition, copies of the API that had been made during the granting period were distributed to interested parties as long as the supply lasted.

Between 1983 and 1984, the Idaho and Oregon group found creative ways to maintain support for work on the instrument. The API was modified considerably by reducing the number of test items from more than 600 to less than 300 and extending the developmental range to 36 months. Most items were rewritten and the presentation format changed. The modifications were so extensive that the measure was renamed the Comprehensive Early Evaluation and Programming System. A dissertation conducted by E.J. Bailey (Ayers) at the University of Oregon examined the psychometric properties of the modified instrument and was completed in August, 1983.

Using the Bailey (Ayers) dissertation data as a base, a research grant was written and submitted to the field-initiated research program of the Division of Innovation and Development, Office of Special Education Programs. In October, 1984, a 3-year grant was awarded to the University of Oregon. During the ensuing 3 years, another extensive revision was conducted on the instrument and the name was changed to the Evaluation and Programming System: For Infants and Young Children (EPS). In addition, an associated curriculum was developed and field tested.

From 1984 to 1989, extensive data were collected and published on the EPS Birth to Three Years (Bailey & Bricker, 1986; Bricker, Bailey, & Slentz, 1990; Cripe, 1990; Notari & Bricker, 1990). In 1993, the EPS Test for Birth to Three Years and its associated curriculum were published by Paul H. Brookes Publishing Co., and the name was changed to the Assessment, Evaluation, and Programming System (AEPS) for Infants and Children to reflect accurately its purpose and use. In the first edition, the AEPS for Birth to Three Years was composed of a test *(AEPS Measurement for Birth to Three Years)* and an associated curriculum *(AEPS Curriculum for Birth to Three Years)*. The success of the AEPS Test and Curriculum for the developmental range from birth to 3 years served as the major impetus for expanding the AEPS to cover the developmental range from 3 to 6 years.

From the time of the first field testing of the AEPS for Birth to Three Years, there was pressure to expand the system to cover the entire preschool age range. In 1985, work was begun on the development of a test and associated curriculum to address the developmental range from 3 to 6 years. The first version was field tested by Slentz (1986). The results from this study served as a basis for extensive revisions of the test. The revised test was called the Evaluation and Programming System for Young Children—Assessment Level II: Developmentally 3 Years to 6 Years (Bricker, Janko, Cripe, Bailey, & Kaminski, 1989). Selected psychometric properties of the revised test were examined by Hsia (1993). The findings from this study were encouraging and suggested only minor modifications in test items were needed. The revised test was titled the *Assessment, Evaluation, and Programming System Test for Three to Six Years* (Bricker, Ayers, Slentz, & Kaminski, 1992).

Between 1992 and 1995, a curriculum linked to the 3–6 years test was developed. In 1996, Volumes 3 and 4 of the AEPS series were published by Paul H. Brookes Publishing Co. Volume 3 was titled *AEPS Measurement for Three to Six Years* (Bricker & Pretti-Frontczak, 1996) and Volume 4 was titled *AEPS Curriculum for Three to Six Years* (Bricker & Waddell, 1996).

As the AEPS became commercially available, requests for training on its use became frequent. AEPS training efforts have been extensive and have been supported through four outreach grants from the U.S. Department of Education, Office of Special Education Programs. The first outreach project was funded in 1988 and addressed the needs of personnel in individual programs. Training was provided to more than 1,000 participants in 50 sites across 19 states. The second outreach project, from 1991 to 1994, also provided training to more than 1,000 participants in 54 sites across 16 states. The third outreach project, initiated in 1996, changed the focus of training from individual programs to a train-the-trainer model. This change was instituted in an effort to 1) meet the growing requests for AEPS training and 2) produce systematic change throughout states. Training on the AEPS has been done by a cadre of experts located across the country and includes Kristie Pretti-Frontczak at Kent State University, Kent, Ohio; J.J. Johnson at the University of Nevada, Reno; Kristine Slentz at Western Washington University, Bellingham; Elizabeth Straka of New England Early Intervention Consulting, Wells, Maine; and Betty Capt and Misti Waddell at the University of Oregon, Eugene. The fourth outreach project began in 1999 and also employs a train-the-trainer model. Individuals trained by these last two outreach projects have provided services to approximately 1,500 individuals in 50 sites across 13 states.

In addition to providing training to hundreds of AEPS users, Kristie Pretti-Frontczak, J.J. Johnson, Kristine Slentz, Elizabeth Straka, Betty Capt, and Misti Waddell met at the University of Oregon, Eugene, during the summers of 1999 and 2000 and, led by Diane Bricker, discussed changes in the AEPS. In addition, Jane Squires, Natalya McComas, and doctoral students enrolled in the Early Intervention Program, College of Education, University of Oregon, provided additional insight and expertise. At the first meeting in 1999, data gathered on the AEPS Test and information garnered from outreach training sessions were studied and discussed. Based on these discussions, a series of changes and modifications to the AEPS were proposed. Each of the participants left the meeting with a set of assigned tasks. During the ensuing year, the group completed changes and circulated them to other participants. At the second meeting held in the summer of 2000, additional changes and refinements were discussed and participants left again with a set of tasks to be completed for the second edition of the AEPS. The results of those discussions and their crystallization are contained in this second edition of the AEPS.

A DESCRIPTION OF THE FIRST EDITION OF THE AEPS

The AEPS is an assessment/evaluation system with associated curricula. The AEPS is more than an assessment measure; it is a comprehensive and linked system that includes assessment/evaluation, curricular, and family participation components. As shown in Figure 1, the first edition of the AEPS was divided into two developmental ranges: birth to 3 years (Volumes I and II) and 3–6 years (Volumes III and IV). Each developmental range was covered by two volumes, one that contained measurement information and a second that contained associated curricular information. The test and associated measurement materials were contained in Volumes I and III, whereas the curriculum materials were contained in Volumes II and IV.

Volume I, AEPS Measurement for Birth to Three Years, was divided into three sections. Section I provided a comprehensive description of the AEPS. Section II presented the AEPS Test items, which were divided into six areas that covered the developmental period from 1 month to 3 years. Section III described how to involve families in the assessment/evaluation process as well as how to provide specific strategies and guidelines for doing so.

Volume II, AEPS Curriculum for Birth to Three Years, was also composed of three sections. Section I described the relationship between the AEPS Test described in Volume I and the Curriculum. The numbering system for the AEPS Test and Curriculum permitted efficient movement between the two volumes. Procedures for general use of the AEPS Curriculum were also described in Section I. Section II explained in detail how to use the AEPS Curriculum separately or in conjunction with the AEPS Test. Section III presented the AEPS curricular activities, covering the Fine Motor, Gross Motor, Adaptive, Cognitive, Social-Communication, and Social Domains. For each item on the AEPS Test, an associated set of curricular activities was described, including cross-references to the AEPS Test, the item's importance to a child's development, procedures for using an activity-based intervention approach, as well as more structured approaches, cautions, and teaching suggestions.

Volume III, AEPS Measurement for Three to Six Years, was divided into three sections. Section I provided a comprehensive description of the AEPS. Section II presented the AEPS Test items organized into six areas that covered the developmental period from 3 to 6 years. Section III described how to involve families in the assessment/evaluation process as well as specific strategies and guidelines for doing so. The content of Volume III was focused on assisting interventionists and caregivers in assessment/evaluation activities. It described a program-relevant assessment and evaluation system designed for interventionists to use on a regular basis. Use of this system ensured the accurate assessment and ongoing monitoring of infants and children at risk for or who have disabilities and their families.

Volume IV, AEPS Curriculum for Three to Six Years, was composed of five sections. Section I described the relationship between the AEPS Test for Three

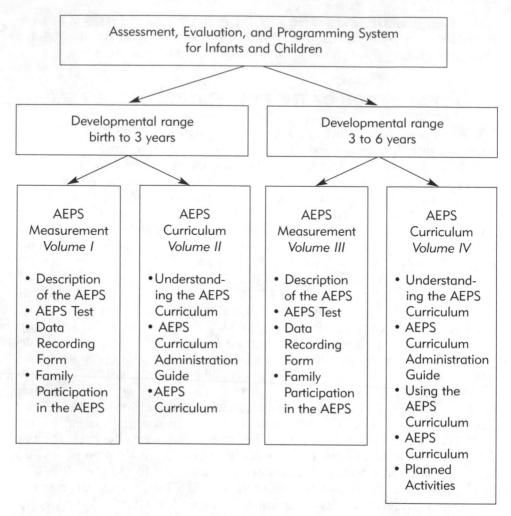

Figure 1.   Four volumes of the *Assessment, Evaluation, and Programming System for Infants and Children, First Edition.*

to Six Years and the Curriculum. The numbering system for the AEPS Test and Curriculum permitted efficient movement between the two volumes. Section II explained how to use the AEPS Curriculum separately or in conjunction with the AEPS Test. Section III described the use of the AEPS Curriculum in the context of an activity-based intervention approach. Section IV presented the AEPS curricular activities, covering the Fine Motor, Gross Motor, Adaptive, Cognitive, Social-Communication, and Social Domains. For each item on the AEPS Test, an associated set of curricular activities was described, including cross-references to the AEPS Test, procedures for using an activity-based intervention approach, as well as more structured approaches, cautions, teaching suggestions, and cross-references to other early childhood curricula with similar goals/objectives. Finally, Section V presented a series of planned activities appropriate for young children that could be used to embed individual children's goals/objectives.

A DESCRIPTION OF THE SECOND EDITION OF THE AEPS

Since the publication of the first edition of the AEPS Test and Curriculum for Birth to Three Years in 1993 and the AEPS Test and Curriculum for Three to Six Years in 1996, data and information on the usefulness of the AEPS system to professionals and caregivers have been collected. Studying this information has led to a number of changes in the second edition of the AEPS. These changes are of three types—organization, content, and format—and are described next. The two most significant changes for the second edition were 1) combining the Birth to Three Years and Three to Six Years Administration materials into one volume and 2) combining the Birth to Three Years and Three to Six Years Test items into one volume. These changes occurred for reasons of efficiency (i.e., elimination of redundancy) and ease of use. A combined administration guide permitted the deletion of significant redundancy because the guidelines are the same for both test levels. Combining the Birth to Three Years and Three to Six Years Test items into one volume permits test users to easily move across tests when children's repertoires cut across both levels. It is important to note that the basic purpose and content of the AEPS remain the same; that is, the AEPS remains a curriculum-based measurement system linked to intervention. Figure 2 presents the four volumes that compose the second edition of the AEPS.

A review of Figure 2 highlights the second edition organizational changes. To reduce redundancy, the foundational information for understanding and using the AEPS has been combined into one volume. *Volume 1, AEPS Administration Guide,* presents information on the conceptual and organizational structure of the AEPS, how to get started using the system, components of a linked system, interpretation of test outcomes, family involvement in the assessment/evaluation process, and team collaboration when using the system. This volume also contains a description of the Psychometric Properties of the AEPS Test (Appendix A); IFSP/IEP Goal and Objective Examples (Appendix B); Child Observation Data Recording Form (Appendix C); Family Report (Appendix D); Child Progress Record (Appendix E); and Corroborating Eligibility Scores (Appendix F).

Volume 2, AEPS Test, contains the test items for Birth to Three Years and Three to Six Years, divided into six developmental areas: Fine Motor, Gross Motor, Adaptive, Cognitive, Social-Communication, and Social. The majority of AEPS Test items have remained unchanged from the first editions; however, a few items were subjected to minor rewrites to improve their clarity. A few items were eliminated because of redundancy, and a few items were added to eliminate important developmental content gaps (e.g., emergent literacy). Finally, the content in the Cognitive Area for Three to Six Years was combined to significantly reduce the number of items. Volume 2 also contains general administration guidelines as well as Assessment Activities (Appendix A). The assessment activities are simple scripts that guide the assessment of a range of AEPS Test items during specific activities.

Volume 3, AEPS Curriculum for Birth to Three Years, and *Volume 4, AEPS Curriculum for Three to Six Years,* of the second edition contain the curricular material for the developmental range birth to 3 years and 3 to 6 years, respec-

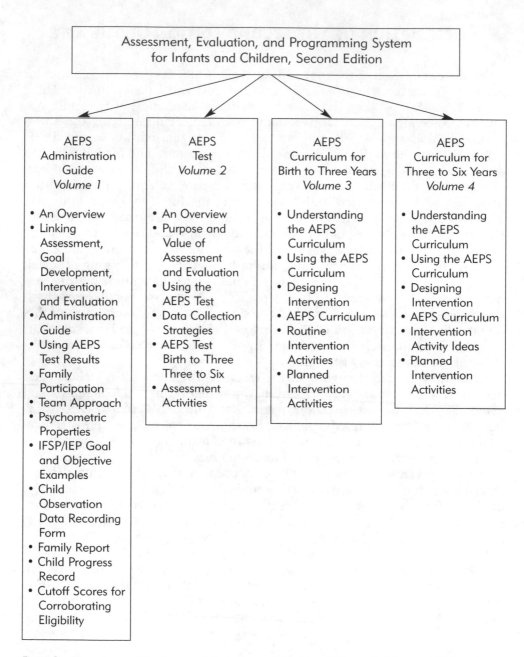

Figure 2. Four volumes of the *Assessment, Evaluation, and Programming System for Infants and Children, Second Edition*.

tively. In these volumes, the major changes were in formatting and the addition of intervention strategies and activities.

The changes introduced in the second edition of the AEPS are designed to improve its usefulness to interventionists and caregivers and to clarify procedures for its use. The underlying philosophy of the AEPS and its basic goals remain unchanged.

The AEPS: An Overview

Chapter 1 provides important contextual information to users or potential users of the *Assessment, Evaluation, and Programming System for Infants and Children (AEPS)*™. In particular, the what, why, and who of using the AEPS is addressed. In addition, a Quick Start section on how to use the AEPS is offered to assist new users of the AEPS. The AEPS has a number of components, and new users of the system may experience difficulty in deciding where to begin and how to orchestrate the many pieces into a cohesive approach. Previous users of the AEPS will find few procedural changes.

WHAT IS THE AEPS?

The AEPS is more than an assessment/evaluation measure and more than a curriculum. The approach of the AEPS is counter to the use of standardized and normed measures, which yield scores or outcomes that do not provide information that can be used to develop educational goals or outcomes and intervention content. In contrast to standardized norm-based tests, the AEPS is a comprehensive system that ties together assessment, goal development, intervention, and ongoing monitoring and evaluation. The test components of the AEPS yield educationally relevant, meaningful, and functional information that can be used to formulate developmentally appropriate goals/outcomes and objectives/benchmarks for children. These goals and objectives, in turn, link directly to intervention content and procedures offered in the curricular components of the AEPS. The test and curricular components of the AEPS form a comprehensive and linked system that permits using assessment results to develop intervention content and to monitor child progress.

The AEPS is not a screening tool nor is it a norm-referenced measure that yields a developmental age or IQ score. The primary purpose of the AEPS is to assist professionals and parents/caregivers in identifying and monitoring children's developmentally appropriate educational targets and planning individualized intervention; for this reason, the AEPS can be of enormous assistance in assessing children's functional repertoires, developing quality goals, formulating intervention content, and monitoring child progress over time.

WHY USE THE AEPS?

There are four essential reasons to use a linked assessment, goal development, intervention, and evaluation system such as the AEPS:

1. The test portions of the AEPS yield functional and educationally relevant developmental information that can be used effectively and efficiently to develop individualized plans and intervention content.

2. The AEPS Test results make the formulation of goals/outcomes and objectives/benchmarks and intervention activities straightforward and accurate.

3. The AEPS provides materials that permit and encourage the active input and participation of family members in the assessment, goal development, intervention, and evaluation processes for their children.

4. The AEPS supports placement of children in inclusive environments and fosters collaboration among teachers, specialists, family members, and other caregivers.

Ms. Jones, the teacher, and Mr. Robart, the county early intervention specialist, jointly completed an AEPS Test on 4-year-old Michael upon his entry into the Acme Child Care Program by observing him across several days and many classroom activities. In addition, Ms. Martinez, the speech-language pathologist, assisted with the completion of the Social-Communication Area of the AEPS. Soon after Michael's entry in the child care program, Michael's parents were asked to complete the Family Report while observing Michael at home. Ms. Jones, Mr. Robart, Ms. Martinez, and Michael's parents did not have to ask Michael to engage in activities that were meaningless for him, nor did they have to use irrelevant and unhelpful information to formulate his individualized education program (IEP). The information gathered during typical daily routines provided information about Michael's skills and abilities in important developmental areas, and, therefore, formulating appropriate and functional IEP goals/objectives for Michael was straightforward. In addition, Michael's parents were able to actively contribute to the selection of goals/objectives. Because the AEPS permits a direct link between the selected goals and curricular content, Ms. Jones had significant help in choosing daily intervention activities and procedures that would appeal to Michael and target his IEP goals/objectives.

By using the AEPS, members of Michael's IEP team (i.e., Ms. Jones, Mr. Robart, Ms. Martinez, Michael's parents) saved valuable time because they were able to select appropriate and functional goals and intervention content for Michael without having to remove him from his usual daily activities. The selection of developmentally appropriate and meaningful IEP goals and intervention content helped ensure that Michael will make timely developmental progress.

WHO SHOULD USE THE AEPS?

The previous vignette makes clear that the AEPS was designed to be used by teachers, specialists, and caregivers. The caregiver[1] components of the AEPS are written in straightforward language that avoids jargon and complicated descriptions. Caregivers are asked to observe the children as they engage in daily activities and then indicate the children's ability to perform important behaviors.

Using the AEPS enhances interventionist and caregiver understanding of development in young children. The layout of the AEPS provides basic information about developmental milestones and the general sequence in which they appear. The AEPS, however, does require that some members of each professional team have adequate training in child development and child learning to correctly interpret child performance in critical areas.

The AEPS is designed to be used by specialists as well as early childhood, early intervention, or special education teachers and interventionists. Items and curricular activities are divided into six areas so that, for example, a communication specialist can assist in completing the Social-Communication Area and a physical or occupational therapist can assist in completing the Fine and Gross Motor Areas. Division into areas permits efficient test completion by team members, whereas commonalities across areas and cross-referencing provide a solid basis for collaboration.

A QUICK START ON HOW TO USE THE AEPS TEST

At first glance, the AEPS may seem to contain an overwhelming amount of material because there are hundreds of items across six developmental areas in two age ranges of assessment and curriculum, as well as family components. Once you begin using the AEPS, however, its advantages will quickly become evident and the structure of the system will provide a clear and systematic framework for initial and ongoing assessment, intervention planning, and evaluation. Taking the time to learn the AEPS can, in fact, stimulate and organize major improvements in existing assessment procedures, team roles, and service delivery environments.

The following suggestions provide directions for a quick start to the AEPS system for first time users. There are separate sections for home- and center-based settings that provide a stepwise summary of AEPS Test administration procedures for regular users of the test and should be considered a supplement, rather than a replacement, for the detailed AEPS Test administration guidelines contained in subsequent chapters of this volume.

---

[1] The term *caregiver* is preferred over parent because young children may interact with a variety of caregivers.

Specific Steps for AEPS Test Administration:
Center-Based Settings

- **Identify the child or children to be assessed.** Review existing information to familiarize yourself with each child's age, developmental performance across areas, medical history, family concerns, and behavioral characteristics.

- **Review AEPS Test items for the areas that you plan to address.** Read through the specific goals/objectives in Volume 2 to clarify the content and criteria for each skill that you plan to assess. Some users find it useful to make notations about criteria.

- **Organize the testing environment.** Determine if you will be using the AEPS Test to observe one or more children during play, planned activities, and/or regular routines such as opening circle or snack time in the classroom. Use the Assessment Activities in Volume 2, Appendix A to develop a list of necessary materials and to schedule time and set up space for assessment in the classroom accordingly.

- **Select the data recording form that matches your assessment procedure.** The AEPS provides a variety of recording forms to meet individual users' needs. After organizing the environment, identify and reproduce the form that matches your situation; for example, if you have decided to observe a single child in a single area of development, then you may want to use the Child Observation Data Recording Form found in Appendix C of this volume. If you have decided to assess a group of children, then you may want to use the Assessment Activities found in Appendix A of Volume 2.

- **Prepare for data collection.** Designate someone to monitor play or facilitate the assessment activity and someone else to record data. Complete the Child Observation Data Recording Form cover sheet for each child, and bracket the child's performance level by eliminating goals that are clearly too easy or difficult. Score items that are developmentally below the child's current level of performance as 2R and items that are demonstrably too difficult as 0R. The R, which stands for Report, is found in the Notes section of the Child Observation Data Recording Form.

- **Record assessment data using the three-point scoring options (2 = consistently meets criterion; 1 = inconsistently meets criterion; 0 = does not meet criterion).** Observation is the preferred method of data collection. Score each goal, and then score all associated objectives for goals scored 1 or 0. Add notes and comments to qualify and explain scores.

- **Summarize child's performance across areas.** Users may summarize AEPS information numerically, narratively, or visually. Be sure that enough information has been collected to make sound decisions, and look for patterns in how a child demonstrates various skills. Many teams working in center-based programs generate narratives that can be used as the child's present level of performance or as quarterly progress reports.

Specific Steps for AEPS Test Administration:
Home-Based Settings

- **Review existing information about the child to be assessed.** Familiarize yourself with each child's age, medical history, family concerns, and behavioral characteristics. Explain the importance of caregiver input in the assessment process, assist caregivers in completing the Family Report, and review developmental performance across AEPS assessment areas.

- **Review AEPS Test items for the areas that you plan to address.** Read through the specific goals/objectives in Volume 2 to clarify the content and criteria for each skill that you plan to assess. Discuss the content of assessment items with the parents or other caregivers, and answer any questions that they might have.

- **Organize the testing environment.** Talk with the caregivers to determine the best time of day to gather assessment information during a home visit and to clarify the role that they would like to take in the process. Use the Assessment Activities in Volume 2, Appendix A, and plan to identify materials and events with the caregivers for the assessment home visit(s) accordingly.

- **Select the data recording form that matches your assessment procedure.** The AEPS provides a variety of recording forms to help meet individual users' needs. The forms can be purchased separately from Paul H. Brookes Publishing Co. The CD-Rom containing these forms includes a bonus Child Observation Form with Criteria for Birth to Three Years and Three to Six Years. After organizing the environment, identify and reproduce the form that matches your situation; for example, if you are observing a single child in his or her home environment, then you may want to begin with the Family Report and then complete the Child Observation Data Recording Form found in Appendix C of this volume.

- **Prepare for data collection.** Complete the cover sheet for the child's Observation Data Recording Form, and use results of the Family Report to bracket the child's performance level. Eliminate goals that are too easy or difficult by scoring items that are clearly below the child's current level of performance as 2R and items that are demonstrably too difficult as 0R. Discuss with the participating caregivers how they will be interacting with the child during the various assessment activities. Encourage caregivers to facilitate activities as much as possible. The R, which stands for Report, is found in the Notes section of the Child Observation Data Recording Form.

- **Record assessment data using the three-point scoring options (2 = consistently meets criterion; 1 = inconsistently meets criterion; 0 = does not meet criterion).** Observation is the preferred method of data collection. Score each goal, and then score all associated objectives for goals scored 1 or 0. Use notes and comments to qualify and explain scores. Encourage caregivers to add explanatory comments. Review and discuss the child's performance with the caregivers as you assess.

- **Summarize child's performance across areas.** Users may summarize AEPS information numerically, narratively, or visually. Be sure that enough information has been collected to make sound decisions, and look for patterns in how a child demonstrates various skills. Teams working in home-based programs may summarize the child's performance visually by completing the Child Progress Record found in Appendix E of this volume.

Optional Strategies for Using the AEPS Test

- **Start with a single activity or center that is designed specifically for exploring use of the AEPS Test.** Select a few assessment activities from Volume 2, Appendix A for use in either home or classroom settings; for example, set up the Washing Babies activity in the dramatic play area or at home. Use the assessment activities to experiment with administering the AEPS Test. Identify the specific goals/objectives associated with each activity and practice embedding opportunities for children to perform the skills during the activity. Once you are comfortable and confident with facilitating the activities, begin collecting data on children's performance of the skills using the Child Observation Data Recording Form in this volume, Appendix C.

- **Identify a single child for whom existing assessment information is inadequate, and use a portion of the AEPS Test to gather additional information.** Select one or two areas of the AEPS Test that seem to address specific areas of interest to caregivers and professionals; for instance, both the Cognitive and Social-Communication Areas will provide detailed information for a child with identified delays in language. Read the section on scoring in Chapter 3 of this volume. Read through the test items in Volume 2 for each selected area, and observe the child engaging in activities where he or she will have opportunities to perform the skills (e.g., during free play with peers, during parent–child interactions). Use the Child Observation Data Recording Form from Appendix C in this volume to record your observations of specific skills in each area using the three-point scoring options and notes. Refer to Volume 2 for detailed information on test items (e.g., specific item criteria) and consult the assessment activities in Volume 2, Appendix A for ideas on activities that can be used to observe target skills.

- **Use the AEPS Test to assess a child who enters the program in the middle of the year.** Give the child time to acclimate to the home visitor or the classroom setting, and then arrange to observe during the next few consecutive home visits or classroom activities. Use the Child Observation Data Recording Form from Appendix C in this volume to record your observations of specific skills across all areas using the three-point scoring options and notes. Ask caregivers to complete the Family Report to gather additional information on the child's performance, and compare your observations with their ratings. Refer to Volume 2 for detailed information on individual items and to the Assessment Activities (Appendix A) for assessment activity ideas.

Optional Strategies for Curriculum Implementation

- **Start with a single activity or center that is designed specifically for using the AEPS Curriculum.** Use the Routine and Planned Intervention Activities from Volumes 3 or 4 to design intervention activities for use in either home or classroom settings that may provide an opportunity to address a number of existing IFSP/IEP goals for children in your program. Facilitate each activity several times to practice embedding a range of specific goals/objectives within a single activity. Once you are comfortable with facilitating the activities, try using the Child Observation Data Recording Form from Appendix C in this volume to record observations of children's performance on specific IFSP/IEP goals/objectives.

- **Use the AEPS Curriculum items to address existing IFSP/IEP goals/objectives within daily activities.** Compare existing IFSP/IEP goals/objectives for children in your program with the IFSP/IEP Goal and Objective Examples in Appendix B of this volume; for example, review the Balance and Mobility strands in the Gross Motor Area of Birth to Three Years to find functional skills associated with goals such as "Walks without support," or "Runs." Select AEPS skills that match existing goals/objectives, and use the curriculum items to identify teaching strategies in the context of daily activities. Use the Routine and Planned Intervention Activities from Volumes 3 or 4 to design intervention activities at home or in the classroom.

SUMMARY

This chapter has presented a range of overview information designed to assist the user or potential user of the AEPS in understanding what the system is, who might use it, and why. This information addresses the essential issues that potential users of any curriculum-based measure should address prior to adopting an approach. A final section lays out step-by-step procedures for beginning users of the AEPS. For additional information about using the AEPS, please see http://www.brookespublishing.com/tools.

2

Linking Assessment, Goal Development, Intervention, and Evaluation

The use of the AEPS Test or other similar curriculum-based measures (CBMs) is fundamental to the adoption of intervention models that link assessment, goal development, intervention, and evaluation processes. These linked intervention models are the most appropriate and effective approaches available to early intervention and early childhood special education personnel. In this chapter, a linked assessment, goal development, intervention, and evaluation approach to early intervention is described. Two outcomes for the reader are anticipated: 1) an understanding of a linked approach and 2) an understanding of the importance of using a CBM tool to employ a linked approach.

An explanation of linked assessment–goal development–intervention–evaluation systems in early intervention and early childhood special education programs is important for at least three reasons. First, many personnel who operate programs have not received adequate preparation on topics of assessment and evaluation or on methods for linking assessment, goal development, intervention, and evaluation. Second, descriptions of linked systems seldom appear in the literature. With few exceptions (e.g., Bagnato & Neisworth, 1991; Bagnato, Neisworth, & Munson, 1997; Bricker, 1989a; Bricker, Pretti-Frontczak, & McComas, 1998), descriptions focus on one element (e.g., assessment or intervention) and fail to extend the linkage to other program elements at the theoretical level or to provide practical ideas for linking assessment, goal development, intervention, and evaluation activities. Third, many norm- and criterion-referenced instruments yield results that are not helpful for program planning for young children who are at risk for or who have disabilities. The items are often chosen because they discriminate between children of different developmental levels versus their educational relevance or functional importance. In addition, outcomes yield scores or a developmental/cognitive age, which does not help target important skills for future intervention goals. Finally, items may be narrow in focus (e.g., "Child can stack three blocks"), making it challenging for interventionists to develop

meaningful individualized family service plans (IFSPs)/individualized education programs (IEPs).

The assessment and evaluation of individual change and programmatic
impact require that intervention methods and systems be supported with procedures appropriate to evaluating their efficacy. Assessment and evaluation
should determine the format and success of intervention for individual children and determine the effect that programs have on groups of children. These
objectives require that assessment and evaluation procedures serve three dis-
tinct but complementary functions: 1) providing essential content for the development of educational and therapeutic goals/objectives and intervention
activities for individual children, 2) monitoring child progress toward targeted
goals/objectives, and 3) determining the value of an intervention program for
groups or subgroups of children (e.g., at risk; having mild, moderate, or severe
disabilities). Underlying these three functions is the important concept that
these separate assessment/evaluation objectives are linked into a unified systems approach.

The linked approach is composed of four basic processes: assessment, goal
development, intervention, and evaluation. *Assessment* refers to the process
of establishing a baseline or entry-level measurement of the child's skills and
desired family outcomes and assumes that a child's eligibility for services has
been established. The assessment process should produce the necessary information for appropriate and relevant *goal development. Intervention* refers to
the process of arranging and individualizing the physical and social environment to produce the desired growth and development specified in the formulated intervention plan for the child and family. *Evaluation* refers to the
process of comparing the child's performance on selected intervention goals/
objectives before and after intervention and comparing the family's progress
toward selected family outcomes.

Figure 3 provides an illustration of the linked assessment, goal development, intervention, and evaluation approach. The major components are rep-
resented by boxes linked by arrows to indicate the sequence in which they typically occur. In addition, the diagonal arrows indicate the need for professional
collaboration and family participation in each of these components.

The assessment, goal development, intervention, and evaluation linked
system approach is described next. As indicated in Figure 3, family and caregiver input and participation should be encouraged throughout all of these
processes. The more caregivers become involved in the assessment, goal development, intervention, and evaluation processes, the greater the likelihood of
improved outcomes for their children. Family participation, however, should
always be tailored to meet individual family values, priorities, and needs.

PROGRAMMATIC ASSESSMENT

The links among assessment, goal development, intervention, and evaluation
begin after children's eligibility for services has been established and they have
entered into a program. The major objective of programmatic assessment is to
formulate a realistic and appropriate IFSP/IEP. As shown in Figure 4, program-

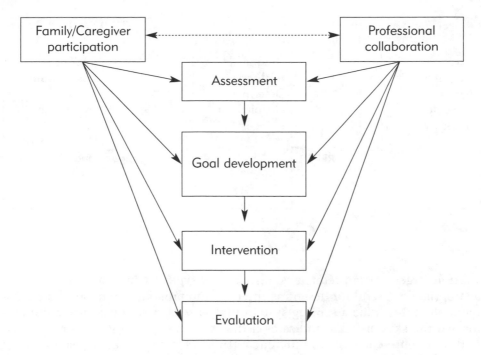

Figure 3. Schematic of a linked assessment–goal development–intervention–evaluation approach to early intervention with collaborative professional and family/caregiver participation.

matic assessment should be preceded by screening (Step 1) and a diagnostic evaluation (Step 2).

For Step 1, screening (a quick assessment of the child), the purpose is to determine if the child requires a comprehensive diagnostic evaluation, which is generally performed by a professional team. For children referred to Step 2, diagnostic evaluation, standardized norm-referenced tests are typically used to determine whether the child performs in a manner similar to his or her peers. In addition, specialty tests that attempt to document specific impairments may be given. The purposes of diagnostic evaluation are to determine if a child is eligible to receive early intervention services and, when options exist, to refer the child to the most appropriate intervention program. Once a child has been determined to be eligible for services, Step 3 is to administer program-relevant or programmatic (e.g., curriculum-based) assessments to the child to determine IFSP/IEP and intervention content. The content of the IFSP/IEP provides the road map for moving children from their beginning skills repertoires to the acquisition of skills specified as annual goals on their IFSPs/IEPs (Benner, 1992). During Step 3, families can be encouraged to participate by completing an appropriate formal or informal assessment of their child.

The formulation of the IFSP/IEP is crucially dependent on an accurate assessment of the child's beginning skill level. In addition, the assessment strategies employed should yield information that precisely describes the child's behavior in the following ways. First, the assessment should include information about the child's performance of skills that are appropriate inter-

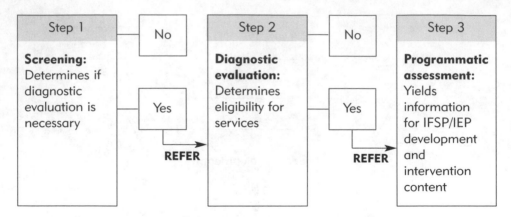

Figure 4.   Three-step screening, diagnostic evaluation, and programmatic assessment process.

vention targets. Norm-referenced tests do not typically include items that are appropriate or useful for designing intervention programs. Second, the assessment should include a scoring system that is sensitive to how the child performed the skill and that indicates if the skill was performed independently, with different people, or in different settings. A standard binary scoring system only provides information on whether the child's response was "correct" or "incorrect"; therefore, important information for developing educational programs may be lost. Third, the assessment measure should be designed to be administered by intervention personnel in the child's typical environments. Individuals working with the child should be able to use the test in the home or other environments in an unobtrusive manner. Fourth, the assessment should have some procedure for the formal inclusion of input from caregivers. Finally, and most important, the information generated by the test should be directly usable in the development of an IFSP/IEP.

A programmatic assessment that measures functional skills and is sensitive to the conditions in which a child is most likely to perform the skills will facilitate the development of appropriate and realistic IFSPs/IEPs. This, in turn, will encourage child growth and development and will yield a sensitive measure of child progress throughout the intervention process.

Formulation of an IFSP requires specification of family outcomes as well as children's goals. Family assessment should yield program-relevant information that will aid in developing functional outcome statements, but it should not be seen as intrusive by family members.

GOAL DEVELOPMENT

The initial IFSP/IEP should be based primarily on information accumulated during the initial assessment period, although this assessment information should be validated at the first quarterly evaluation or sooner. Relevant information should be obtained from caregivers' knowledge of the children as well as professional observation and testing. The initial information should be used to develop a plan of action for the interventionists and family to identify the specific content areas that the IFSP/IEP will address. The child's portion of the IFSP/IEP should contain goals or outcomes, objectives or benchmarks, strategies for reaching objectives, and a time frame for meeting selected goals or outcomes. The IFSP/IEP should be straightforward so that it can be used as a working guide for interventionists and caregivers. The IFSP/IEP can also be used as a criterion for evaluating the success of the intervention.

The family portion of the IFSP should contain a statement of family strengths and needs related to enhancing the child's development. This statement is based on information obtained from the family's assessment of their interests and needs. Priorities can be collaboratively established during a structured interview—meaning that the interventionist has developed a set of open-ended questions to which caregivers can respond (e.g., "How can program staff be most useful to you and your child?"). A set of outcome statements will evolve from these priorities, and activities and resources necessary for reaching outcomes, as well as a timeline, should be indicated.

INTERVENTION

Once the IFSP/IEP has been formulated by caregivers and interventionists, intervention activities can be initiated. The child's performance on the program assessment indicates where teaching should begin; items that the child is beginning to perform should become the skills targeted for intervention. Many children who are at risk or who have disabilities have challenges that affect their behavior in more than one developmental area. Consequently, a program assessment may reveal delays or impairments in several skill areas. Given a variety of needs, it may be appropriate to have multiple goals/objectives. Although targeting multiple goals/objectives may be appropriate, most programs and caregivers have genuine limits on the time and resources that can be directed to intervention efforts for individual children. Therefore, goals/objectives should be prioritized. The intervention team should select the two to four most important goals for intervention for each child.

Once goals/objectives are selected, the intervention team is ready to develop an intervention plan. In a system such as the AEPS, goals/objectives are directly linked or tied to curricular content. Interventionists can easily locate the intervention activities that were designed to facilitate acquisition of specific goals/objectives. There is a direct correspondence between the assessment items (skills) in the AEPS Test identified as goals/objectives and the intervention content and strategies specified in the associated AEPS Curriculum.

EVALUATION

A useful IFSP/IEP specifies both the tasks to be completed and the manner in which the success of the intervention will be evaluated. A variety of strategies may be used for daily or weekly monitoring of child progress (e.g., trial-by-trial data, brief probes during or after intervention activities, narrative notes, portfolios). The strategies selected should be determined by the specific goals/ objectives, the program resources, and the need for daily or weekly monitoring as a source of feedback to keep intervention efforts on track. Weekly monitoring may enhance the prospects of demonstrating individual improvement and program efficacy at quarterly and annual evaluations by providing ongoing feedback that will allow interventionists to detect and remedy ineffective intervention strategies that impede child progress. Ongoing monitoring also allows timely identification of child progress (e.g., reaching the specified criteria) so that children can proceed with subsequent objectives in the most efficient manner.

The IFSP requires specifications of activities and associated evaluation procedures to be conducted for the family as well as the child. Caregivers and staff should arrive at mutually agreed-upon procedures for monitoring progress toward selected family outcomes. Family priorities and interests may change and, therefore, should be reviewed and updated periodically.

Quarterly evaluation should focus on determining the effect of intervention efforts on children's objectives as specified in the IFSP/IEP. This can be done by using the initial assessment measures in conjunction with the weekly data. Quarterly evaluations should be used to compare the child's progress with some standard or expectation for progress. Without assigning an expected date of completion for objectives, it may not be possible to determine if the progress made by the child is acceptable or unacceptable; for example, quarterly IFSP/IEP objectives should have accompanying timelines (e.g., the child is expected to reach criterion on objectives within 3 months).

By frequently reviewing the child's progress toward the established objectives, interventionists can establish more realistic timelines and outcomes. In addition, comparisons between expected and attained outcomes will generate information that may eventually allow the establishment of relevant and useful norms for subgroups of children who are at risk for or who have disabilities.

Quarterly evaluations may also provide information for revising program intervention efforts. If all children fail to reach their established objectives in the Gross Motor Area, then program staff or caregivers may not be providing enough intervention time in this area, or the teaching strategies employed may be ineffective. In either case, quarterly evaluations may suggest that modifications of the program content or emphasis is in order. Information from quarterly evaluations provides feedback about the child's progress and clarifies where modifications or revisions in the IFSP/IEP or intervention efforts may be necessary.

Procedures should also be employed for monitoring family progress. Effective strategies for helping families and professionals monitor progress toward established outcomes should be used; for example, Goal Attainment Scalings may help determine if progress is better than expected, as expected, or not up to expectations. The type of system employed should be useful for monitoring change but also should be nonjudgmental of the family's participation or progress.

In addition to quarterly evaluations, annual or semi-annual evaluations can be used to monitor the progress of individual children and subgroups of children and families. Without subgroup comparisons, it is difficult to know how to improve intervention strategies for subgroups of children and families. Methodological design and measurement problems facing the field of early intervention make subgroup evaluations difficult; however, analyses of subgroups may yield important findings on the generalization of impact for certain groups of children and families.

JESSE

An example of applying a linked assessment, goal development, intervention, and evaluation approach follows. This example describes how Jesse, an active 3-year-old, and his parents move through each process.

Programmatic Assessment. Following a preschool screening round-up, Jesse's parents were advised to seek a comprehensive evaluation to examine his development. A diagnostic evaluation found that Jesse had a mild motor delay and a behavior disorder that met the state's criteria for receiving early intervention services. Jesse and his parents were referred to a special preschool program in their neighborhood. The family found the program acceptable, and Jesse was enrolled. During his first days at school, Jesse was assessed using the AEPS Test: Three to Six Years by the professional staff. His performance across settings, people, and events was observed, and the teachers, speech-language pathologist, and physical therapist scored AEPS items. For the purpose of this example, only results from the Social Area on the Child Observation Data Recording Form are shown in Figure 5.

Jesse met the criteria for all items in Goal 1 of Strand A. Jesse was able to perform some of the easier objectives in Goal 2 and Goal 3; for example, Jesse met the objectives of sharing or exchanging objects and was beginning to cooperate with others (see items in Strand A, Goal 2). Jesse was beginning to demonstrate skills in resolving conflicts with others by using a variety of strategies, often with assistance from adults (see items in Strand A, Goal 3). In Strand B, he would sometimes initiate and complete age-appropriate activities and was beginning to participate in small and large group activities more consistently (see items in Strand B, Goals 2 and 3). In Strand C, Jesse met the criteria for two of the simplest items regarding meeting physical needs and was beginning to follow context-specific rules outside of the home and the classroom. In Strand D, Jesse selected preferred activities and knew his full name, age, gender, the gender of others, and the names of his brothers but did not meet criteria for the other objectives nor the associated goals. Jesse's parents completed the Family Report as they observed their child at home. The parents' findings shown in Figure 6 are similar to the interventionists' AEPS Test results.

Goal Development. The AEPS Test and Family Report assessment information provided Jesse's parents and interventionists with an accurate picture of what he can currently do, what he is starting to do, and what skills might be appropriate on his IEP. For the Social Area, Jesse's parents selected the goal: Initiates cooperative ac-

SOCIAL AREA

S = Scoring key	N = Notes
2 = Consistently meets criterion	A = Assistance provided
1 = Inconsistently meets criterion	B = Behavior interfered
0 = Does not meet criterion	D = Direct test
	M = Modification/adaptation
	Q = Quality of performance
	R = Report

Name: Jesse

	Test period:	1							
	Test date:	8/02-9/02							
	Examiner:	DM							

	IFSP/IEP	S	N	S	N	S	N	S	N
A. Interaction with Others									
1. Interacts with others as play partners (p. 194)		2							
1.1 Responds to others in distress or need		2							
1.2 Establishes and maintains proximity to others		2							
1.3 Takes turns with others		2							
1.4 Initiates greetings to others who are familiar		2							
1.5 Responds to affective initiations from others		2							
2. Initiates cooperative activity (p. 195)		0							
2.1 Joins others in cooperative activity		0							
2.2 Maintains cooperative participation with others		1	A						
2.3 Shares or exchanges objects		2							
3. Resolves conflicts by selecting effective strategy (p. 196)		1							
3.1 Negotiates to resolve conflicts		1	A						
3.2 Uses simple strategies to resolve conflicts		1	A						
3.3 Claims and defends possessions		2							
B. Participation									
1. Initiates and completes age-appropriate activities (p. 198)		1	A						
1.1 Responds to request to finish activity		1	A						
1.2 Responds to request to begin activity		1							
2. Watches, listens, and participates during small group activities (p. 198)		1	A						

Figure 5. Strand A, B, C, and D of Jesse's Child Observation Data Recording Form II, Social Area, Three to Six Years. The page numbers listed after each goal indicate where that particular goal can be found in Volume 2.

Child Observation Data Recording Form II: Social Area

Name: _Jesse_

Test period:	1			
Test date:	8/02-9/02			
Examiner:	DM			

	IFSP/IEP	S	N	S	N	S	N	S	N
2.1 Interacts appropriately with materials during small group activities		1							
2.2 Responds appropriately to directions during small group activities		1							
2.3 Looks at appropriate object, person, or event during small group activities		1							
2.4 Remains with group during small group activities		1							
3. Watches, listens, and participates during large group activities (p. 199)		1							
3.1 Interacts appropriately with materials during large group activities		1							
3.2 Responds appropriately to directions during large group activities		1							
3.3 Looks at appropriate object, person, or event during large group activities		1							
3.4 Remains with group during large group activities		1							
C. Interaction with Environment									
1. Meets physical needs in socially appropriate ways (p. 201)		1							
1.1 Meets physical needs when uncomfortable, sick, hurt, or tired		1							
1.2 Meets observable physical needs		2							
1.3 Meets physical needs of hunger and thirst		2							
2. Follows context-specific rules outside home and classroom (p. 202)		0							
2.1 Seeks adult permission		1							
2.2 Follows established rules at home and in classroom		1	R						
D. Knowledge of Self and Others									
1. Communicates personal likes and dislikes (p. 203)		1							
1.1 Initiates preferred activities		1							
1.2 Selects activities and/or objects		1							
2. Understands how own behaviors, thoughts, and feelings relate to consequences for others (p. 203)		1							

Figure 5. (continued)

AEPS Three to Six Years

	Test period:	1							
Name: *Jesse*	Test date: Examiner:	8/02-9/02 DM							
	IFSP/ IEP	S	N	S	N	S	N	S	N
2.1 Identifies affect/emotions of others		1							
2.2 Identifies own affect/emotions		1							
3. Relates identifying information about self and others (p. 204)		1							
3.1 States address		O	B/R						
3.2 States telephone numbers		O	B/R						
3.3 States birthday		O	B/R						
3.4 Names siblings and gives full name of self		2	R						
3.5 States gender of self and others		2	R						
3.6 States name and age		2	R						

Figure 5. *(continued)*

tivity (Strand A, Goal 2), and two of the associated objectives (i.e., 2.1 and 2.2). Table 1 shows the relationship between the selected AEPS Test items and their wording as IFSP/IEP Goal and Objective Examples found in Volume 1, Appendix B.

Intervention. The next step was to develop an intervention plan for Jesse focused on the selected IEP goals and their associated objectives. For each selected priority goal and its associated objectives, in our example a social goal, an intervention plan should be developed and written. An intervention plan can follow a number of formats but should contain the following information: 1) identifying information such as the child's name, intervention team, dates for initiation of intervention, and expected completion; 2) intervention area or outcome; 3) goals/objectives/benchmarks and program steps, if necessary; 4) intervention strategies and teaching considerations; 5) curricular modifications; 6) child progress evaluation procedures; and 7) decision rules to be used.

A sample intervention plan addressing Jesse's social goal and its associated objectives is contained in Figure 7. As shown in Figure 7, intervention plans contain more detail and specification than IFSP/IEP documents and provide caregivers and interventionists with a framework for choosing and developing individualized intervention activities. Using the intervention plan as a guide, Jesse's parents and interventionists can design an array of daily activities to address his targeted

Social Area

Social skills are those that involve interactions and participation with others as well as meeting bodily needs. These skills include playing with others, managing conflict, taking part in group activities, following rules, showing preferences, identifying emotions, and knowing personal information.

1. Does your child play with other children? (A1)

date	8/02		
Y			

2. Does your child begin activities and encourage friends to join in? For example, your child says to friends, "Come on, let's build a house" and then gives them jobs to do. (A2)

S		

3. Does your child find ways to stop conflicts? (A3)
   NOTE: Place a "Y," "S," or "N" by items a through c:

S		

   _S_ a. Does your child try to find a solution to disagreements with playmates? For example, when your child is not getting along with a friend, your child says, "I'll play with the ball first, and then it's your turn." (A3.1)

   _S_ b. Does your child tell an adult when he or she is having trouble with a friend? (A3.2)

   _S_ c. Does your child claim a toy that belongs to him or her by taking the toy back or by saying, "That's mine!" (A3.3)

4. Does your child begin playing with toys and finish the activity without being told? For example, your child gets out a puzzle, puts it together, and puts is away. (B1)

5. Does your child take part in a *small* group activity with adult supervision? (B2)

?		

6. Does your child take part in a *large* group activity with adult supervision? (B3)

?		

7. Can your child meet his or her physical needs? (C1)
   NOTE: Place a "Y," "S," or "N" by items a through c:

S		

   _S_ a. Does your child ask for help when uncomfortable, sick, hurt, or tired? (C1.1)

   _Y_ b. Does your child take care of his or her own physical needs? For example, your child washes his or her dirty hands or takes off wet clothes. (C1.2)

   _Y_ c. Does your child ask for or get food or drink when hungry or thirsty? (C1.3)

Note: ? means parents were unable to observe this item.

(continued)

Figure 6.　A portion of the Family Report II, Social Area, Three to Six Years, completed by Jesse's parents.

Figure 6. *(continued)*

8. Does your child follow rules in places outside of his or her home or school? For example, your child follows rules to stay seated during a bus ride or follows directions to not touch food in the grocery store. (C2)

S			

9. Does your child tell you what he or she likes and does not like? For example, your child says, "I love chocolate cake," or "I don't like to play football." (D1)

Y			

10. Does your child understand how his or her behavior affects others? For example, after pushing another child, your child says, "I'm sorry," or your child chooses to play with a child who is alone. (D2) NOTE: Place a "Y," "S," or "N" by items a and b:

S			

  _S_ a. Does your child correctly identify the emotions of others when they are hurt, sad, angry, or happy? (D2.1)

  _S_ b. Does your child correctly identify his or her own emotions when he or she is hurt, sad, angry, or happy? (D2.2)

11. Does your child know personal information about self and others: (D3) NOTE: Place a "Y," "S," or "N" by items a through f:

S			

  _N_ a. Does your child know own address, including number, street, and town? (D3.1)

  _N_ b. Does your child know own telephone number? (D3.2)

  _Y_ c. Does your child know own birthday, including the month and the day? (D3.3)

  _Y_ d. Does your child know brother's and sister's first names *and* own first and last name? (D3.4)

  _Y_ e. Does your child know whether he or she and others are boys or girls? (D3.5)

  _Y_ f. Does your child know own first name and age? (D3.6)

What social skills do you want your child to learn? _____

To play with other children his age.

Table 1. Correspondence between AEPS Test items and IFSP/IEP Goal and Objective Examples for Social Area, Strand A

AEPS Test items	IFSP/IEP Goal and Objective Examples
G2 Initiates cooperative activity	**G2** The child will use verbal or nonverbal strategies to initiate cooperative activities and encourage peer(s) to participate (e.g., the child says, "Come on, let's build a house," to a group of peers).
2.1 Joins others in cooperative activity	**2.1** The child will use socially appropriate verbal or nonverbal strategies to join others engaged in cooperative activities (e.g., the child approaches a group of peers building a sand castle, sits next to them for a while, then begins to help peer who is digging a tunnel).
2.2 Maintains cooperative participation with others	**2.2** The child will maintain jobs, roles, or identities that supplement other children's jobs, roles, or identities during cooperative activities (e.g., the child holds two blocks together while a peer puts a third block on top to build a house).
2.3 Shares or exchanges objects	**2.3** During daily activities, the child will share or exchange objects with others engaged in the same activity (e.g., the child shares a glue bottle with a peer when both are gluing leaves and flowers onto paper).

Note: AEPS Test items taken from Strand A, Social Area, Three to Six Years and IFSP/IEP Goal and Objective Examples taken from Strand A, Social Area, Three to Six Years, Volume 1, Appendix B.

goals/objectives. This process is greatly facilitated when using a CBM tool such as the AEPS. The intervention activities described in the AEPS Curriculum correspond directly to the AEPS Test items, making it straightforward to relate intervention activities for Jesse directly to his selected goals/objectives. For each AEPS Test item, the AEPS Curriculum contains an associated section that lists sample concurrent goals, and provides a series of suggested intervention activities. An AEPS Curriculum page associated with Jesse's selected social goal is shown in Figure 8.

Evaluation. Once intervention has begun, it is essential for Jesse's intervention team to monitor his progress toward the selected IEP goals/objectives. Without systematic documentation of change, interventionists and caregivers cannot determine the effects of the intervention efforts. It is important to conduct both weekly and quarterly evaluations.

Given adequate staff or caregiver time, the use of observational systems to collect weekly child progress data is recommended. Continuing with the example, progress toward Jesse's selected social goal and objectives can be monitored by conducting daily observations at his center-based program and weekly observations at home.

The interventionist can frequently conduct these brief observations by watching Jesse during daily activities, noting his response, and prompting a response if necessary. These data can be plotted on a graph (as shown in Figure 9). Using this or a similar procedure can alert parents and interventionists to when Jesse has met the established criteria for a particular goal/objective. Once the criterion is met, training should begin on the next goal/objective. If, according to specified decision rules,

INTERVENTION PLAN

Child: _Jesse_ Team members/Interventionist: _Ms. Husesta_
Date initiated: _9/02_ Expected date of completion: _12/02_
Type of setting: _x_ Group ____ Individual ____ Home

SOCIAL AREA
Target Goal and Objectives

AEPS Test: Social Area Strand A, Goal 2

Initiates cooperative activity using verbal or nonverbal strategies once a day for 2 weeks. For example, Jesse may say, "It's time to clean up" to a group of friends, assign jobs to be done, and encourage peers to carry them out.

AEPS Test: Objective 2.1

Joins others in cooperative activity using verbal or nonverbal strategies such as requesting items, sitting and watching, and giving objects to peers twice a day for 2 weeks. For example, Jesse approaches group of friends building a sand castle, sits next to them for awhile, then begins to help friend who is digging a tunnel to the castle.

AEPS Test: Objective 2.2

Maintains cooperative participation with others (i.e., maintains job, role, or identity that supplements another's job, role, or identity during a cooperative activity) six times a week for 2 weeks. For example, Jesse's friend may say "You hold these," and Jesse holds two blocks together while his friend puts a third block on top to build a house.

Intervention Strategies and Teaching Considerations

List of strategies that will be used to provide an opportunity for Jesse to practice the targeted goals and objectives	List of possible child behaviors: targeted and expected (+) or nontargeted and unexpected (–)	Consequences or what will be done following Jesse's targeted behaviors (+) or nontargeted behaviors(–)
· Set up activities that require more than one child and the sharing of materials · Model cooperative play by drawing attention to when other children join or initiate · Read stories about children playing together and sharing toys · Encourage Jesse to join or stay in cooperative activities · Ask Jesse to select a friend and an area in which to play · Assign roles or tasks to Jesse and a partner during clean-up	· Initiate (verbally or non-verbally) (+) · Join (verbally or non-verbally) (+) · Maintain (verbally or nonverbally) (+) · Ignore request or model (–) · Grab toys (–) · Walk away when peer extends invitation to play (–)	· Comment on how well children are working on playing together (+) · Smile or praise Jesse (+) · Continue modeling (–) · Make request again or encourage again (–) · Remind Jesse how to initiate/join/maintain cooperative play (–)

Figure 7. Intervention plan for Jesse's priority social goal and associated objectives.

Figure 7.   *(continued)*

Curricular Modifications

1. Start with small group activities (i.e., fewer than four children)
2. Select activities and materials of high interest to Jesse

Child Progress Procedures			
Who	Where	When	How

· Ms. Husesta
· Family
	· Snack
	· Circle
	· Free play
	· Home
		· Once a day at home
		· Twice a day in three
		  different activities
			· Family will keep notes
			  on how Jesse plays
			  with brother
			· Classroom staff will
			  record number of
			  verbal responses

Decision Rule

If adequate progress does not occur in ___3 weeks___ (specify time frame), then
the team will:
_x_ modify intervention strategies
___ modify curricular content (i.e., targeted goals, objectives)
___ other (describe)_____
_____
_____

progress is nonexistent, slow, or variable, then some form of intervention change is likely to be in order.

Re-administration of the AEPS Test and Family Report at 3- to 4-month intervals can provide an important record of Jesse's progress toward his selected IEP goals and overall changes in development. Results for quarterly evaluations can be displayed on a graph as shown in Figure 10.

SUMMARY

The linked system approach to early intervention exemplifies the need to directly relate the processes of assessment, goal development, intervention, and evaluation. Employing such systems allows for efficiency of effort and use of resources, accountability in terms of program impact over time, and individualization through the design of programs specific to the needs of children and their families. Fundamental to the operation of such a system is an assessment/evaluation tool that yields the information necessary to devise appropriate goals, intervention plans, and permits ongoing evaluation. The content, organization, and scoring for the AEPS Test are described in Chapter 3.

STRAND A

Interaction with Others

GOAL 2 Initiates cooperative activity

Objective 2.1 **Joins others in cooperative activity**
Objective 2.2 **Maintains cooperative participation with others**
Objective 2.3 **Shares or exchanges objects**

CONCURRENT GOALS

GM B:2 Bounces, catches, kicks, and throws ball
Cog F Play (all goals)
SC A Social-communicative interactions (all goals)
SC B Production of words, phrases, and sentences (all goals)
Soc B Participation (all goals)

DAILY ROUTINES

Routine events that provide opportunities for children to initiate cooperative activities include the following:

- Circle time

- Snack time

- Unstructured playtime (indoors and outdoors)

Figure 8. Page from the AEPS Curriculum for Three to Six Years, Social Area, Strand A, Goal 2.

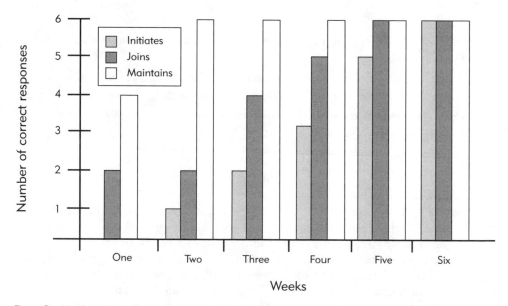

Figure 9. Number of correct responses noted for Jesse's targeted social goal (Initiates cooperative activity) and associated objectives (Joins others in cooperative activity and Maintains cooperative participation with others) during weekly observations.

Summary of AEPS Results

Child's Name: _Jesse_

Date: _____

Test Period 1 = 9/02–10/02
Test Period 2 = 10/02–12/02

For each area, plot the percent correct for each test period (1–4) to determine if the child's performance is improving over time.

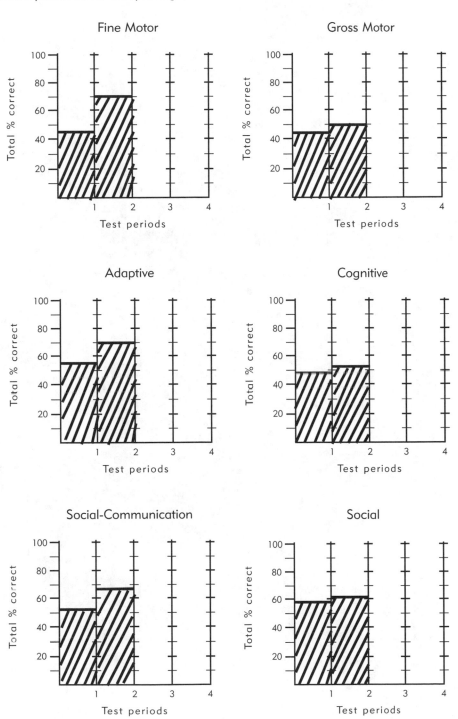

Figure 10.   AEPS Test summary graph for Jesse for two test periods.

3

Administering the AEPS
Content, Organization, and Administration Guidelines

The key to an approach that links assessment, goal development, intervention, and evaluation is a measurement instrument that permits the collection of program-related performance data that can be used to formulate children's IFSPs/IEPs, guide intervention efforts, and monitor child progress. The assessment/evaluation instrument should meet certain recommended practice guidelines to be appropriate for use with infants, toddlers, and preschool children who are at risk for or who have disabilities (e.g., Bagnato & Neisworth, 1991; Bagnato, Neisworth, & Munson, 1997; Bricker, 1989a; McLean & McCormick, 1993). In particular, the instrument should

- Contain content reflective of the philosophy and goals of the intervention program

- Be usable by a range of team members (e.g., interventionists, specialists, families), particularly those who interact with the child on a regular basis in familiar settings

- Offer a logical developmental sequence of items that can be directly linked to intervention content

- Specify a range of performance criteria that indicate if a child has a particular skill and if the skill is a functional part of the child's usual repertoire

- Permit adaptations and modifications for a variety of disabling conditions

- Provide procedures for family participation

- Have reliability and validity data to support its use

The *Assessment, Evaluation, and Programming System for Infants and Children (AEPS)*™ meets these recommended guidelines and provides useful programming and evaluation information. The AEPS Test is a curriculum-based measure (CBM) designed to assist teams in 1) determining a child's present level of functioning, 2) developing meaningful IFSP/IEP goals/objectives,

35

3) planning intervention, and 4) evaluating a child's performance over time. Teams comprised of family members, direct services personnel (e.g., classroom interventionists, home visitors, child care providers, assistants) and specialists (e.g., speech-language pathologists, occupational and physical therapists, psychologists) can use the AEPS Test to assess and evaluate the skills of infants and young children who are at risk for or who have disabilities. The test was specifically developed to link assessment, goal and objective development, intervention, and evaluation activities.

The AEPS Test has two separate developmental levels, Birth to Three Years and Three to Six Years, which cover six broad curricular areas including Fine Motor, Gross Motor, Adaptive, Cognitive, Social-Communication, and Social. Items on the AEPS Test for Birth to Three Years cover the developmental period from birth to 36 months. Items on the AEPS Test for Three to Six Years cover the developmental period from 36 to 72 months. For children with significant delays, the AEPS Test can be used up to age 9. Significant modification may be necessary in the wording of the items and criteria to make items appropriate for a child who is 6 years of age and older.

The AEPS Test has been used successfully with children who have a wide range of diagnoses or conditions, including Down syndrome, cerebral palsy, autism spectrum disorder, seizure disorders, sensory impairments, and general developmental delays. The test has been used successfully with children who are environmentally at risk (e.g., those with adolescent parents, those in foster care). The AEPS Test has also been used successfully with typically developing children in identifying center-based/classroom goals and monitoring children's performance over time as a key part of program evaluation activities.

ADVANTAGES OF THE AEPS TEST

Personnel working with infants, toddlers, and young children who are at risk for or who have disabilities are often frustrated when they use traditional instruments to assess children's development and to measure child progress. Frequently, outcomes from standardized measures are not reflective of a child's actual abilities and do not aid the selection of appropriate intervention goals/ objectives. The progress made by children with disabilities may be slow and gradual, and the increments between items on traditional assessment instruments may not reflect small changes in behavior. Traditional standardized assessments can penalize children with communication, sensory, or motor disabilities by allowing only a single correct response to narrowly framed items. To counter these and other problems in assessing children who are at risk for or who have disabilities, the AEPS Test diverges from other available instruments in a number of ways and presents several advantages:

- The AEPS Test measures functional skills and abilities thought to be essential for young children to function independently and cope with environmental demands. The focus on functional skills and abilities ensures that each test item is potentially an appropriate intervention target.

- The AEPS Test is comprehensive in nature. The content of the AEPS Test covers the major developmental areas of Fine Motor, Gross Motor, Adaptive, Cognitive, Social-Communication, and Social, making it valuable both as an initial assessment tool and in monitoring children's subsequent progress.

- The primary and preferred method of obtaining assessment/evaluation information is through observing the child in familiar and usual environments. This feature of the AEPS Test provides the team with critical information about what responses the child uses in a functional manner and when and how they are used.

- Administration of the AEPS Test is flexible and allows the user to adapt or modify either the presentation format of items or the stated criteria to maximize the child's functional performance; for example, teams are encouraged to use sign language with children with hearing impairments and to allow children with motor impairments to use prosthetics to complete items such as self-feeding. Flexibility in the presentation and in the child's response are acceptable because test results are used primarily to generate appropriate intervention targets for individual children and monitor subsequent progress, not for comparing a child with a normed standard of performance.

- The items on the AEPS Test are written to reflect conceptual or broad response classes rather than the singular, specific responses usually found on standardized tests; for example, an item asks about reaching and grasping rather than the ability to insert pegs in a pegboard.

- The AEPS Test has associated curricula (*AEPS Curriculum for Birth to Three Years* and *AEPS Curriculum for Three to Six Years*). Results from the AEPS Test can be used to locate and select intervention content using the associated curricula.

- A parallel family assessment/evaluation form (Family Report) for both levels is available for caregivers to assess their child and to help promote involvement in the IFSP/IEP and intervention process. In addition, the IFSP/IEP Goal and Objective Examples assists the family in preparing for IFSP/IEP meetings. Asking caregivers to complete an assessment form regarding their child's development clearly conveys that the professional staff considers caregiver knowledge an important contribution to the assessment, goal development, intervention, and evaluation processes.

- An associated set of written IFSP/IEP goal/objective examples for each AEPS Test level are available in Appendix B. These can be used as guides, models, or examples for developing meaningful IFSP/IEP goals/objectives and intervention plans for individual children.

These advantages make the AEPS Test an appealing choice for teams interested in obtaining comprehensive information on children's behavioral repertoires and implementing an approach that links assessment, goal development, intervention, and evaluation.

CAVEATS FOR USING THE AEPS TEST

Several characteristics of the AEPS Test are addressed in anticipation of questions that may arise about administration and interpretation of information gained from the AEPS Test.

1. The AEPS Test was not designed as a normed-based measure but rather as a CBM, which is a type of criterion-referenced measure. The content of CBMs is focused on important functional skills, whereas the content of norm-based tests is focused on skills generally selected because they discriminate between different age groups. Norm-based tests are appropriate to use for comparative purposes (e.g., determining eligibility for services), whereas CBMs are appropriate to use for selecting intervention content. Goals/objectives, as well as intervention content, should be selected by comparing the child's current repertoire against the next appropriate developmental targets; age norms provide little functional information that can be used to determine intervention content. In addition, for children with significant discrepancies between their chronological age and developmental level—which is often true for many children who are at risk and who have disabilities—using age norms to select intervention content is, at best, questionable. Many interventionists, however, would like to use AEPS Test results to corroborate information gathered from standardized, norm-referenced tests to determine a child's eligibility for services. Consequently, in this second edition, tables containing cutoff scores for establishing eligibility for services have been included. The cutoff scores for the Birth to Three and Three to Six levels of the AEPS Test are not age norms and should only be used to assist in corroborating decisions regarding a child's eligibility for services. Use of the AEPS Test results to corroborate eligibility decisions is described in Appendix F of this volume. The procedures used to create the cutoff tables also is explained.

2. Gathering data using the AEPS Test requires an initial time investment. Users of the AEPS Test have found the administration time to vary as a function of 1) familiarity with the test (e.g., the more familiar the assessor is with the AEPS Test, the more quickly assessments can be completed), 2) familiarity with the child (e.g., familiarity with the child's behavioral repertoire speeds administration), and 3) the child's level of functioning (e.g., children with more advanced behavioral repertoires may take longer to assess). Such variations make it difficult to state precise administration time for the AEPS Test. Interventionists familiar with the test and children report that initial assessments require several hours to score the AEPS Test in its entirety, whereas subsequent assessments usually take one quarter of that time. Assessment/evaluation, however, should not be viewed as a discrete activity that can be completed in a predetermined period of time but as a continuous process that occurs across time and situations and allows for a comprehensive developmental profile of a child to be created. Comprehensive, detailed assessments are fundamental to the development of appropriate IFSPs/IEPs and to the quality of subsequent intervention. If IFSPs/IEPs are not based on comprehensive, accurate assessment data, then they will be of questionable value and relevance to children and families.

3. Users of the AEPS Test should be familiar with the content and organization of the instrument. The AEPS Test is not a simple checklist that can be examined briefly prior to its use. The assessor should have read each item and studied its associated criteria and notes. In addition, the user should be familiar with the various data recording forms. Use of the AEPS Test without sufficient preparation may yield inaccurate and misleading results. Hastily completed assessments or evaluations that do not include information about a child's performance across time, activities, materials, people, and settings will yield results that are incomplete and often inaccurate.

4. Individual interventionists can complete the AEPS Test; however, the accuracy and quality of the outcomes will be greatly enhanced if specialists (e.g., communication specialists, occupational therapists, physical therapists) and caregivers participate in the assessment process. It is particularly important to involve a motor specialist if the child has a motor disability, a sensory specialist if the child has a sensory disability (e.g., hearing or visual impairment), and a communication specialist if the child has a communication delay or disorder. Caregivers can provide information about children's skills in the home or other community settings that may not be observed by interventionists or specialists.

CONTENT AND ORGANIZATION OF THE AEPS TEST

Using the AEPS Test allows teams to generate a comprehensive profile of children's behavior in familiar environments. To collect comprehensive information on developmental status, six broad curricular or developmental areas are included: Fine Motor, Gross Motor, Adaptive, Cognitive, Social-Communication, and Social. Each developmental area encompasses a particular set of skills, behaviors, or information that is traditionally seen as related developmental content. Categorization of behavior into areas sometimes results in the somewhat arbitrary placement of skills into one area rather than another (e.g., emergent writing is in the Fine Motor Area rather than the Cognitive Area).

Each developmental area is divided into strands. Table 2 provides an overview of the six areas for both AEPS Test levels along with associated strands. Strands consist of related groups of behaviors organized under a common category; for example, behaviors relating to large muscle movements used in play are grouped in the Play Skills strand of the Gross Motor Area. Each strand contains a series of test items called *goals and objectives*. These items can be used to write IFSPs/IEPs. The objectives represent components of the goals or more discrete skills (i.e., building blocks to the goals) and enable the user to accurately pinpoint a child's developmental level within a specific skill sequence. AEPS Test items within a given strand are sequenced to facilitate the assessment of a child's ability to perform a particular behavior within a developmental sequence of skills.

Whenever possible, strands and goals have been arranged from easier or developmentally earlier skills to more difficult or developmentally more advanced skills. The objectives associated with each goal are arranged in a reverse sequence—that is, generally the most difficult items occur first and the less difficult items follow sequentially. The strands, goals, and objectives were

Table 2. Overview of the areas and strands for the two levels of the AEPS Test

Areas	Birth to Three Strands	Three to Six Strands
Fine Motor	A. Reach, Grasp, and Release B. Functional Use of Fine Motor Skills	A. Bilateral Motor Coordination B. Emergent Writing
Gross Motor	A. Movement and Locomotion in Supine and Prone Position B. Balance in Sitting C. Balance and Mobility D. Play Skills	A. Balance and Mobility B. Play Skills
Adaptive	A. Feeding B. Personal Hygiene C. Undressing	A. Mealtime B. Personal Hygiene C. Dressing and Undressing
Cognitive	A. Sensory Stimuli B. Object Permanence C. Causality D. Imitation E. Problem Solving F. Interaction with Objects G. Early Concepts	A. Concepts B. Categorizing C. Sequencing D. Recalling Events E. Problem Solving F. Play G. Premath H. Phonological Awareness and Emergent Reading
Social-Communication	A. Prelinguistic Communicative Interactions B. Transition to Words C. Comprehension of Words and Sentences D. Production of Social-Communicative Signals, Words, and Sentences	A. Social-Communicative Interactions B. Production of Words, Phrases, and Sentences
Social	A. Interaction with Familiar Adults B. Interaction with Environment C. Interaction with Peers	A. Interaction with Others B. Participation C. Interaction with Environment D. Knowledge of Self and Others

arranged to facilitate test administration; for example, if a child performs a more advanced objective within a sequence of objectives, then the assessment of earlier objectives within the sequence is generally unnecessary. The arrangement also provides a framework for understanding children's behavioral repertoires (i.e., which skills they have mastered, which are emerging, and which will they likely acquire next). There are instances, however, in which associated objectives are of equal difficulty and do not represent a developmental sequence from easier to more difficult. Furthermore, there are instances when a child's behavioral repertoire appears to be uneven (i.e., the child performs a variety of splinter skills). In these cases, assessment of a broader range of items is in order.

The contents of the AEPS Test for Three to Six Years are less hierarchical than that of the Birth to Three Years, reflecting an increase in the influence of individual experience and environmental factors on the preschool child's development. As children approach school age, they show increasing individuality and variability as they learn new skills.

The hierarchical nature of strands, goals, and objectives is shown in Figure 11. The identification system associated with the strands (e.g., A, B, C), goals (e.g., 1, 2, 3), and objectives (e.g., 1.1, 1.2, 1.3) reflects this sequential arrangement and can assist the test user in locating and referring to items. The

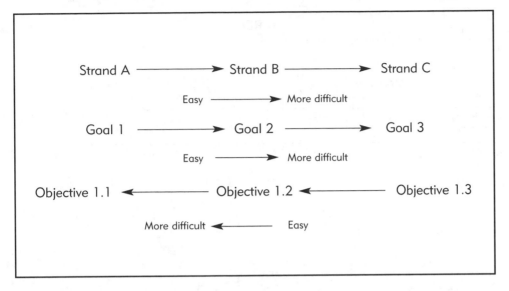

Figure 11.   Hierarchical arrangement of strands, goals, and objectives on the AEPS Test.

organizational structure of the strands, goals, and objectives is presented in Figure 12. Users are encouraged to become familiar with the administration guidelines prior to using the AEPS Test. Test administrations that do not follow the guidelines are likely to be inefficient and may yield inaccurate child performance outcomes. Administration procedures are discussed next.

ADMINISTRATION PROCEDURES

Order of Test Administration

The user can choose to assess one area at a time or assess across areas as items are observed. The latter procedure is more efficient but requires greater familiarity with the AEPS Test. Users may obtain more accurate results by observing and recording information by area for the first few times that the AEPS Test is administered. The user should begin with the first item and observe whether the child meets stated criteria before moving to the next item.

As familiarity with the AEPS Test increases, the user can shift to assessing children across areas; for example, clusters of skills can often be observed during the occurrence of daily activities in the classroom or at home. During large-group time in the classroom, the user may be able to observe cognitive skills (e.g., understanding of concepts, recalling events), gross motor skills (e.g., running, jumping), social skills (e.g., following established rules), and social-communication skills (e.g., using of words and phrases to describe past events). During mealtime at home, the user may be able to observe fine motor skills (e.g., manipulating objects), adaptive skills (e.g., using a knife to spread food, assisting in clearing the table), cognitive skills (e.g., grouping objects on the basis of function), and social skills (e.g., seeking adult permission, meeting physical needs of hunger and thirst). Finally, the more experienced user may

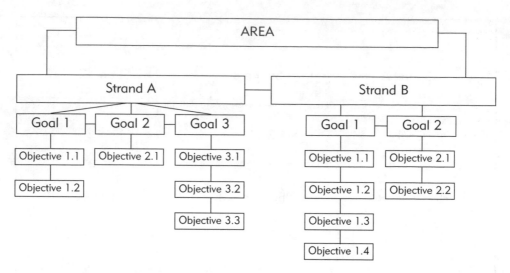

Figure 12. Organizational structure of items on the AEPS Test.

be able to assess several children simultaneously; for example, when three children are engaged in an outside activity, the user may be able to observe and record the social interactions, communication, and play skills of all three children. The AEPS Test provides assessment activities that permit assessment/evaluation of groups of children simultaneously. Procedures for using these activities are described in Volume 2. Appendix A of Volume 2 contains sample Assessment Activities for both AEPS Test levels.

Collecting Assessment and Evaluation Information

The AEPS Test includes three methods of collecting assessment and evaluation information: observation, direct test, and report. Observation is the preferred method. Observation allows the user to view the topography, or form, of the behavior; when and how frequently the behavior is performed; and the environmental factors that may influence the child's performance (e.g., antecedents, consequences). Although observation is the preferred method of data collection, when a user does not have an opportunity to observe a behavior during play or a routine activity, a situation may be created to directly elicit the behavior (i.e., direct test). The third method of obtaining assessment and evaluation is through the use of report. Sources of reported information may be the parents, caregivers, therapists, child care providers, classroom assistants, or written documentation (e.g., evaluation reports, medical reports).

Recording and Scoring Child Performance

The AEPS Test has data recording forms to assist users in assessing initial child performance and recording subsequent change over time. The forms

Table 3.   AEPS data recording forms, locations, primary user(s), and purpose(s) for each form

Form	Location	Primary user(s)	Purpose(s)
Child Observation Data Recording Form		Professional staff	Tracks individual child perfor-mance across four time periods
• I: Birth to Three Years	Vol. 1 Appendix C		
• II: Three to Six Years	Vol. 1 Appendix C		
Social-Communication Observation Form	Vol. 1 Appendix C	Communication specialist	Summarizes child's communica-tion skills to complete portions of the Social-Communication Area of the Child Observation Data Recording Form
Social-Communication Summary Form	Vol. 1 Appendix C		
Family Report		Caregiver and professional staff	Allows caregivers to track their child's performance across four time periods
• I: Birth to Three Years	Vol. 1 Appendix D		
• II: Three to Six Years	Vol. 1 Appendix D		Allows professional staff to ob-tain information from care-givers and in other settings
Child Progress Record		Caregiver and professional staff	Provides visual summary of child's progress on acquisition of goals and objectives
• I: Birth to Three Years	Vol. 1 Appendix E		
• II: Three to Six Years	Vol. 1 Appendix E		
Child Observation Data Recording Form with Criteria		Professional staff	Tracks individual child perfor-mance across four time periods
• I: Birth to Three Years			Forms contain item criteria
• II: Three to Six Years			
Assessment Activities		Professional staff	Permits assessment of multiple children's performance simul-taneously using planned activities
• I: Birth to Three Years	Vol. 2 Appendix A		
• II: Three to Six Years	Vol. 2 Appendix A		

Note: All of these forms, except the Assessment Activities, can be purchased in a packet or on a CD-Rom from Paul H. Brookes Publishing Co. The CD-Rom includes a bonus Child Observation Data Recording Form with Criteria for Birth to Three Years and Three to Six Years.

were designed for different purposes (e.g., monitoring individual child change, monitoring change in groups of children) and for different users (e.g., professional staff, caregivers). Table 3 provides an overview of the six data recording forms and accompanying assessment activities, where they are located, the primary users, and the purpose of each form. All six forms are described next.

Child Observation Data Recording Form

This is the primary form used to record the child's initial performance on the AEPS Test and subsequent performances across test administrations (up to four test periods). This form was designed for use in conjunction with AEPS Test by professional staff and includes each of the six areas for both AEPS Test levels. Space is provided on the cover sheet that accompanies the recording form to indicate the child's name, his or her date of birth, the family's name and address, and the name of the person(s) completing the form. Directions for completing the data recording form are also provided. An example of the recording form for the Gross Motor Area, AEPS Test Three to Six Years is shown in Figure 13. Copies of the Child Observation Data Recording Form for both levels of the AEPS Test are contained in Appendix C of this volume. An explanation of the numbered items on the data recording form shown in Figure 13 follows.

① GROSS MOTOR AREA

② S = Scoring key ③ N = Notes

2 = Consistently meets criterion
1 = Inconsistently meets criterion
0 = Does not meet criterion

A = Assistance provided
B = Behavior interfered
D = Direct test
M = Modification/adaptation
Q = Quality of performance
R = Report

④ Name: _____

⑤ Test period: _____
Test date: _____
Examiner: _____

Strand →
Goal
⑦
Objective →

Refers to adaptation or modification of behavior

⑥	⑧ IFSP/IEP	S	N	S	N	S	N	S	N
A. Balance and Mobility									
1. Runs avoiding obstacles (p. 136)		⑨							
1.1 Runs									
2. Alternates feet walking up and down stairs (p. 136)									
2.1 Walks up and down stairs									
B. Play Skills									
1. Jumps forward (p. 137)									
1.1 Jumps in place									
1.2 Jumps from platform									
1.3 Balances on one foot									
2. Bounces, catches, kicks, and throws ball (p. 137)									
2.1 Bounces ball									
2.2 Catches ball									
2.3 Kicks ball									
2.4 Throws ball									
3. Skips (p. 138)									
3.1 Hops									
4. Rides and steers two-wheel bicycle (p. 138)									
4.1 Pedals and steers two-wheel bicycle with training wheels									

An Area Raw Score can be computed by adding all of the 2 and 1 scores entered in the S column for specific test period. To compute the Area Percent Score: divide the Area Raw Score by the Area Raw Score Possible, then multiply by 100.

RESULTS	⑩ Test date	_____	_____	_____	_____
	Area Raw Score	_____	_____	_____	_____
	Area Raw Score Possible	34	34	34	34
	Area Percent Score	_____	_____	_____	_____

EXAMINER: _____ DATE: _____

⑪ COMMENTS: _____

Figure 13. An example of a Child Observation Data Recording Form II for the Gross Motor Area, Three to Six Years. The page numbers listed after each goal indicate where that particular goal can be found in Volume 2.

1. The developmental area is listed at the top of the Child Observation Data Recording Form.

2. Scoring options used to assess items are listed under the Scoring Key. Numbers are placed in the scoring boxes directly under the S on the data recording form.

3. Scoring note options that further describe a child's performance are listed under Notes. Letters can be placed in the scoring boxes directly under the N on the data recording form.

4. The child's name or initials is recorded on each page.

5. Testing information including the test period (e.g., 1, 2, 3, 4), the date of assessment (i.e., month, year), and the examiner's initials are also recorded on each page.

6. The strands for each area are shaded and appear alphabetically (i.e., A, B, C).

7. The assessment items in abbreviated form are listed below each strand. In addition, the corresponding page number for each goal from Volume 2 is provided for quick references to item criteria and examples.

8. The IFSP/IEP column provides a place to check when an AEPS Test item (goal and/or objective) has been targeted for intervention.

9. Performance data and notes are recorded in the next eight columns (two columns per testing period). Performance data (i.e., 2, 1, 0) are recorded in the box under the S on the form and notes (i.e., A, B, D, M, Q, R) are recorded in the space under the N on the form.

10. AEPS Test results (i.e., Area Raw Score, Area Percent Score) are recorded at the end of each area at the bottom of the form.

11. Additional comments can be written at the end of each area for each test period to provide critical information regarding the circumstances under which a child performed a particular skill.

Scoring the Child Observation Data Recording Form   Items on the AEPS Test are scored with a 2, 1, or 0. When the child consistently meets the criterion as specified in Volume 2, the item is scored 2. Scoring the item with a 2 indicates that the child performs the item independently; that the behavior is a functional part of the child's repertoire; and that the child uses the skill across time, materials, settings, and people. When the child inconsistently meets the criterion, the item is scored 1. Scoring the item with a 1 indicates that the child performs the item with assistance, that the child does not perform all components of the item or does not meet all aspects of the specified criterion (i.e., the behavior is emerging), or that the child performs the item only under specific situations or conditions (i.e., with certain people, in certain settings). When a child does not meet the criterion, the item is scored a 0. Scoring the item with a 0 indicates that the child does not yet perform the item when given repeated opportunities, assistance, or when modifications and adaptations are made, or that the child was not observed performing the item because it is not expected based on knowledge of development (e.g., the

Table 4. Example of how an AEPS Test item would be scored when comparing a child's performance with stated AEPS Test criteria

AEPS Test item and criterion	Score	Child's performance
Goal: **Alternates feet walking up and down stairs**	2	Child independently and consistently walks up and down a variety of stairs alternating feet
Criterion: **Child walks up and down stairs, alternating feet without holding handrail or wall.**	1	Child walks up stairs at home but does not walk up stairs at school or Grandma's house **OR**
	1	Child walks up stairs independently but needs to have help when coming down stairs **OR**
	1	Child does not alternate feet going up or down stairs
	0	Child does not walk up or down stairs with or without assistance

Gross Motor Area, Strand A, Goal 2 from the AEPS Test, Three to Six Years.

child's chronological age is 6 months and he or she would not be expected to perform such items as categorizing similar objects, copying simple shapes, or walking up and down stairs). It is important to ensure that the child has had sufficient opportunities to demonstrate the behavior (i.e., three or more occasions when the behavior could be used) and that modifications and assistance have been provided before scoring an item as 0.

To determine whether the child's response should be scored 2, 1, or 0, specific criteria are provided for each AEPS Test item (i.e., for each goal/objective). It is essential to compare children's performance with each item's criterion before recording a score. Table 4 provides an example of how an item would be scored when comparing a child's performance with stated criteria. If the user must directly test the item, then the child must demonstrate the behavior on at least two out of three trials to receive a score of 2 and one out of three trials to receive a score of 1. Table 5 presents a summary of scoring differences when information is collected through direct test procedures versus observation.

It should be emphasized that arranging antecedent conditions to help elicit responses from children does not necessarily constitute direct testing; for example, placing silverware within a child's reach to assess eating skills is not direct testing. Having available and accessible objects of different colors, sizes, and configurations to assess a child's early concept understanding would not be considered direct testing. Rather, *direct testing* refers to conducting specific trial-by-trial procedures generally apart from routine or play activities in which specific and direct antecedents are given; for example, the child is repeatedly shown a set of pictures and asked to name them.

Adding Notes to the Child Observation Data Recording Form   In addition to the three-option scoring codes, notes are provided to allow users to record other important information about a child's performance on AEPS Test items; for example, a child may use adaptive equipment such as a communication board to perform an item of labeling objects and events. Because the child can demonstrate the concept of labeling independently and consistently, the item is scored 2, but it is also scored with a note (i.e., M = modification/

Table 5.   Scoring guidelines for observation and direct test procedures

Score	Description of performance
Observation	
2 = Consistently meets criterion	Child consistently performs the item as specified in the criterion. Child performs the item independently. Behavior is a functional part of the child's repertoire. Child uses the skill across time, materials, settings, and people.
1 = Inconsistently meets criterion	Child does not consistently perform the item as specified in the criterion. Child performs the item with assistance. Child does not perform all components of the item or does not meet all aspects of the specified criterion (i.e., the behavior is emerging). Child performs the item only under specific situations or conditions (i.e., with certain people or in certain settings).
0 = Does not meet criterion	Child does not yet perform the item as specified in the criterion when given repeated opportunities or assistance or when modifications and adaptations are made. Child was not observed performing the item because it is not expected based on knowledge of development (e.g., the child's chronological age is 6 months and he or she would not be expected to perform such items as categorizing similar objects, copying simple shapes, or walking up and down stairs).
Direct test	
2 = Consistently meets criterion	Child performs the item as specified in the criterion on at least two out of three trials. Child performs the item independently on two out of three trials. Child uses the skill on two out of three trials across time, materials, settings, and people.
1 = Inconsistently meets criterion	Child performs the item as specified in the criterion on one out of three trials. Child performs the item with assistance on one out of three trials. Child performs only portions of the item or certain aspects of the specified criterion on one out of three trials. Child performs the item under one situation or one set of conditions.
0 = Does not meet criterion	Child does not yet perform the item as specified in the criterion on zero out of three trials when assistance is provided or when modifications and adaptations are made. Child was not observed performing the item because it is not expected based on knowledge of development (e.g., the child's chronological age is 6 months and he or she would not be expected to perform such items as categorizing similar objects, copying simple shapes, or walking up and down stairs); thus, no trials are given.

adaptation in this case). Notes alert teams to important information that should be considered when interpreting AEPS Test information, designing subsequent intervention plans, and conducting future evaluations. Modifications of items for children with disabilities is encouraged; however, when such modifications occur, they should be noted. A description of the six notes and associated scoring guidelines is contained in Table 6.

Table 6. Notes, definitions, and scoring guidelines

Note	Definitions and scoring guidelines
A	**Assistance provided** When a child is provided with some form of *assistance*, an A should be noted in the space next to the performance score box. If assistance is provided, then the only scores allowed are 1 and 0 because a score of 2 indicates full independent performance. Assistance includes any direct verbal or physical prompt, cue, or model that assists the child in initiating or performing the desired behavior. A general direction given to the child to initiate the behavior is not considered assistance. For example, the directive, "Put on your coat" is not considered assistance, but physically holding out the coat and helping the child insert his or her arms is assistance for the AEPS Test item Puts on Front-Opening Garment.
B	**Behavior interfered** At times, a child's *behavior* may interfere with the demonstration of the desired skill. In such cases, the item may be scored 1 or 0 with a B noted next to the performance score. This note indicates that the child may have the skill, but disruptive or noncompliant behavior interfered with its demonstration.
D	**Direct test** When the examiner *directly elicits* a behavior, a D is noted next to the performance score and the guidelines for determining the score presented in Table 5 should be followed.
M	**Modification/adaptation** At times, an examiner may need to *modify* the stated criteria (e.g., rate or mode of response) or *adapt* the environment/materials (e.g., adaptive equipment is necessary) to assess children with sensory or motor disabilities. When *modifications* are made in gathering child performance information, an M is noted next to the performance score and a 2, 1, or 0 is used.
Q	**Quality of performance** At times, a child is able to perform a skill independently, but the team feels the *quality of the performance* hinders the ability to meet criteria. At other times, a child is able to meet or partially meet the stated criteria, but the team wishes to continue strengthening the quality of performance. When the quality of the performance is in question, teams are encouraged to use a Q in the notes accompanied by a score of 2 or 1.
R	**Report** When an item is assessed by *report*, an R is noted next to the performance score. Report is used under one of three conditions: • When assessment information is collected by another person or documented source (e.g., written evaluation), the item is scored 2, 1, or 0, and an R is noted. • When the item is judged inappropriate because it assesses a primitive or developmentally easier response (e.g., sucking on a nipple when the child is able to drink from a cup), the item is scored 2 and an R is noted. • When the item is judged inappropriate because it is too advanced or beyond the child's developmental level (e.g., walking when the child is unable to stand), the item is scored 0 and an R is noted.

Social-Communication Forms

The Social-Communication Area of the AEPS requires special attention be paid to how children communicate with others and that additional information be collected primarily through language samples and language observations. In particular, comprehensive information on children's communication is needed to score Strands B and D of Birth to Three Years and Strand B of Three to Six Years. Two forms were created to assist professional staff in scoring these strands of the Social-Communication Area: Social-Communication Observation Form (SCOF) and Social-Communication Summary Form (SCSF). How to gather information about children's communication and how to use these forms is described in the following sections. These forms are found directly following the Social-Communication Area of the Child Observation

Data Recording Form for Birth to Three Years and Three to Six Years in Appendix C of this volume.

The purpose of collecting and recording a sample of a child's communicative behavior is to determine how the child typically communicates, both verbally and nonverbally. Language sampling and *observation* techniques allow the assessment of a child's comprehension and production of words and sentences, communicative functions and intentions, and interactions with the social environment. Following are guidelines for collecting samples of communicative behavior. Be sure that the observation is typical or representative of the way that the child usually communicates.

1. **Become familiar with the child.** Get to know the child before you record a sample of communicative behavior. Children usually do not communicate at the same frequency or in the same way with strangers as they do with familiar people. It is not always possible to establish rapport with a child in an hour or even in a day or two. Allow several days, if necessary, before recording a communication sample, and allow time for the child to warm up at the beginning of an *observation* session before you begin to record the child's communicative behavior. The extra time invested will yield more accurate and useful information for programming.

2. **Collect several communicative samples.** Collect three or four short samples (e.g., 10–20 minutes) of the child's communicative behavior over several days in several settings, rather than one long sample in a single setting. The frequency of communicative responses may differ greatly for children at different times and under different conditions. Even several recording sessions may not yield an adequate sample of behavior for those children who use language infrequently. Make an effort to collect at least 50 separate communicative utterances (e.g., 50 vocalizations, 50 gestures, 50 single words, 50 word combinations) for a single child. If two of the total number of samples recorded are collected in similar settings (e.g., two free-play activities with the same materials and same children present), then the sample should appear similar in frequency of words and phrases used and in the forms used by the child. If the two samples are not similar, then collect a third sample in the same setting to determine which of the samples is more representative of the way that the child usually communicates in that setting. Samples collected in different settings may differ in frequency of word and phrase use and in form use and may accurately reflect the child's typical performance in each respective setting; for example, most children communicate differently with adults than with peers. Hence, a child might use shorter, less complex language with a younger sibling in one setting than with a parent in another setting, yet both samples of behavior are accurate and representative. The task is to determine how the child communicates in a variety of settings typical for the child.

3. **Select routine and familiar settings and materials.** Settings used for sampling communicative behavior should be familiar to the child (e.g., a free-play activity in the classroom, a parent–child or sibling–child dyad versus a structured activity with one adult and one child in a therapy room). Ma-

terials and activities should be centered around play with age-appropriate toys or around usually occurring activities (e.g., eating, dressing). Adult-directed classroom activities will probably not yield an accurate picture of how well the child usually communicates. Some materials that may encourage social-communicative interactions include dish sets, dress-up clothes, water and sand, and toy buildings with people and vehicles.

4. **Techniques for interacting with children.** While taking the sample, you may interact with the child or you may observe the child's interactions with another adult or peer. In addition to verbatim recording at the time of the interaction, audiotaping and videotaping may be useful for the collection and analysis of the child's communicative behavior. Children who use rudimentary gestures may be videotaped so that the context of their communicative behaviors can be observed, the meanings of the gestures inferred, and the patterns of interactions between the child and the environment discerned. Verbatim recording can be employed for children who use a formalized system such as American Sign Language or a communication board. Each word that the child signs or points to should be written down just as if the child used the word verbally.

Allow the child to direct the activity and interactions. You may find it helpful at the beginning of the sampling to engage in play alongside the child while you describe your actions, the actions of your toys, and occasionally the actions of the child in a monologue fashion. Frequent, prolonged pauses will allow the child opportunities to request objects or actions, participate in your activity, or talk about the activity. Avoid questions that require only a yes/no or single-word response, a manual gesture, or a head shake (e.g., adult asks, "Doggie outside?" and the child nods head affirmatively; adult asks, "Where is the doggie?" and the child says, "Outside"). Listen to what the child says, and base your responses on the content of the child's verbal and gestural behavior.

A Note on Bilingual Language Learners   Young children from bilingual homes or who are learning English as a second language should always be assessed for comprehension in both languages and, if possible, in multiple settings. Children may use the family's native language predominantly at home and English at a center-based program, even if they have more sophisticated skills in the native language. An accurate measure of comprehension, therefore, includes presenting AEPS Test items in any language to which the child is regularly exposed.

To assist in the collection and summary of social-communicative data, an observation and a summary form are provided for both levels of the AEPS. Directions for using these forms are described next.

Birth to Three Years Social-Communication Observation Form   The SCOF for Birth to Three Years was designed to assist in the collection of data on children's prelanguage and language responses that can be used to complete Strands B and D of the Social-Communication Area of the Child Observation Data Recording Form. The SCOF is composed of two sections: I—Transition to Words and II—Production of Social-Communicative Signals, Words, and Sentences. A copy of the SCOF can be found in Appendix C of this volume following the Social-Communication Area of the Child Observation Data Recording Form.

Section I: Transition to Words (Strand B)   Use this section of the SCOF to record the child's gestures and vocalizations that are not words or word approximations. Record each occurrence of the child's gestures and vocalizations by entering a hash mark (/) in the appropriate box on the recording form. Use the column designated "Interpretable," "Partially Interpretable," or "Not Interpretable," depending on whether the general meaning of the child's gesture and/or vocalization is understandable. If the gesture or vocalization is interpretable or partially interpretable, then make a hash mark in the appropriate box under "Communicative Function" on the recording form, depending on how the child used the gesture or vocalization to communicate (e.g., gain attention, refer to an object, greet). If the communicative function of a vocalization or gesture is not apparent, then do not score the box under "Communicative Function." For specific examples of communicative functions, refer to the Social-Communication Area, Strand B, Goal 1 through Objective 1.4 of the AEPS Test.

Interpretable Signals: If the child's communicative intention is apparent to the other participant in the communicative interaction, then the communication should be noted as an Interpretable Signal. For example,

- Child reaches for juice when asked, "Do you want juice?" and adult hands juice to child (Interpretable Gesture, Responds to Questions).

- Child makes a negative noise and turns away when offered food (Interpretable Vocalization/Gesture, Protests/Refuses).

Partially Interpretable Signals: If the child's communicative intention is not completely understood by the other participant in the communicative interaction, then the communication should be noted as a Partially Interpretable Signal. For example,

- Child points to a shelf with many toys on it but does not point to one specific toy (Partially Interpretable Gesture, Refers to Objects/People).

- Child looks at adult and vocalizes using a rising pitch that sounds question-like, but the adult does not understand what the child wants (Partially Interpretable Vocalization, function is not scored).

Not Interpretable Signals: If the child's vocalizations and gestures are not understood by an observer or a participant in an interaction with contextual cues, then the communication should be noted as a Non Interpretable Signal. For example,

- Child approaches adult and vocalizes, but the adult does not understand the meaning of the child's vocalization (Not Interpretable Vocalization, function is not scored).

- Child makes eye contact with adult and bangs on table (Not Interpretable Gesture, function is not scored).

Section II: Production of Social-Communicative Signals, Words, and Sentences (Strand D)   Use this section of the SCOF to record verbatim the child's understandable word approximations and word combinations and the context in which they occur. Information that should be recorded in the context column of the SCOF includes brief descriptions of objects and events that occur immediately before, during, or immediately following the child's verbalization. Information recorded should be comprehensive enough to allow interpretation of the child's words and sentences, but it should not be so detailed that it interferes with the accurate recording of the child's responses. If portions of the child's phrases or sentences are not understandable, then use a line in place of the word or words that you do not understand (e.g., child says, "Me go _," or "_doggy").

A section is included on the SCOF to record the communicative function of the signal used by the child (i.e., initiation, response to a comment, response to a question, imitation). An additional column is included for recording child responses that are inappropriate (e.g., responses that do not relate to the topic or situation or are repetitive or perseverative). A checkmark should be recorded in the appropriate column at the time that the child's response is recorded. As soon as possible after recording the child's communicative behavior, review the sample of recorded words and word combinations on the SCOF and score the SCSF.

A note on bilingual language learners: Young children acquiring more than one language simultaneously learn vocabulary without distinguishing between languages. The number of words in a child's vocabulary, therefore, should be counted as the total number of words or word approximations that the child is using in both languages. This principle holds for toddlers learning English as a second language, as well as for children from bilingual or multilingual homes. Typically developing children do not reliably and consistently sort languages into separate systems until they acquire cognitive skills of categorization and classification, usually after their third birthday.

Birth to Three Social-Communication Summary Form   The purpose of the SCSF is to provide a summary of the child's social-communicative behavior from the sample of prelanguage and language responses that were collected and recorded on the SCOF. The sample of behavior recorded on the SCOF should be reviewed and the SCSF completed as soon as possible after the child's communicative behavior is collected. Directions for scoring the SCSF are described next. The summarized information contained on the SCSF can be used to complete Strands B and D of the Social-Communication Area of the Child Observation Data Recording Form. The SCSF can be found in Appendix C of this volume.

Section I: Transition to Words (Strand B)   Transfer the data from the SCOF to the summary form using the following directions:

1. Total the number of hash marks from each separate box under the section labeled "Communicative Signal" on the SCOF, and enter the totals in the

appropriate boxes labeled Interpretable Gestures, Partially Interpretable Gestures, and Not Interpretable Gestures on the SCSF.

2. Add the total number of gestures from each category (Interpretable, Partially Interpretable, Not Interpretable), and enter that total in the space labeled "Total Gestures."

3. Enter the total number of Interpretable Gestures from the observation form in the boxes labeled "Interpretable Gestures" on the SCSF.

4. Divide the total number of Interpretable Gestures by the total number of Gestures. Multiply that number by 100 to determine the percentage of the child's gestures that are understood by others.

5. Repeat Steps 1–4 for Vocalizations and Vocalizations/Gestures.

6. Use the information from the boxes in the section labeled Communicative Function on the SCOF to score individual items on the Social-Communication Area of the Child Observation Data Recording Form. Each category (Gains Attention, Responds to Questions, Refers to Objects/People, Greets, and Protests/Refuses) directly corresponds to an item in Strand B, Goal 1 through Objective 1.4.

Section II: Production of Social-Communicative Signals, Words, and Sentences (Strand D)   Record the frequency with which specific types of word approximations, words, and word combinations occur by entering a hash mark in the appropriate space on the SCSF. Some word combinations will be scored in more than one space (e.g., a two-word descriptive utterance also will be scored in the space for single descriptive words and single object and/or event labels). For example:

*   If the child says, "My shoe," then enter one mark in the space labeled Objective 2.2 "Two-word possession" (my), one mark in the space labeled Objective 1.3 "Pronouns" (my), and one mark in the space labeled Objective 1.4 "Object/event labels" (shoe).

*   If the child says, "Go car," then enter one mark in the space labeled Objective 2.1 "Action–object" (go car), one mark in the space labeled Objective 1.2 "Action words" (go), and one mark in the space labeled Objective 1.4 "Object/event labels" (car).

For additional examples of individual items, see Strand D, Goals 1, 2, and 3 and associated objectives. Each labeled space on the SCSF directly corresponds to an item on the AEPS Test. Use the frequencies recorded on the SCSF to score all goals/objectives in Strands B and D on the Social-Communication Area of the Child Observation Data Recording Form I: Birth to Three Years.

Three to Six Years Social-Communication Observation Form   Specific directions for recording social-communicative behavior using the SCOF are described in the following sections. Directions correspond to items on the Social-Communication section of the Child Observation Data Recording Form for Strand B of the AEPS Test for Three to Six Years.

Use the SCOF to record verbatim the child's word approximations and word combinations and the context in which they occurred. The child's name and a brief description of the activities in which the language sample was collected should be indicated at the top of the SCOF. The amount of time that each language sample took should also be recorded. It may also be helpful to indicate on the form when the activity changed; for example, if utterances 1–11 were recorded during snack time (15-minute activity) and then utterances 12–22 were recorded during circle time (10-minute activity). Then, an asterisk could be placed at numbers 12 and 23 to indicate a change in activity. This information may be useful when interpreting the results.

When using the SCOF, record verbatim in longhand all child communications. For spoken responses, begin a new line each time the child begins a new utterance. A new utterance occurs when the child addresses a new person, when the child pauses for at least 2 seconds, or when the child uses intonation that signals the end of an utterance. If you cannot understand a word that the child says, then use the letter "u" in place of the unintelligible word. Information recorded in the column under the heading Context includes brief descriptions of objects and events that occur immediately before, during, or immediately after the child's communication. Information recorded should permit accurate interpretation of the child's words and sentences but it should not be so detailed that it interferes with the accurate recording of the child's communication. Under the Functions heading are columns that provide space to note the way that the child's communication was used in relation to others. The headings include Initiation, to indicate that the child initiated an appropriate topic; Response to Comment, to indicate that the child responded to another's comment with a related comment; Response to Question, to indicate that the child responded to a question with a related answer; Imitation, to indicate that the child repeated another person's words or sentences; and Unrelated, to indicate that the child's response appeared to be unrelated to the activity or conversational context.

If time permits after you record each utterance, and if the function of the utterance is clear, then place a checkmark in the appropriate columns to the right of the recorded utterance, indicating the function that the child's utterance served. If the frequency of the child's utterances makes it difficult to check and record the type and the actual utterance, then it is more important to concentrate on recording the actual utterance word for word. Many times a lull in the conversation later in the session will allow you to return to categorize the child's utterances. If you are not sure about the function and/or meaning of a child's utterance, then leave the column blank.

Three to Six Years Social-Communication Summary Form   After recording a child's language on the SCOF, the language samples may be analyzed so that the AEPS Test items in Strand B can be compared with specific criteria and scored.

The SCSF is completed by reviewing each utterance for its categorization; for example, if the child's first utterance was, "I'm going outside," then hash marks would be placed next to Item 4.1: Uses subject pronouns (for the word "I" in "I'm"); next to 1.2: Uses copula verb "to be" (for the "am" part of "I'm"); next to 1.6: Uses present progressive "ing" (for the verb "going"); and next to 5.3: Uses adverbs (for the word "outside"). The number of tally marks per objective does not translate directly to a score (i.e., 0, 1, 2). The number of tally marks should be compared with the specific item criterion listed on the item page in Volume 2. As the complexity of the child's language increases, it may become difficult to categorize some words; for example, the word "outside" can be a noun, adjective, adverb, or preposition depending on its use. Resources such as a dictionary or basic English grammar text can be of help in categorizing language. If there is a speech-language pathologist on the child's team, then this portion of the AEPS should be analyzed in conjunction with him or her.

After an adequate number of utterances (at least 50 separate utterances) have been categorized on the SCSF, the information can be used to score Strand B of the Social-Communication Area of the Child Observation Data Recording Form. The AEPS Test should be consulted and individual item criteria should be compared with data from the SCSF when determining an item's score.

Family Report

The Family Report was developed to obtain information from parents and other caregivers about their children's skills and abilities across major areas of development. The Family Report is divided into two sections. Section 1 is designed to help gather information from families regarding their daily routines and the child's participation in family activities. Section 2 of the Family Report has items that parallel AEPS Test items. As shown in Table 7, items in Section 2 of the Family Report are simply reworded statements that correspond directly to each goal (and in some cases, each objective) from the corresponding AEPS Test level. The Family Report provides spaces to enter data across four test intervals and a space for caregivers to enter priority goals for their child. Caregivers are asked to score each item on Section 2 of the Family Report by selecting one of three responses that most accurately describes their child's current level of functioning: "yes," "sometimes," and "not yet." Professional staff can translate caregiver's scores to 2, 1, and 0 if they prefer. If caregivers are unable to observe an item, then a question mark can be inserted in the box. Caregivers should be informed that they should not expect their child to perform all of the skills listed on the form and be encouraged to observe their child in situations that are likely to elicit each skill before scoring items they are not sure about. Discussion of how to use the Family Report; the importance of including caregivers in the initial assessing and subsequent monitoring of their child's progress; and how to actively involve families in the assessment, goal development, intervention, and evaluation process are contained in Chapter 5 of this volume. Copies of the Family Report for both levels of the AEPS are contained in Appendix D of this volume.

Child Progress Record

The Child Progress Record was developed to monitor individual children's progress over time. The simplicity of the form makes it appropriate for use by caregivers or professional staff. Each AEPS Test age level has a Child Progress Record. Figure 14 contains a portion of Strand A from the Fine Motor Area of

Table 7. Examples of AEPS Test items and corresponding Family Report items from the AEPS Test: Three to Six Years

	AEPS Test items	Family Report items
Area	Social	Social
Strand	A: Interaction with Others	
Item	Goal 1: Interacts with others as play partners	1. Does your child play with other children? (A1)
Strand	D: Knowledge of Self and Others	
Item	Goal 1: Communicates personal likes and dislikes	9. Does your child tell you what he or she likes and does not like? For example, your child says, "I love chocolate cake," or "I don't like to play football." (D1)

the Child Progress Record I: Birth to Three Years. As children meet the stated criteria for a goal (ovals) or objective (arrows), progress can be indicated by striking or shading through the particular skill. Teams often signify a child's specific performance by shading arrows and ovals completely when scored 2, partially or with stripes when scored 1, and leaving ovals and arrows blank when scored 0. Teams may also use an asterisk to signify which skills are targeted for intervention or may use different colors to signify different levels of performance. The Child Progress Record provides caregivers with a visual record of the child's accomplishments, current targets, and future goals/objectives.

The Child Progress Record can be updated quarterly in conjunction with subsequent administrations of the AEPS Test. For children with severe disabilities, teams may wish to add items to the Child Progress Record by scaling back the objectives to smaller, more discrete targets. Copies of the Child Progress Record for both levels of the AEPS are contained in Appendix E of this volume.

Child Observation Data Recording Form with Criteria

The Child Observation Data Recording Form with Criteria serves the same purpose as the Child Observation Data Recording Form described previously.

FINE MOTOR AREA

Strand A: Reach, Grasp, and Release

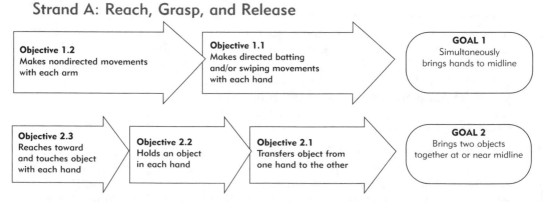

Figure 14.   A portion of the Fine Motor Area of the Child Progress Record I: Birth to Three Years.

It is for use by professional staff but can be made available to interested caregivers. All AEPS Test items have associated criteria in abbreviated form. The Child Observation Data Recording Form with Criteria differs from the Child Observation Data Recording Form in that the criteria for each item is included on the data form itself for easy reference. However, items are scored in the same manner (i.e., by using 2, 1, 0 for scores and A, B, D, M, Q, or R for notes). Although this form requires considerably more paper, it releases personnel from frequent referral to Volume 2 and helps to ensure that children's performance is compared with the stated criterion each time. This form is available on CD-Rom and can be purchased separately from the publisher.

Assessment Activities

A set of Assessment Activities were developed to assist professional staff when information is needed across multiple developmental areas and for multiple children. Assessment Activities have been developed for use with both levels of the AEPS Test and are described in Appendix A of Volume 2. Each activity is composed of a set of events designed to elicit an array of skills (i.e., AEPS Test items) from groups of children; for example, a sandbox activity may provide the team the opportunity to assess a variety of fine motor skills (e.g., grasping and releasing), social skills (e.g., sharing toys), communication skills (e.g., asking for an object), gross motor skills (e.g., walking to the sand box), cognitive skills (e.g., finding a buried toy), and adaptive skills (e.g., washing hands after leaving the sand box) across three to five children. Each assessment activity lists the AEPS Test items by area and strand that can be observed during the activity in the order that they are likely to be observed if the script is followed. Groups of children can be assessed during a period of several days by organizing assessment stations. A different activity can be conducted at each station and small groups of children can rotate from station to station throughout the day. The activities conducted at each station should be designed to ensure that target goals/objectives occur frequently. It is important to remember that modification in plans and format will be likely if the individual needs of children are to be met.

Administration Guidelines

The AEPS Test has six developmental areas, each composed of a series of test items designated as goals and their associated objectives. Although no specific sequence for administration is mandated, several guidelines should be considered when administering the AEPS Test. Additional strategies for data collection are described in Chapter 4 of Volume 2.

Guideline 1: All goals should be assessed and scored. Users are not required to assess and score all areas of the AEPS Test, but when a deficit area(s) has been identified the user should gather information and score all associated goals; for example, if information about a child's development is needed from the Fine Motor and Adaptive Area, then all goals from the two areas should be assessed and scored.

A strategy for reducing administration time is to review items in areas of interest and eliminate the need to assess goals that are clearly below and above a child's development level. These items may be scored without observing or directly testing the items; for example, if a child is observed walking and running, then there is no need to observe or directly test the child's ability to perform earlier developmental items such as rolling over or pulling to a stand. Likewise, if a child is just beginning to hold up his or her head, then there is no need to assess his or her ability to kick a ball. Instead, the user may score the item that is below the child's current developmental level (or that they mastered previously) a 2 in the score (S) column and an R in the scoring notes (N) column. Items that are significantly above the child's developmental level can be scored a 0 in the score (S) column and an R in the scoring notes (N) column. Because the behavioral repertoires of children with disabilities are often uneven, it may be advisable to gather information (e.g., conduct observations and conversations with others) on all goals that appear to be above the child's present level of functioning.

Guideline 2: If a goal is scored as 0 or 1, then all associated objectives should be assessed and scored. If the child does not perform a goal (indicated by a score of 0) or if the child inconsistently performs the goal as stated in the criterion (indicated by a score of 1), then it is necessary to determine the level at which the child is able to consistently and independently perform associated objectives; for example, if the child is not yet able to dress and undress (an AEPS Test goal from the Adaptive Area), then it is necessary to determine where in the sequence of related skills the child is able to consistently perform (indicated by a score of 2). Failure to assess the objectives under a goal that has been scored 0 or 1 does not give the child credit for mastering small increments of skills, nor does it provide a comprehensive picture of the child's strengths. As with goals that are clearly below or above a child's developmental level, users can score objectives as 0 or 2 by report as long as this is indicated in the scoring note column with an R.

Guideline 3: The three-point scoring options (2, 1, 0) should be used with all items scored. AEPS Test items that were assessed (i.e., information collected through observation, direct test, and report) should be scored using the three-point scoring options (i.e., 2, 1, 0). Using a consistent coding system enhances interpretation of findings across interventionists and programs. A consistent coding system also enhances a team's ability to interpret changes in a child's development over time.

Guideline 4: When items are directly tested or information is obtained through report, corresponding scoring notes should be so indicated on the Child Observation Data Recording Form. Most items should be assessed through observation and may not, therefore, have any accompanying note. In order to discriminate among those items assessed through observation and those through direct test or report, the user should add either D or R when appropriate, under the N column on the Child Observation Data Recording Form. The use of two or more scoring notes may be appropriate at times.

Assessment and Evaluation Procedural Modifications

Standardized tests require that items be presented following a specified format and that responses also meet specific criteria. The AEPS Test was designed to be used with children who are at risk for or who have disabilities, many of whom will not be able to respond to a standard presentation or produce a typical response. Rather than penalize children who are unable to respond as do children who are typically developing, the AEPS Test encourages modifications or adaptations to items that will increase the likelihood that the child will be successful. It is more important that the child communicates than it is for the child to communicate in a specific manner. It is more important that the child develops mobility skills than he or she learns to move following a set pattern that may be unattainable. In particular, children with sensory and motor disabilities may require modifications to successfully perform test items.

The AEPS Test allows teams to modify the materials, child's position, or administration procedures for all items. Teams are encouraged to use adaptive equipment (e.g., a built-up spoon), adaptive positions (e.g., positioned over a wedge), or special procedures (e.g., providing photographs for a child with autism to use when making choices of what to eat and drink for snack). It is important for the user to accurately record the types of modifications that are used in order for future evaluations to be valid. Without indicating the types of adaptations that occurred, accurately monitoring child progress is not possible. When modifications are made, the user should place the note M in the N column next to the performance score and indicate the modification used in the Comments section at the end of each Area.

Teams will find that they are able to use the AEPS Test in determining strengths and emerging skills even for children with severe disabilities. Interventionists have the option of using the AEPS Test objectives as goals and developing new, simpler objectives to meet the adjusted goals. Alternatively, teams working with children who are chronologically 3–6 years old may find it necessary to use items from the AEPS Test for Birth to Three Years in determining a child's current level of functioning. Finally, for children whose chronological age exceeds 6 years, items should be carefully evaluated to ensure their appropriateness.

A useful and accurate child assessment and evaluation will be obtained by employing a team of professionals whenever possible. It is particularly important to consult and involve a specialist when children have motor or sensory impairments. Specialists are mandatory when assessing and evaluating children with severe and multiple disabilities.

General test modification guidelines are provided for three types of disabilities: visual impairments, hearing impairments, and motor impairments.

Visual Impairments

- When working with children with limited functional vision, the examiner should present each stimulus item within the child's field of vision (the visual field will need to be established for each child). It may be necessary to move objects close to the child; however, a large object placed too close may fill the child's entire visual field and obscure distinguishing features.

- The examiner should attend to the background-foreground contrast when evaluating a child with a visual impairment; for example, if working at a table with a dark surface, then lighter color objects should be used.

- Objects that provide more than one type of sensory feedback to the child, such as sound- or light-producing objects and tactilely interesting materials should be used. Objects that have high visual contrast (e.g., black, white, red, fluorescent orange) may be useful to maximize the child's residual vision.

- A child who cannot see certain materials should be made aware of all materials through physical contact with the objects. Guiding a child's hand over objects to be grasped, for example, may assist the child's performance of the task. The child may not be aware of the desired behavior because there has been no prior visual experience with the object or task. Physical manipulation of the child through the movements will provide a model of the desired behavior and may give needed kinesthetic feedback to perform the task.

Hearing Impairments

- Positioning the child is critical for optimal use of sensory information. The examiner should ensure that the child is facing the speaker and is in a proper position to see lips, gestures, or signs.

- If the child wears a hearing aid, then the examiner should make certain that the aid is operating at the optimal level.

- The examiner must know the communication system of the child and be able to respond appropriately (e.g., understand and use sign language).

Motor Impairments

- The child with a motor impairment may have difficulty sequencing motor behaviors and may reverse steps in a sequence; for example, when requested to imitate a series of motor behaviors, the child may have difficulty either producing all of the actions or correctly sequencing the actions. The examiner may need to assist the child (through cues or prompts) to remember what behavior is next in the sequence.

- The use of adaptive equipment or alterations in the types of objects used may be beneficial for the child. A physical or occupational therapist should be consulted when selecting adaptive equipment.

- When attempting to complete a task, if the child's movements appear awkward, unstable, or uncoordinated, then the child may benefit from positioning equipment (e.g., specialized chair, wedges, pillows).

- The child's environment may require alteration to facilitate movement and allow the child to function more independently (e.g., stairs replaced by ramps, hand railing placed by toilets).

Criterion Modifications

Modifications in stated criteria are also allowed and encouraged. In other words, to best represent a child's performance and individual needs, teams may modify the standard criteria for acceptable child performance (e.g., change the rate or manner of response). The criteria for Gross Motor Area, Strand C, Goal 1, Walks avoiding obstacles, states "When walking unsupported, child moves to avoid obstacles (e.g., toys, furniture, people)." The criteria may be changed to "When using a wheelchair, child moves to avoid obstacles," allowing a child with a motor disability to demonstrate mobility and locomotion. The goal, Uses 50 single words can be changed to Uses 50 single signs for a child who uses sign language as his or her primary mode of communication.

Summarizing Assessment Information

Using the information obtained from the AEPS Test to develop an appropriate IFSP/IEP for a child is an important activity to be accomplished prior to beginning intervention. The development of IFSPs/IEPs from AEPS Test information is described in Chapter 4; however, before developing an IFSP/IEP, a child's performance should be summarized following the administration of the AEPS Test. The AEPS Test permits summarization of results numerically, by narrative, and visually. Each summary strategy is discussed next.

Numerical Summary

The most commonly computed score is a raw score for each of the six areas. To obtain an Area Raw Score, all of the items on which the child received a 2 and a 1 are summed and recorded at the end of each area on the Child Observation Data Recording Form. Interventionists may also want to calculate a child's Total Raw Score. A Total Raw Score is computed by counting all of the items scored with 2s and 1s **across** all six developmental areas; for example, if a child received a total of 330 when all of the scores of 2 and 1 are added across areas, then the child's Total Raw Score is 330. Table 8 indicates the number of items for each area, the Area Raw Scores possible, and the area Total Raw Scores possible for both the AEPS Test for Birth to Three Years and Three to Six Years.

In some instances, personnel may find it useful to convert raw scores to percent scores for areas and/or for total raw scores. To convert area raw scores to area percent scores, divide the area raw score by the total area raw score possible. To convert the total raw score to a total percent score, divide the total raw score by the total overall score possible. It should be emphasized that raw and percent scores are not age equivalents, nor do they reflect any type of standardized score.

It is important that children's performances on the AEPS Test be summarized so child progress can be monitored over time. Children should be making steady progress toward targeted goals/objectives, which, in turn, should be reflected in the number of items given a score of 2 across test periods. The AEPS Test should be administered quarterly so that assessment/evaluation information can be summarized and plotted three to four times per year.

Table 8. Number of items per area, total number of items, Area Raw Scores possible, and Total Raw Scores possible on the AEPS Test, Birth to Three Years and Three to Six Years

Area	Number of Items		Area Raw Scores Possible	
	Birth to Three Years	Three to Six Years	Birth to Three Years	Three to Six Years
Fine Motor	33	15	66	30
Gross Motor	55	17	110	34
Adaptive	32	35	64	70
Cognitive	58	54	116	108
Social-Communication	46	49	92	98
Social	25	47	50	94
Total Number of Items	**249**	**217**	—	—
Total Raw Scores Possible	—	—	**498**	**434**

Narrative Summary

A narrative summary can be written by examining a child's performance on the AEPS Test. The child's performance in each area can be summarized by identifying items that the child performs independently and consistently (i.e., received a score of 2) and items that are emerging (i.e., received a score of 1). The purpose of a narrative summary is to paint a picture of the child's strengths and interests by describing the child's functional skills using examples from the team's observations of the child.

Traditionally, test results are summarized from a deficit model, whereas a narrative summary written from the AEPS Test emphasizes the child's strengths, interests, and emerging skills. The summary should assist teams in better understanding the child's behavioral repertoire and in selecting goals/objectives for the IFSP/IEP. A positively written summary of the child's skills does not ignore the areas in which the child may need intervention; rather, it provides the team with an accurate picture of the child's current skill level and highlights those skills that are emerging and will be the target of intervention efforts. When constructing a narrative summary from AEPS Test results, teams are reminded to

- Use objective language

- Record emerging and functional skills

- Use examples to describe and personalize

- Use nontechnical language

- Include information and comments from all team members

- Describe the relationship between behaviors and events and avoid describing isolated events

Visual Summary

A third way to summarize AEPS Test information is visually. Area or Total Percent Scores for each test period can be plotted on a graph to monitor a child's

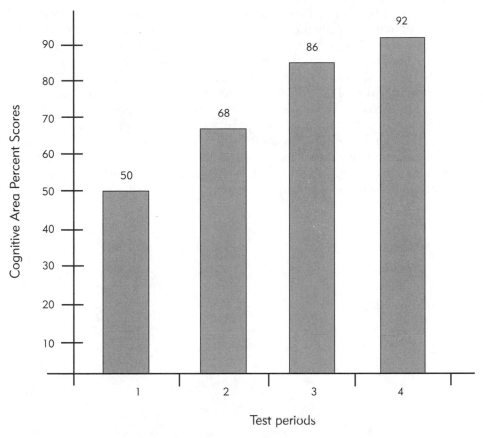

Figure 15. AEPS Test Cognitive Area Percent Scores for one child plotted across four test periods.

performance over time. An example of how a graph can be used to summarize a child's performance using Cognitive Area Percent Scores across four test periods is contained in Figure 15. Children's performance on the AEPS Test can also be visually summarized using the Child Progress Record (Appendix E of this volume).

SUMMARY

The information in this chapter is designed to assist teams in understanding the general features of the AEPS Test that distinguish it from other available instruments. The overall content, organization, and administration procedures of the AEPS Test were described to assist in use of the AEPS Test. The AEPS Test is governed by a set of general principles that should be followed; however, these principles provide only broad guidelines within which users are encouraged to individualize for children, particularly those with sensory or motor impairments.

Collection of educational and intervention-relevant assessment/evaluation data is critical to developing functional IFSPs/IEPs, planning intervention, and monitoring children's developmental progress. The AEPS Test is designed to provide information to the user about children's functional behavioral repertoires. The type of data generated by the AEPS Test is particularly appropriate for designing useful IFSPs/IEPs and intervention content. In addition, results from the AEPS Test can be used to provide teams with supporting or corroborating evidence in determining the eligibility of children for services.

In the following chapters, the inclusion of families throughout the assessment/evaluation process (see Chapter 5) and a team's use of the AEPS Test (see Chapter 6) are discussed. Chapter 4 offers information on using AEPS Test results to develop IFSPs/IEPs and intervention plans.

4

Using AEPS Test Results

In Chapters 2 and 3 the importance of using assessment information to guide intervention with young children is discussed. If intervention efforts are to be effective, assessment information should provide information regarding children's interests, present level of functioning, and developmental needs. When team members gather comprehensive assessment information that directly lends itself to the development of goals/objectives, intervention planning, and evaluation efforts, children's needs are better met (e.g., Bagnato et al., 1997; Bricker, 1989a; Bricker et al., 1998).

This chapter describes how AEPS Test results can be used to provide services to children at risk or with disabilities, from eligibility decisions and planning intervention to monitoring child progress and program efficacy. The chapter is divided into five sections that discuss using the AEPS Test results to

- Develop individualized education program (IEP) goals/objectives or benchmarks: The first section describes a five-step process for developing children's IEP goals/objectives or benchmarks using AEPS Test information.

- Develop individualized family service plan (IFSP) outcomes and intervention plans: The second section addresses using AEPS Test results to develop IFSP outcomes and to create intervention plans.

- Use the AEPS curriculum: The third section addresses linking assessment information, goal development, intervention efforts, and evaluation.

- Monitor child progress: The fourth section describes how repeated administrations of the AEPS Test can be used to monitor children's performance over time (e.g., provide information for progress reports), assist in re-evaluating children, and examine program effects.

- Corroborate eligibility decisions: The fifth section describes how AEPS Test results can be used to corroborate eligibility decisions.

As discussed previously, the AEPS Test has three features that make it useful for developing children's IFSPs/IEPs. First, most items from the AEPS

Test are written to reflect conceptual or generative response classes rather than singular, specific responses (e.g., target wrist rotation across conditions rather than target a specific response such as removing a jar lid). Second, AEPS Test items target skills and abilities essential for young children to function independently and to cope with environmental demands. Third, the AEPS Test contains example IFSP/IEP goals/objectives that can serve as models or guides for using AEPS Test items to develop IFSPs/IEPs. In addition, it is important to note that use of the AEPS Test to develop IFSPs/IEPs is supported by research on its utility and a growing body of evidence regarding the treatment validity of the AEPS Test (e.g., Hsia, 1993; Notari & Bricker, 1990; Notari & Drinkwater, 1991; Pretti-Frontczak & Bricker, 2000, 2001). The AEPS Test's psychometric properties are discussed in Appendix A of this volume.

When developing IFSPs/IEPs, teams are required to adhere to federal and state mandates. The Individuals with Disabilities Education Act (IDEA) requires teams to conceptualize IEP intervention targets as goals/objectives or benchmarks and IFSP targets as outcomes (Huefner, 2000). The terms *goal, objective, benchmark,* and *outcome* are used throughout the law. For the purposes of this chapter and throughout the AEPS volumes, we primarily use the terms *goals* and *objectives.* However, because it is important that teams reach consensus on the use of terms to improve communication about the focus of intervention, we have provided the following brief definitions of these key terms.

Goals are defined as measurable skills targeted for a child to acquire or master within 1 year. Goals often represent general or broad classes of behaviors that are demonstrated by the child across settings and are often performed independently. Most goals are composed of a set of discrete skills referred to in some state regulations as objectives or benchmarks. *Objectives* or *benchmarks* represent intermediate or measurable steps toward the goal or are the prerequisites, milestones, or building blocks of a goal. *IFSP outcomes* are statements of changes that family members want to see for their child or themselves. Outcomes should be written to be understandable to the family and should represent their priorities and concerns.

DEVELOPING IEP GOALS/OBJECTIVES: A FIVE-STEP PROCESS

The development of IEP goals/objectives can be conceptualized as a five-step process: 1) gathering information, 2) summarizing information, 3) selecting potential intervention targets, 4) prioritizing the selected targets, and 5) writing goals/objectives that will be used to guide subsequent intervention and evaluation efforts.

Step 1: Gathering Information

The first step in developing IEP goals/objectives is to gather data over time from a variety of sources, using multiple measures, in order to collect sufficient information for making sound decisions. Federal/state mandates and recommended practice indicate that teams should collect information that can be used to directly link the IFSP/IEP to intervention efforts. The AEPS Test and Family Report serve as key sources for assessment information. Please refer to Chapter 3 for how to gather information on children's development using the AEPS Test and to Chapter 5 for how to gather family information using the Family Report.

Step 2: Summarizing Information

The second step in developing IEP goals/objectives is to summarize the information collected in Step 1. In particular, teams should review AEPS Test information for each developmental area by focusing on what a child can do, is beginning to do, and is interested in doing. Teams are encouraged to look for patterns in how a child demonstrates skills (e.g., with or without assistance; consistently or inconsistently; in certain locations, but not others) and for the relationship between the child's performances across areas of development; for example, teams may look for a common feature that impedes the child from performing related tasks. Summaries should clearly describe a child's present level of performance, strengths, interests, and needs.

Step 3: Selecting Potential Intervention Targets

Based on the information summarized in Step 2, the team should then select skills that 1) are developmentally appropriate, 2) are aligned with the child's current level of functioning, 3) promote a child's ability to participate in daily activities, and 4) promote independence. The AEPS Test is appropriate for this step because it meets each of these criteria. In most cases, teams will identify more goals as potential intervention targets than can be reasonably addressed. Consequently, in Step 4 it is necessary to select the most critical goals through prioritization.

Step 4: Prioritizing the Selected Targets

The fourth step in developing IEP goals/objectives is for the team to prioritize the meaningful skills identified in Step 3. Children with disabilities often show impairments in several or all of the major developmental areas. Attempting to select several skills from each problem area may be unproductive and overwhelming if caregivers and interventionists are responsible for intervening and tracking child progress on 10–15 skills. All too often, each member of a team composes or prioritizes a set of skills that align with their discipline; for example, the classroom teacher may write several goals regarding the child's participation in classroom activities (e.g., follows directions, plays cooperatively), and the speech-language pathologist may write goals regarding articulation and production of words, and the motor specialist may write goals dealing with play skills (e.g., improve bilateral motor coordination). There are at least three limitations to this approach. First, the role of the family is minimized as well as collaboration among other team members. Second, too many skills become targeted for intervention, often leading to a lack of progress by

children and overwhelmed team members. Lastly, by targeting numerous, unrelated skills, teams find it challenging to individualize and monitor each with
enough regularity and reliability to use in making future decisions.

An alternative and recommended approach is for caregivers and interventionists to prioritize skills together and to select only the highest priorities.
Furthermore, teams should find ways to develop goals/objectives that address
multiple areas of need at the same time. Prioritizing is made easier when
teams select goals/objectives in Step 3 that directly or indirectly address multiple areas of development. For a child with delays in adaptive, language,
motor, and social functioning, a skill that addresses all areas simultaneously
can offer greater efficiency; for example, learning to self-feed (an adaptive behavior) can also provide opportunities for a child to work on motor, social, and
communication skills. Picking up pieces of food requires eye–hand coordination, biting and chewing addresses motor coordination of the tongue and lips,
gaining attention is a social behavior, and if a child wants more or something
different, then communication is necessary.

When prioritizing, teams should select goals/objectives that 1) are not
likely to develop without intervention, 2) will significantly enhance a child's
behavioral repertoire, 3) enable the child to be involved in the general cur-
riculum/daily activities, and 4) match a child's developmental level of performance; for example, the goal of learning to make requests has the potential
of enhancing a child's entire behavioral repertoire more than learning to label
pictures on flashcards. By learning to make requests, children are able to get
their needs met, interact with adults and peers, and engage in age-appropriate
activities and play, whereas labeling pictures on flashcards is limited to a single activity that is not as likely to be interesting to the child or to promote independence and problem solving.

Step 5: Writing IEP Goals/Objectives

After prioritizing skills, team members are ready to write the IEP goals/ob-
jectives. The next portion of the chapter focuses primarily on issues related to
writing IEPs. The process for writing and targeting IFSP outcomes is described
in the following section.

As mentioned previously, an advantage of the AEPS Test is that it contains a list of goals/objectives (see Appendix B in this volume) that can serve
as guides or examples for writing IEPs. The guides or models are provided to
assist teams in writing meaningful goals/objectives as well as intervention
plans. These goal/objective examples, however, should not be used as actual
targets without modifying them to meet the needs of individual children. Furthermore, every AEPS item may not meet criteria for inclusion as a target for
intervention (e.g., labeling colors may not be seen by the team as a priority or
a skill considered critical to the child's participation in daily activities). Four
criteria are often used when determining if a skill is meaningful including
whether it is 1) functional, 2) generative, 3) measurable, and 4) understandable
by all team members (Pretti-Frontczak & Bricker, 2000).

When modifying or revising the AEPS goal/objective examples, a simple,
straightforward method involving the use of an ABC formula is suggested in

which A represents an antecedent, B stands for the target behavior, and C represents the criterion or level of acceptable performance. The ABC formula is compatible with legal mandates and also allows teams to write target skills in an understandable and usable manner. When using the ABC formula, each goal or objective that is written should contain the conditions under which the behavior is to be performed, a measurable behavior, and performance criteria. Two examples are presented next.

Antecedent:	When needing to move from location to location at home and in the classroom,
Behavior:	Millie will walk using alternative left–right stepping
Criteria:	without support or without falling for at least 2 weeks.

Antecedent:	When asked or initiated spontaneously,
Behavior:	Georgie will use three or more words to describe an action or event that occurred recently
Criteria:	6 times per day for 2 weeks. The words should accurately reflect the action or event, should occur in the proper order, and should be intelligible to the listener.

Prioritized IEP goals/objectives should be selected and written cooperatively by members of the team. All too often, as mentioned previously, they are developed by individual team members, then shared with one another. In this scenario, the child's caregivers may be handed a "draft" IEP and may be asked for input, may be informed of the skills that will be targeted, or may only be asked for their signature. At other times, IEPs are updated at the end of the year and are passed to the next year's teacher, leaving the recipient no opportunity for input. The list of targeted skills may not be appropriate for intervention approaches they will be using and such IEPs do not guide intervention or ensure individualized efforts. Another ill-advised procedure for selecting IEP goals/objectives is taking them from a computerized bank or list of skills. Members of the team gain access to a computerized list, select or mark desired skills (typically those that a child did not demonstrate during testing), and produce a child's "individualized" plan. Little consideration is given to how meaningful the skills are (e.g., if they are developmentally appropriate, if they promote a child's ability to participate in daily activities, if they meet a child's individual needs).

Using information from the AEPS Test, as well as working closely with team members, can help reduce many of the problems associated with developing meaningful IEP goals/objectives. Further, using the five-step process described previously should assist teams in ensuring appropriate intervention targets are selected and written.

DEVELOPING AN IEP FOR SOPHIE

Sophie is a 5-year-old who stacks blocks, runs and jumps, and swings on the monkey bars. Sophie received a diagnosis of autism at the age of 3 and attends an inclusive preschool for 3 hours per day. Occupational and speech-language therapy services are provided within the context of Sophie's preschool classroom. In addition, Sophie attends a playgroup twice per week. In the fall, Sophie will be moving to a kindergarten program, so it is time for her team to review her IEP. The five-step process described previously was used by the team to examine and modify Sophie's IEP. The team was composed of the family (Sophie's mom, dad, and grandparents), Sophie's preschool interventionist, next year's kindergarten teacher, the occupational therapist, and the speech-language pathologist.

Step 1: Gathering Information

The team gathered information by administering the AEPS Test: Birth to Three Years and Three to Six Years and the Family Report II: Three to Six Years. They gathered information during routine activities at the home, preschool, and playgroup. Dad talked to the playgroup coordinator to get additional information regarding Sophie's skills across settings and time. The preschool teacher reviewed Sophie's medical files, particularly the latest report from Sophie's neurologist. Finally, Sophie and her mom visited the new kindergarten classroom several times to see how she would respond to the new environment.

Step 2: Summarizing Information

The team reviewed all of the information that they had collected and reviewed changes in Sophie's strengths, interests, and areas of need. Sophie has learned to run around obstacles, play with balls, and climb on playground equipment. Her favorite activities continue to include movement and music; she also enjoys watching Walt Disney movies and her favorite book is *The Little Engine that Could*. The team looked for patterns and relationships between skills and across developmental areas; for example, they noticed that Sophie's comprehension of words and sentences (i.e., Social-Communication Area), and interactions with familiar adults (i.e., Social Area) had changed little. They looked to see which skills she performed independently and those that she still needed assistance to perform.

Step 3: Selecting Potential Intervention Targets

Based on the information collected and summarized, the team identified a list of new behaviors as potential intervention targets for Sophie in kindergarten:

- Use a variety of art materials
- Use a fork and spoon to feed herself
- Dress and undress herself

- Categorize objects, people, and events
- Participate in group activities
- Establish joint attention
- Acknowledge when people greet her or say good-bye
- Seek out and select desired toys or objects
- Respond to familiar adults' affective initiations
- Use words to describe and inform
- Meet physical needs of hunger and thirst
- Play with or near peers

As is the case for most children, Sophie's team identified more behaviors than could be reasonably addressed as intervention targets, thus requiring the prioritization that occurs at Step 4.

Step 4: Prioritizing the Selected Targets

The list of potential behaviors that could be addressed during Sophie's year in kindergarten required that the team first combine related behaviors wherever possible and then to prioritize them. For Sophie, this process produced two target behaviors:

1. Increase Sophie's interaction with others (e.g., respond to greetings, play with or near peers, use words to describe and inform)
2. Seek out and select toys/objects, manipulate toys/objects (e.g., color with crayons, feed self with fork or spoon, dress and undress)

Step 5: Writing IEP Goals/Objectives

After gathering information, summarizing the information, and selecting and prioritizing behaviors, the team was ready to write the targeted IEP goals for Sophie. The team consulted Appendix B (in this volume) and reviewed the goal/objective guides. The team proceeded to write two target goals for Sophie's IEP. The first targeted goal addressed the team's priority of increasing Sophie's interactions with others. The second targeted IEP goal addressed her need to learn to manipulate materials. These goals and their associated objectives were developed by modifying the goal/objectives guide provided in Appendix B in this volume. One of her targeted goals and associated objective appears next.

Goal: During daily activities, Sophie will manipulate a variety of objects/toys/materials that require use of both hands at the same time, while performing different movements, five times per day for 2 weeks; for example, Sophie will tie shoes, color with crayons, button clothes, cut out shapes with curved lines, and use a spoon and fork to feed herself.

Objective: During daily activities, Sophie will perform any two-handed task using one hand to hold or steady an object/toy/material while the other hand manipulates the object/toy/material or performs a movement, five times per day for 2 weeks; for example, Sophie will hold paper and draw with a crayon, hold paper and cut paper in half, hold a bowl and spoon up food or liquid, thread and zip a zipper, and turn the pages of a book.

After the IEP goals/objectives were written, the team re-examined them to ensure that they were 1) functional, 2) generative, 3) measurable, and 4) understandable by all team members and 5) to ensure that objectives were hierarchically related to the goals. Once this was completed, the team was ready to begin planning intervention and evaluation activities.

DEVELOPING IFSP OUTCOMES AND INTERVENTION PLANS

In principle, the five-step process described for developing IEPs using AEPS Test results can be followed to develop IFSPs; however, a number of important conceptual as well as practical modifications are necessary. These modifications are described next.

Rather than goals/objectives, IFSPs generally refer to outcomes. *Outcomes* are defined as statements of the changes that a family wants to see for their child and themselves and are written in a language understandable to caregivers. One family may indicate that it is important for their child to learn to walk; therefore an outcome statement might read: "We would like Kennedy to walk by herself so that she can play with toys and friends, move around the house, and go places with the family." The following recommendations should be considered when writing IFSP outcomes:

- Be sensitive to the cultural and social environment of the child and family.
- Consider the unique abilities and disabilities of each child as well as concerns, resources, and priorities of the family.
- Avoid professional jargon.
- Select a small number of outcomes from the family's stated priorities.
- Target outcomes that reflect the child's current level of need but are not too narrow or too broad.
- State specific strategies, materials, and personnel, as well as criteria for mastery.
- Design outcomes to enhance the child's participation in daily activities.
- Write outcomes that combine targets across developmental areas.

Even when teams follow these recommendations, it is critical that IFSP outcomes be accompanied by an intervention plan that contains measurable goals/objectives so progress toward IFSP outcomes can be measured. Teams are encouraged to use information provided by the AEPS curricula when constructing intervention plans.

Intervention plans (sometimes referred to as *treatment plans* or *program plans*) serve as systematic guides for planning interventions. Intervention plans allow teams to ensure that daily activities and events are individualized to meet the needs of specific children. Developing intervention plans is necessary to ensure that targeted outcomes are addressed throughout a child's daily activities.

The successful development of useful and effective intervention plans is dependent on 1) a linked assessment, goal development, intervention, and evaluation process; 2) meaningful and clear outcomes; and 3) team planning and decision making. Given the realities in which most interventionists and families operate, it may be difficult to find time to plan together, but teams should use creative strategies to ensure that they have time to discuss intervention content and strategies and how to evaluate intervention efforts once initiated.

Ensuring an effective choice of intervention content requires not only planning time but also a comprehensive assessment. When intervention targets are functional and operationally defined, intervention efforts become clear, and the selection of activities or routines as well as the reinforcement of child-initiated activities becomes straightforward. Without appropriate and functional target skills, interventionists and caregivers cannot confidently select activities that will enhance learning. Thus, the manner in which IFSPs are written has a direct and critical impact on subsequent intervention.

After writing meaningful IFSP outcomes, the next step is to develop an intervention plan. When developing intervention plans, teams may use different procedures for writing the goals/objectives section for children on IEPs than on IFSPs. When developing an intervention plan for a child on an IEP, team members should take the goals/objectives directly from the IEP and place them in the goals/objectives section of the intervention plan. When developing intervention plans for a child's IFSP outcomes, team members may want to refer to the IFSP/IEP Goal and Objective Examples in Appendix B of this volume to specify the conditions under which the outcome will occur, to designate the actual measurable behaviors that compose the outcome statements, and to identify data collection procedures.

Intervention plans should include information found on the IFSP but should expand that information in two significant ways. First, intervention plans are developed after the IFSP is written. As a result, teams have a foundation for planning intervention as well as additional time to develop activities and events that will support a child's acquisition of targeted skills. Second, an intervention plan is a malleable planning guide that can be altered and modified as a child's and family's interests and needs change. The plans are the link between what a team agrees on for a child and actual day-to-day practice and are designed to ensure that multiple opportunities are provided for children to work on targeted skills. Intervention plans can follow a number of formats but they should contain the following information:

- Basic information (e.g., child's and team members' names, dates for initiation and expected completion, type of setting where intervention occurs)

- Intervention area or outcome
- Goal(s)/objective(s) listed **and** program steps if needed
- Intervention strategies and teaching considerations
- Curricular modifications
- Child progress procedures
- Decision rules

An example of developing IFSP outcomes for a toddler with significant disabilities follows.

DEVELOPING AN IFSP FOR HANNAH

Hannah, an 18-month-old child, was born at 41 weeks' gestation through emergency cesarean section. Hannah suffered from a lack of oxygen to the brain that resulted in increased muscle tone. She received a diagnosis of cerebral palsy and was referred for early intervention services due to concerns with motor, communication, and feeding skills. She was evaluated by a team that included the family, an occupational therapist, and a speech-language pathologist. The team noted serious oral-motor and swallowing problems for Hannah (e.g., unable to coordinate tongue–lip movements, only able to swallow liquids without choking) as well as poor upper body balance and coordination problems with her arms and hands. After her eligibility was established, the team engaged in a five-step process to develop IFSP outcomes.

Step 1: Gathering Information

Using the AEPS Test: Birth to Three Years, the team gathered information about 1) what Hannah can do, likes to do, and is starting to do; 2) how Hannah uses her skills to participate in daily activities; 3) Hannah's typical interactions with friends and family, and 4) how successful or how much difficulty Hannah and her caregivers have during daily routines. The Family Report I: Birth to Three Years was used to gather vital information regarding Hannah's family's needs around daily routines and where they may need help to address Hannah's changing developmental needs. It was important to identify the environments in which Hannah spends most of her time and how she participates in daily activities. This information was used to decide whether a particular environment should be selected for intervention purposes and what interventions were necessary. In other words, it helped the team determine "where" and "when" intervention might occur, "who" would need to develop and/or use intervention strategies, and if Hannah would have access to materials necessary to target identified outcomes. Thus, the AEPS Test: Birth to Three Years and the Family Report I: Birth to Three Years were used to gather relevant information across settings, people, material, and time.

Step 2: Summarizing Information

The team compiled all of the information that they had gathered and discussed what Hannah was able to do and what she was beginning to do. The team talked about which routines were frustrating for the family (e.g., mealtimes), where they needed assistance (e.g., how to help Hannah swallow without choking), and what daily activities were going well (e.g., bedtime). During the conversation, members of the team gained a better understanding of what the family's resources, priorities, and concerns were. When summarizing what they learned, the team noted the family's strengths, including a strong affectionate bond between Hannah and her parents, excellent visual tracking skills, responsiveness to oral communication and visual expressions of adults, and frequent smiles and laughter. Areas in which needs were noted included Hannah's coordination of arms and hands to midline, oral–motor coordination, vocal and consonant sound production, and swallowing.

Step 3: Selecting Potential Outcomes

Hannah's strengths as well as her needs in the area of motor coordination, oral–motor coordination, sound production, and swallowing were examined by the team. Potential outcomes for Hannah and her family were developed and listed. As is often the case, the list of potential target outcomes exceeded the team's resources, making prioritization a necessity. The team then developed intervention strategies making use of all team members' expertise, but focusing on a single outcome:

1. Occupational therapist will work with caregivers on best positioning for feeding and create a support system to help keep Hannah's body and head in midline during feeding.

2. Speech-language pathologist will provide direct services that show caregivers how to provide oral–motor exercise to increase the mobility and coordination of the tongue and lips.

3. Occupational therapist and speech-language pathologist will develop a procedure to assist Hannah in swallowing.

The team also discussed ways to measure Hannah's progress in this area:

1. Evaluate over time Hannah's ability to maintain her head position.

2. Evaluate over time improvements in her oral–motor coordination and swallowing.

Step 4: Prioritizing the Selected Outcomes

Often, team members need to assist each other in establishing priority outcomes in order that the areas most critical to the child and family be addressed. In the ensuing discussion, Hannah's parents made clear their continuing frustration with mealtime because Hannah seemed to "choke often" and "her tongue doesn't seem to be working right." Given this parental concern, the speech-language pathologist's priority to address Hannah's oral–motor and swallowing problems, and the occupational therapist's desire to focus on Hannah's positioning and swallowing needs, the following IFSP outcome was given priority: "We want Hannah to be more successful in eating." This one outcome could address the family's major concern (i.e., ingesting food), as well as the priority targets of the professional staff (i.e., oral–motor coordination and positioning).

Step 5: Writing IFSP Outcomes
and Associated Intervention Plans

After the IFSP priority outcome was selected (and in this case, one outcome was able to address three critical areas of need), Hannah's team was ready to create an associated intervention or treatment plan. Using information gathered from the AEPS Test and Family Report I: Birth to Three Years, the team developed an intervention plan that contained specific goals/objectives used to ensure that the outcome targeted was addressed throughout Hannah's daily activities.

USING THE AEPS CURRICULUM

As described in the Introduction to Volume 1, the AEPS is a curriculum-based assessment and evaluation measure with an associated curriculum that consists of a set of intervention activities designed to link assessment information, goal development, intervention efforts, and evaluation. The curricular items in *Volume 3: AEPS Curriculum for Birth to Three Years* and *Volume 4: AEPS Curriculum for Three to Six Years* correspond directly to AEPS Test items, clearly relating intervention activities to children's selected goals/objectives for each area and strand. The *AEPS Curriculum for Birth to Three Years* lists goals/objectives (including programming steps), importance of the skills, lists of concurrent goals/objectives, teaching suggestions (activity based, environmental arrangement, instruction sequence), and teaching considerations for each area and strand. The *AEPS Curriculum for Three to Six Years* contains a general developmental introduction and is divided into four sections: 1) intervention considerations, 2) suggested activities, 3) using activity-based intervention, and 4) area goals.

The AEPS Curriculum follows an activity-based intervention (ABI) approach. *ABI* is "a child-directed, transactional approach that embeds children's

Table 9. Activity-based intervention (ABI) elements linked to key features of the AEPS Test

Elements of activity-based intervention (ABI)	Key features of the AEPS Test
1. ABI is a child-directed transactional approach.	• Children's interactions during daily activities (e.g., play, dressing, meals, outside time) and across settings (e.g., home, school, community) are observed. • Interactions in social and physical environment are observed. • Items that build on children's interests and allow interventionists and caregivers to follow children's lead can be targeted.
2. ABI embeds goals/objectives in routine, planned, and child-initiated activities.	• AEPS Test items are educationally relevant and functional and can therefore be embedded into a range of meaningful activities. • AEPS Test items can be targeted in a variety of settings by caregivers, interventionists, and/or specialists (e.g., occupational therapist).
3. ABI uses logical antecedents and consequences.	• AEPS Test items are observed during routine, planned, and child-initiated activities that ensure the occurrence of logical antecedents and consequences.
4. ABI targets functional and generalizable skills.	• AEPS Test items are functional and generalizable. • AEPS Test items represent broad response classes rather than discrete skills.

From Bricker, D., Pretti-Frontczak, K., & McComas, N. (1998). *An activity-based approach to early intervention* (2nd. ed.). Baltimore: Paul H. Brookes Publishing Co.; reprinted by permission.

individual goals/objectives in routine, planned, or child-initiated activities and uses logically occurring antecedents and consequences to develop functional and generative skills" (Bricker et al., 1998, p. 11). ABI consists of four major elements:

1. Uses child-initiated transactions

2. Embeds children's goals/objectives in routine, planned, or child-initiated activities

3. Uses logically occurring antecedents and consequences

4. Develops functional and generalizable skills

Table 9 shows the link between the four elements of ABI and key features of the AEPS Test. The ABI approach enhances the link between assessment, targeted skills, and intervention; for example, multiple skills (e.g., fine motor, gross motor, adaptive, cognitive, social-communication, social) can be addressed in a water play activity in which children are sailing boats. Teams can use the water play activity to promote communication skills ("Where is my boat?"), social skills (taking turns), adaptive skills (drying hands), fine motor skills (manipulating two hand-size objects at the same time), and cognitive skills (comparing boats of different materials, sizes, colors, and shapes). Another example can be seen during an art activity in which children are given the opportunity to manipulate paper, tissue, and cellophane. This kind of art activity addresses the fine motor skill of cutting out shapes, the communication skill of informing others about what is being cut (e.g., "I'm cutting purple circles"), the cognitive skill of grouping the paper according to size/shape, and the social skill of sharing or exchanging objects (e.g., scissors, tissue). The AEPS Curriculum encourages teams to address targeted skills by embedding them into functional daily activities of interest to children; for example, rather than designing an activity in which children sit down and count to 10, they are given opportunities throughout the day to count a variety of objects/events (e.g., counting the number of children at circle time, counting plates during snack time, counting the number of trees while on a nature walk).

There are several advantages to using the AEPS Curriculum. First, the notion of providing relevant antecedents and consequences within an activity is incorporated into teaching functional skills within the child's usual environment. When the antecedents and consequences are relevant or part of an activity, motivation and attention problems tend to be less frequent. Second, a curriculum using an ABI approach addresses the issues of generalization and maintenance. When using the AEPS Curriculum, teaching a particular skill is not limited to one activity but, instead, is taught by a variety of interventionists and/or family members across a range of materials and settings. Third, the AEPS Curriculum helps to keep targeted objectives functional for the child. If the skills targeted for intervention are those used in daily activities, then they are useful to the child in adjusting to and coping with environmental demands. A fourth advantage is that when goals/objectives are embedded into daily activities, a variety of people, such as caregivers and peers, can be used as change agents and teaching resources. Fifth, the AEPS Curriculum can be used with a heterogeneous group of young children. Children can act as peer models for one another and be involved in antecedent and consequent events; for example, in a painting activity, children may be given different color paints and will need to request various colors from one another to complete their paintings. Sally's request for red paint may act as an antecedent event to which Miguel responds. Miguel's response (e.g., looking, smiling, verbalizing, offering paint) may act as a positive consequence to Sally.

For additional information on how to use the AEPS Curriculum to link assessment information, goal development, intervention efforts, and evaluation, teams should review the content found in Volumes 3 and 4 of this series. For additional information on ABI, teams are encouraged to review Bricker, Pretti-Frontczak, and McComas (1998). The next section of this chapter describes how to use AEPS Test information to monitor child progress as the final step in providing quality services to young children and their families.

MONITORING CHILD PROGRESS

Systematic documentation of child change is necessary for interventionists and caregivers to evaluate the effects of their intervention efforts. As discussed in Chapter 2, the AEPS Test can be used for ongoing monitoring as well as quarterly and annual evaluations. The type of child progress monitoring chosen will depend on the background of the professional staff and on program resources. Comprehensive evaluation requires well-trained professionals and ample resources that may exceed the capacity of many programs; however, every program should conduct basic evaluation to ensure that intervention is producing desired outcomes.

Weekly Monitoring

Collecting information on children's weekly progress toward specific goals/ objectives or outcomes is a requisite of quality intervention efforts. The type of weekly child monitoring strategy is less important than ensuring that child change data are systematically collected and used to evaluate the impact of intervention efforts. Data collection procedures should be selected to meet the needs of the child, family, interventionists, setting, and focus of intervention. Given adequate staff or caregiver time, we recommend the use of observational systems to collect weekly child progress data. The use of observation is consistent with the recommended procedures for administering the AEPS Test. In addition, observation permits obtaining information as children go about their daily activities, allowing interventionists to collect progress-monitoring data during ongoing classroom or home activities. This is an efficient strategy that provides information on whether the target response is used independently and is functional for the child.

Other strategies, such as administering probe trials following or before beginning a specific intervention activity, can also be used. In a probe system, one or two opportunities[1] should be offered during daily activities to determine the child's progress; for example, if Aaron is working on walking up and down stairs, he can be observed coming down the steps of a bus, playing on the slide, and other opportunities in the daily environment, and his performance (e.g., no attempt, an unsuccessful or successful attempt) can be noted/documented.

Using probe techniques in center-based programs can be organized in a variety of formats to accommodate the program and individual child needs. The interventionist may choose to collect data on different children's IFSPs/IEPs each day of the week as they participate in group activities. Another option is to collect data for each child during a limited number of activities designed to emphasize targets within a particular area. Thus, gross motor data would be collected during outdoor play, and social-communication data would be collected during circle time for all children who have IFSP/IEP targets in those areas.

Data could also be collected during a specified time within each activity, such as during the first or last 5 minutes of the activity; for example, data could be collected for motor skills as children initiate an activity by gathering materials, or data could be collected for social skills during the last 5 minutes of an activity as children work together to clean up the materials. When, how often, and the procedures teams use to collect data should be guided by both the IFSP/IEP and the intervention plan.

It is equally important that teams use the data that they collect. Thus, teams should summarize and interpret data routinely. The data should be

---

[1] If a "meaningful skill" has been targeted, then one or two opportunities should be sufficient to evaluate child progress on a weekly basis.

summarized in such a way that the information is usable by all team members. Interventionists should work with caregivers to determine how to summarize results over time to make them most useful. Changes in IFSPs/IEPs, intervention strategies, or curricular modifications and adaptations should be guided by the evaluation data collected. After skills are acquired (e.g., criteria are met), behaviors should be observed periodically to determine if target skills continue to be used functionally and if skills are being maintained.

Quarterly and Annual Evaluation

Re-administration of the AEPS Test at 3- or 4-month intervals provides interventionists and caregivers with a systematic record of the child's progress across areas of development, not just on IFSP outcomes or IEP goals/objectives. Quarterly retests on the AEPS Test generally take significantly less time due to the team's familiarity with the child and because only information on skills that were targeted for intervention (i.e., scored 1 or 0 on previous administrations) needs to be gathered; for example, if in a particular area a child received a score of 2 on the first 10 items, then teams do not need to re-administer the AEPS Test for these items.

Caregivers can be encouraged to complete the Family Report at quarterly or yearly intervals. Periodic use of the Family Report may assist in keeping caregivers involved in evaluation activities. Parents and caregivers can also use the Child Progress Record to monitor their child's progress. Results from the AEPS Test or Family Report can be used to score the Child Progress Record on a quarterly or annual basis.

AEPS Test results can be summarized as numeric scores for each developmental area and for the entire test, as described in Chapter 3 of this volume. Although AEPS Test results are best summarized as narrative descriptions of performance, summary scores may offer a useful alternative to standardized test scores or age-equivalency scores for programs required to report child progress data to funding agencies or other external organizations. There are several potential advantages to reporting AEPS summary scores (i.e., area scores or total test scores) as quarterly or annual measures of child progress:

- Reporting summary scores makes use of existing AEPS progress-monitoring data without the necessity of administering an additional standardized, norm-referenced test for each child.

- Changes in summary scores reflect acquisition of functional skills, documenting meaningful change in a child's independent daily performance, rather than tracking comparisons to chronological age standards. Changes in AEPS summary scores are, therefore, consistent with current recommendations for outcome-based evaluation measures.

- AEPS Test summary scores are sensitive to subtle improvements in performance for young children who receive specialized services. The large number of items and the three-point scoring system make it possible to show change as children begin to exhibit emerging skills and move from emergent or inconsistent performance to independence. Tests that compare young children's progress with typically developing peers, however, are likely to yield scores that decrease over time as children with delays and disabilities may fall further behind their peers.

AEPS Test summary scores document progress in mastery of functional skills across developmental areas, but *do not* provide a standard metric (such as age equivalencies) for comparison across groups of children. Our belief is that the efforts of children, families, and interventionists are better evaluated by summary scores that reflect individual acquisition of new skills than by summary scores related to chronological age expectations.

CORROBORATING ELIGIBILITY DECISIONS

The AEPS Test is specifically designed to provide a comprehensive picture of children's behavioral repertoires. The AEPS Test was not designed to determine children's eligibility for services and does not contain age norms for items. Assignment of age norms to items has been resisted for an important reason. A skill should be targeted as an outcome or goal/objective because it is the next developmental step or skill in a teaching sequence for a particular child, not because it is an item for a 3- or 4-year-old child.

Over the years, however, AEPS Test developers have continued to receive requests from professionals using the AEPS Test to develop age norms for the items. A primary impetus for this request comes from state regulations that require evaluation teams to use at least two sources of information to establish a child's eligibility for services. In many states, results from an individualized developmental test (e.g., *Bayley Scales of Infant Development–II* [Bayley, 1993], *The Battelle Developmental Inventory* [Newborg, Stock, & Wnek, 1988]) must be supported by data from at least one other valid source that documents a child's delay or problem.

Many evaluation teams have indicated that it would be valuable to use information from the AEPS Test as the other corroborating source for at least three reasons. First, using AEPS Test information expands both the depth and breadth of developmental information on children. Second, using AEPS Test information would engender significant time-savings because teams would not have to administer two standardized tests. Third, use of the AEPS Test information leads to the development of more functional IFSPs/IEPs (e.g., Pretti-Frontczak & Bricker, 2000). Thus, a middle-ground solution has been created that allows AEPS Test information to be used in corroborating children's eligibility for services without assigning specific age norms to items.

To use the AEPS Test results to corroborate eligibility decisions required developing a procedure for comparing a child's total goal score with total goal scores of typically developing children of the same chronological age. Using Item Response Theory analysis, tables containing cutoff scores were created that showed, by age intervals, the total goal scores expected. Children with a total goal score at or below the cutoff score for their age interval are performing significantly below their age expectations and, therefore, may be eligible for services. Because the cutoff scores have been placed well below the expected total goal scores for specific age intervals, it is highly likely that children whose total goal scores are below cutoff scores will be eligible for services.

Appendix F of this volume contains tables with cutoff scores for the Birth to Three and Three to Six levels of the AEPS Tests. This appendix also contains information on the sensitivity, specificity, percent agreement, overidentification, and underidentification for each age interval. In addition, an expanded explanation of how the tables were developed and how to use them is offered in Appendix F.

SUMMARY

Too frequently in early intervention programs, the relationship between assessment information and intervention planning is disconnected. Often, individuals who will not work with the child or family conduct assessments employing tools that generate information that is not useful for developing IFSPs/IEPs or intervention plans. Using such approaches makes it extremely difficult for interventionists and caregivers to develop appropriate intervention targets and subsequent intervention plans. The AEPS Test offers teams an alternative approach—one that directly links assessment, goal development, intervention, and evaluation efforts.

Quality intervention services require the systematic and direct linking of assessment, goal development, intervention, and evaluation processes. The material contained in this chapter describes a set of practical procedures for forging direct links among assessment information, the development of IFSPs/ IEPs, intervention, and evaluation activities.

When using AEPS Test results to corroborate other standardized, norm-referenced test results, only the total number of goals receiving a score of 2 are used to obtain a total goal score, which then can be used to compare with cutoff scores for the child's age interval.

5

The AEPS
and Family Participation

Caregiver and family input and participation is critically important to a child's assessment, goal development, intervention, and evaluation activities. The greater the involvement in this range of activities, the greater likelihood of improved outcomes for both the child and family. This assumption provides the conceptual basis and motivation for the creation of a process to ensure families' participation and for the development of materials that provide formal mechanisms for gathering information from caregivers. This chapter describes a process designed to ensure family participation and then describes a set of AEPS materials that were specifically developed to be used to ensure and encourage caregiver participation. These materials include

- AEPS IFSP/IEP Planning Guide (see Figure 19)
- Family Report I[a]: Birth to Three Years
- Family Report II: Three to Six Years
- Child Progress Record I: Birth to Three Years
- Child Progress Record II: Three to Six Years

The Family Report is contained in Appendix D, and the Child Progress Record is contained in Appendix E.

Family-friendly measures and procedures specifically designed to obtain assessment/evaluation information from parents and other caregivers are important for several reasons. First, caregivers often have more opportunities to observe their children's behavior than do professionals. Caregivers and other family members have important information on children's current development status and past history. Second, accurate assessment and evaluation is dependent on gathering information from a variety of individuals familiar with the child. The family's perspective about a child is of paramount impor-

---

[a] I and II are used on these forms to be sensitive to families whose children may have significant delays.

tance and should always be included when gathering assessment and evaluation information. Caregivers can identify particular areas of concern for them within normal daily routines that might otherwise be overlooked. Third, caregiver and professional observations can be compared to determine points of agreement and disagreement. The points of agreement can serve as priorities for the development of IFSP/IEP outcomes. The points of disagreement indicate that additional information may be needed. Fourth, asking caregivers to participate in the assessment/evaluation process conveys the message that program personnel believe caregivers can be important contributors to their children's intervention programs. Finally, the use of formal procedures to involve caregivers may assist in their increased participation in the IFSP/IEP process and subsequent monitoring of child progress.

FAMILY PARTICIPATION PROCESS

This section describes a five-step process for helping ensure family participation throughout assessment, goal development, intervention, and evaluation activities. The five steps for family participation described next are initiated once a child has been determined to be eligible for services and are offered only as guidelines. Variations in family values, needs, and circumstances may require significant tailoring of these steps to adequately address the individuality of families. Figure 17 provides an overview of the five steps and their relationship. A brief description of each step follows.

Step 1: Introductory Meeting

The introductory meeting is the first step in the process and should be used to explain a program's philosophy, goals, range of services, and resources available to the family. At this meeting, family members should be encouraged to discuss their general concerns and interests, as well as how they would like to be involved in their child's assessment, goal development, intervention, and evaluation activities.

Step 2: AEPS Test and Family Report Completion

Assuming willingness to participate in assessment activities, families are asked at this step to consider completing the Family Report. At this time, the professional team members complete the AEPS Test. Based on team member feedback, requests for additional information may occur at this step as shown in Figure 17.

Step 3: IFSP/IEP Development and Intervention Planning Meeting

After assessment data are collected, the team—including the caregiver—meets to summarize the results and to develop the IFSP/IEP outcomes or goals/

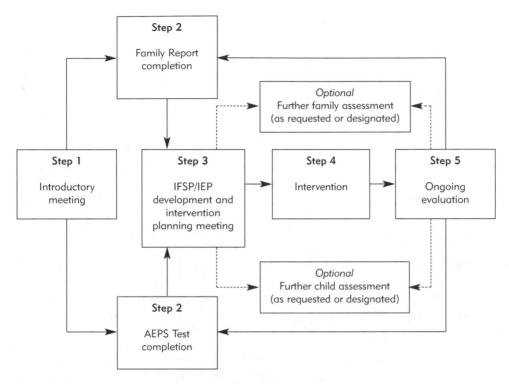

Figure 17. The AEPS five-step process for family participation in assessment, goal development, intervention, and evaluation.

objectives. The IFSP/IEP outcomes or goals/objectives are prioritized, and intervention and evaluation plans are written. As this step concludes, signatures are obtained and copies of the final IFSP/IEP document are distributed. This step may require more than one meeting.

Step 4: Intervention

Using the intervention plans written at Step 3, this step focuses on implementation of those plans. Professional staff and caregivers create activities or use routine activities to provide the child opportunities to acquire targeted goals.

Step 5: Ongoing Evaluation

Ongoing evaluation or review is conducted as specified in the IFSP/IEP. The Child Progress Record can be used to help families monitor their child's progress. Outcome statements and intervention activities are revised as needed based on progress or evaluation information. Over the year, repeated administrations of the AEPS Test and Family Report can provide additional evaluation information. The introductory meeting and IFSP/IEP development and intervention planning meeting are described in greater detail next.

Introductory Meeting

As shown in Figure 17, the first step involving families is an introductory meeting during which intake procedures and program preliminaries are explained to parents and other family members. The setting for this meeting should be comfortable and convenient for the family. The program information needs will vary across families. For some, a brief interview may be sufficient, whereas for other families, considerable time may be needed to obtain information and answer questions. The program representative should be knowledgeable about the program and skilled in interviewing and communicating information.

The introductory meeting has two purposes: 1) to provide information and clarification about the program to families and 2) to decide how programmatic assessments will be completed. Procedures to maintain confidentiality should be discussed and the necessary program forms completed. The program philosophy and goals should be explained to the family, as well as the range of services and program resources.

The family may be ready to consider various program services and resources, or they may need more time to consider their decisions. Supportive print materials can be helpful; however, it is important to avoid providing more information than the family can comfortably manage.

During this meeting, it is also critical that families have the opportunity to describe their concerns, to determine the areas of assessment that they believe are important, and to help decide what assessment information should be gathered. Providing families with choices about their involvement in the assessment process helps to establish their role as decision makers and partners in the program. Some families will choose to complete the Family Report independently, whereas others may prefer to provide the information during a meeting. Some families may want to participate in the child's assessment; others may want to watch and offer comments. Some families may choose to have the professional team complete the assessment. All options are acceptable, and the best way to find out which format the family prefers is to ask.

IFSP/IEP Development and Intervention Planning Meeting

The IFSP/IEP development and intervention planning meeting is scheduled to occur when the child's programmatic assessment (i.e., AEPS Test and additional assessment information that the team chooses to include) and the family's assessment materials (i.e., Family Report) are completed. Prior to the meeting, the assessment information should have been summarized and possible priorities for intervention should have been identified by the family and professionals. The purpose of this meeting is to 1) identify priorities for IFSP/IEP outcomes or goals, 2) design intervention activities, 3) determine an acceptable evaluation plan for each outcome, and 4) produce an IFSP/IEP document.

A program staff member(s) familiar with the child and family and with whom parents or caregivers are comfortable should attend the meeting. The professional primarily responsible for assisting the family may facilitate this meeting. Procedures for this meeting(s) may vary across families; however, each meeting should include the following elements:

- An explanation of the planning process and the tasks to be accomplished
- A summary of available assessment information
- An opportunity to update, change, add, or delete assessment information
- The identification of family priorities
- The development of goals or outcome statements with associated intervention activities and evaluation plans
- A meeting summary and agreement to sign the IFSP/IEP

The meeting can begin with a summary of available assessment information and a summary of the child's abilities. The family should be encouraged to present their information in a manner that they find comfortable. It is critical to let the family identify its strengths and interests. Priorities are established by the family members based on their information and other information presented to them. From these priorities, outcome statements or goals/objectives are developed. For each priority outcome or goal, an intervention and evaluation plan should be developed.

To assist in the development of intervention and evaluation plans, it may be useful to pose a series of exploratory (open-ended) and confirmatory (close-ended) questions. A list of possible questions is contained in Figure 18. The exploratory questions are printed in bold and are followed by the confirmatory questions, which are printed in italic. These questions may be helpful to ensure that the information necessary to achieve the desired outcome is included. The exploratory questions offer opportunities to generate ideas, identify alternatives, and share information. They should be used to initiate discussion about the intervention or evaluation plan. The confirmatory questions are designed to provide clarification and offer a check to ensure that the selected options will be useful in achieving the outcome in a timely and effective manner.

These questions should be used only as a guide. For some goals or outcome statements, the intervention and evaluation plan may be straightforward and not require the generating of options and alternative strategies. Other goals or outcome statements may need considerable discussion to develop an effective and functional plan for the family. It is often useful to ask the family its views first; then after considering the family's response, other participants can add information or suggestions.

Some families may find it useful to write down information as the meeting proceeds or at its termination. The IFSP/IEP Planning Guide may be useful for some caregivers. A completed example of the IFSP/IEP Planning Guide is shown in Figure 19. A blank copy of the IFSP/IEP Planning Guide is contained in Figure 20, and a description of how to complete and use the planning guide is provided in a later section in this chapter.

It may be decided at this meeting that additional information will be useful. At that time, referrals may be initiated for specific family or child assessments,

1. **How would you like to see this outcome achieved? Can you think of some ways you would like to make this happen?**

Purpose: These exploratory questions encourage the family to identify the "ideal" plan for developing this outcome. They encourage the family and the other team participants to think of several strategies and to explore a range of alternatives before identifying specific activities.

2. **Who could participate?**

Purpose: This exploratory question identifies possible participants and agencies.

A. Are these people or agencies willing and able to participate?

B. Will the participation of these individuals or agencies result in the family gaining the information or skills that will improve their ability to enhance their child's development?

Purpose: These confirmatory questions are designed to ensure that the individuals identified are truly potential participants and that their services will be able to produce the outcome as it is stated. This will help the team use their time effectively by encouraging them to choose the best resources before developing the intervention activities.

3. **How would we (you) go about doing this? Where should we (you) start? How shall we (you) proceed?**

Purpose: Brainstorming intervention activities helps to ensure that the activities fit within the structure and values of the family. Exploring a variety of options offers opportunities for all participants to have input and make suggestions. Decisions about the preferred activities should be made collaboratively with the final decision made by the family.

A. Do the activities proceed in a logical or sequential progression?

B. Will the activities selected achieve the outcome?

C. Are the activities compatible with the family's values?

D. Will participation by any family member adversely affect any other family member? If so, is the ratio of cost to benefit acceptable to the family? If not, are there any other alternatives?

Purpose: These confirmatory questions assist the team in planning an effective and efficient intervention plan. These questions provide a check and balance system for developing an innovative and individualized plan. These questions again remind all team members to consider the family first. Be sure the family accepts and agrees with the plan. Be sure that the plan does not isolate any family member from the rest of the family or neglect other family members.

4. **What resources are needed to complete these activities?**

Purpose: The identification of resources is similar to the identification of key participants.

A. Are the resources available?

B. Can they be acquired?

C. By whom?

D. At whose expense?

Purpose: Careful plans often have to be abandoned for lack of resources. To save time and frustration, it is helpful to ensure that the resources necessary to complete the activities are readily available or can be acquired.

5. **How will we (you) know when the outcome is achieved? What are effective evaluation activities? What evaluation activities are the most functional for the desired outcome and the family?**

Purpose: Developing evaluation criteria may be a new and challenging task for many families. Developing evaluation criteria that are written in "family friendly" language may be a new and challenging task for many professionals. The evaluation activities should reflect the needs and interests of the family and the other participants in the intervention plan.

A. Are the timelines acceptable to participants?

B. Who will assume responsibility for monitoring progress?

C. When and how often will progress be monitored?

Purpose: This final set of confirmatory questions focuses on the details of the intervention and evaluation plan to ensure that it will be carried out in a timely manner.

Figure 18. Questions for the IFSP/IEP development and intervention planning meeting. Exploratory questions are printed in bold and confirmatory questions are printed in italic.

AEPS IFSP/IEP Planning Guide

IDENTIFYING INFORMATION

Child's name: Taylor	Birthdate: 1/5/99	Family's name: McClure
Date of IFSP/IEP: 6/6/01	Time: 4:30 p.m.	Location: McClure's home

Family Members/Professionals/Agency Representatives attending:

Mary (grandmother), Ray (classroom interventionist), Kate (communication specialist), Linda (service coordinator)

Strengths and Resources

Child strengths and resources (Include recent progress or changes, favorite activities, special qualities)	Family strengths and resources (Include available resources, special qualities, abilities, supports)
Starting to use two-word sentences	Insurance is okay
Likes to look at books	Good child care
Loves circle time and water activities	

Goals and Priorities

Child goals	Family priorities
1. Playing more with friends	1. Want to know more about services
2. Using longer sentences	2. Want information on language training
3.	3. Want child care teacher to know how to work with Taylor
4.	4.
5.	5.

Comments

Mary is willing to collect weekly data on Taylor's progress.

Linda would like a follow-up meeting in 3 weeks.

Figure 19. A completed example of an AEPS IFSP/IEP Planning Guide.

AEPS IFSP/IEP Planning Guide

IDENTIFYING INFORMATION

Child's name:	Birthdate:	Family's name:
Date of IFSP/IEP:	Time:	Location:

Family Members/Professionals/Agency Representatives attending:

Strengths and Resources

Child strengths and resources (Include recent progress or changes, favorite activities, special qualities)	Family strengths and resources (Include available resources, special qualities, abilities, supports)

Goals and Priorities

Child goals	Family priorities
1.	1.
2.	2.
3.	3.
4.	4.
5.	5.

Comments

Figure 20. Blank AEPS IFSP/IEP Planning Guide.

such as a parent–child interaction scale or an articulation evaluation. The need for additional information may require a follow-up meeting to complete the IFSP/IEP document.

As priorities are established, outcomes are selected, and intervention and evaluation plans are designed to achieve the selected outcomes, the IFSP/IEP takes shape. Team-determined outcomes, goals/objectives, and intervention and evaluation plans are transferred to the formal document along with settings and dates for implementation and review. The IFSP/IEP document may be completed at this meeting; however, for some families an additional meeting may be necessary to develop a comprehensive and useful IFSP/IEP.

A MOTHER'S STORY

"One of the most difficult times for me was the diagnostic process, which was necessary to determine Kiera's eligibility for services. Kiera, who has Down syndrome, is very bright and communicative. To our dismay, her evaluation results showed none of this. She scored even lower than she had on previous tests, and my husband and I were devastated. I was so afraid that with such low scores her teacher would think it was not worth the time to try to teach her. I did not want her to go into the school district with only these horrible scores to introduce her, so we completed the Family Report. This gave her teacher a much better look at Kiera's functional skills as we knew them to be, as well as her participation in our family and the community. I found later that her teacher was thrilled to have any information that would help her know Kiera better."

AEPS FAMILY PARTICIPATON MATERIALS

This section describes the AEPS family participation materials, including the Family Report, IFSP/IEP Planning Guide, and the Child Progress Record.

Family Report

The Family Report has two levels that parallel the AEPS Test: Birth to Three Years and Three to Six Years. In order to be sensitive to families whose children may not be tested at their appropriate chronological age level because of the severity of their developmental delays, the Family Report forms in Appendix D are labeled with a I (for birth to three years) and a II (for three to six years). Each Family Report is divided into two major sections. Section 1 is composed of a series of open-ended items designed to elicit helpful information from caregivers about the child's daily activities, family activities, and community activities. Section 2 is composed of a series of parent-friendly assessment items that parallel the developmental areas and items of the AEPS Test.

Section 1 of the Family Report

Section 1 of the Family Report has two purposes. The first purpose is to assist caregivers in describing their child's participation in daily, family, and community activities and in selecting intervention priorities. The second purpose is to provide professional team members with information on how the child functions in the family and community. This type of information should assist professional staff in helping family members develop appropriate and functional intervention goals/objectives or outcomes.

Section 1 of the Family Report has three features that recommend its use. First, caregivers are asked to provide short responses regarding the child's participation in a variety of caregiving and daily routines that occur throughout the day, as well as family and community activities in which the child participates. Completing Section 1 of the Family Report should assist the family in identifying their priority goals for their child and outcomes for their family.

The second feature is its focus on obtaining information from the caregiver's perspective. Caregivers are asked about the child's participation in daily, family, and community activities; they are asked to identify what activities generally proceed well and where they experience difficulty. Such information should be useful to both professional team members and caregivers as they choose intervention targets and design intervention strategies.

The third feature of this section is its flexibility. Caregivers can complete this section independently; they can choose to answer all areas of the section or only selected areas that they deem relevant. This section can also be used as an interview tool to provide a systematic guide for eliciting important information from caregivers.

Content and Organization of Section 1 of the Family Report   The range of items contained in this section are intended for use with families whose children are between the ages of approximately 3 months and 6 years. Questions are posed and space is provided for describing the child's participation in important daily, family, and community activities.

Administration of Section 1 of the Family Report   This section can be completed jointly by caregivers and other team members in an interview format, by the caregivers independently or as a combination of these two methods. Although this section can be used at any time with families, its usefulness may be maximized by completing it prior to development of the IFSP/IEP and again in midyear.

The purpose of Section 1 should be explained to caregivers and all of their questions should be addressed. Caregivers should be informed that they do not have to answer all questions. An example of questions from the Daily Activities portion of Section 1 from the Family Report is shown in Figure 21. Following the questions in each section, space is available to indicate dates when the questions were reviewed and note changes that permit use of the form on four separate occasions.

Using Information from Section 1 of the Family Report   If completed during the assessment phase, then information from this section can be incorporated into the summarization of assessment results prior to the development of the IFSP/IEP; for example, the information generated by Section I may

Sleeping

1. What is your child's bedtime routine (time, activities)?

2. What is your child's nap routine (time, activities)?

3. Naptime/bedtime is usually enjoyable because

4. Naptime/bedtime can be difficult because

Date reviewed: _____   Noted changes: _____

_____

Date reviewed: _____   Noted changes: _____

_____

Date reviewed: _____   Noted changes: _____

_____

Figure 21. Example questions from the Daily Activities portion of Section 1 of the Family Report.

be useful in rounding out the picture of the child's developmental profile and illustrate areas of significant need, and, as indicated previously, the form can be used on four separate occasions. The date of the first administration is entered on the cover page, with space for noting dates of subsequent reviews located beneath each activity.

During development of the IFSP/IEP, the information gathered using Section 1 may provide important insights about the child's and family's functioning. Information from this section can provide a contextual backdrop for selecting goals/objectives or outcomes. Having completed this section may also assist family members in selecting priority targets for both the child and family and subsequent review may assist in revising the IFSP/IEP.

During development of intervention plans, it is important that the intervention team understand the child's daily activities and how the child participates in those as well as other family activities. Information gathered from Section 1 may suggest activities that would accommodate intervention efforts and those that would not; for example, caregivers may have noted that mealtimes are hectic, and improving the child's self-feeding skills would likely assist in making these times more satisfying and comfortable for all family members. Therefore, a portion of intervention planning might focus on what family members could do at mealtime to assist the child in learning new eating skills.

If caregivers were willing to re-examine needs identified in Section 1 over time, then such comparisons might be useful in monitoring child progress. An indication that the child is participating in more family activities since the initiation of intervention activities may suggest the impact of these intervention efforts for the family.

Section 2 of the Family Report

Using Section 2 of the Family Report can assist caregivers in gaining insights into their child's abilities and help them participate in the development of their child's IFSP/IEP. This section of the Family Report can help to demystify the assessment/evaluation process and clarify for the family the roles of the professionals. Figure 22 presents three items from the Cognitive Area of the Family Report II: Three to Six Years.

Section 2 of the Family Report contains items developed to obtain information from caregivers about their children's current skills, abilities, and behavioral characteristics across major areas of development. Section 2 of the Family Report I: Birth to Three Years and II: Three to Six Years, was designed to be used in conjunction with the AEPS Test. Under each developmental area in Section 2 is a set of assessment items that corresponds directly to a goal or objective on the AEPS Test. An example of the relationship between the AEPS Test and items in Section 2 of the Family Report is shown in Table 10.

Cognitive Area

Cognitive skills are those that involve mental processes and reasoning. These skills include problem solving, counting, recalling, imitating, categorizing, and pre-reading.

11. Does your child pretend play with other children?
(F1) NOTE: Place a "Y," "S," or "N" by items a through c:

date 10/02 — S

___S___ a. Does your child pretend to be someone else and tell other children who they can pretend to be? For example, your child says, "I'll be the bus driver and you be the kid." (F1.1)

___S___ b. Does your child act out a pretend story or event? For example, your child says he or she is going fishing and then pretends to catch some fish and cook them. (F1.2)

___Y___ c. Does your child use pretend objects or motions to play? For example, your child pretends to brush hair without a brush. (F1.3)

12. Does your child play games following rules? (F2) — S

13. Does your child count at least 20 objects? (G1) — N

Figure 22. Cognitive items from Section 2 of the Family Report II: Three to Six Years.

Table 10. Examples of AEPS Test items and corresponding Family Report items from the AEPS Test: Birth to Three Years

	AEPS Test items	Family Report items
Area:	Fine Motor	Fine Motor
Strand:	B: Functional Use of Fine Motor Skills	6. Does your child use a turning motion with either wrist when playing with objects? For example, your child uses a turning motion with his or her wrist to take a lid off a jar or to wind up a toy. (B1)
Item:	Goal 1: Rotates either wrist on horizontal plane	
Area:	Cognitive	Cognitive
Strand:	E: Problem Solving	12. Does your child try different ways to solve a problem? For example, when your child wants something from a container that is hard to open, he or she bangs the container on the floor and asks for your help. (E4)
Item:	Goal 4: Solves common problems	

Section 2 of the Family Report has several important features. First, each Family Report corresponds directly to the associated AEPS Test levels, which are used by professionals (e.g., the Family Report I: Birth to Three Years matches the AEPS Test for Birth to Three Years). As shown in Table 10, the Family Report assessment items are simple paraphrases of the goals and, in some cases, objectives on the AEPS Test. This feature permits a direct comparison between the caregivers' and professionals' assessments of the child.

Second, this section measures skills that are functional for young children; that is, only skills that may enhance the child's ability to cope with and adapt to the demands of his or her social and physical environments are included. This focus on functional skills ensures that all of the items have the potential of being appropriate intervention targets. This feature of the Family Report makes the assessment outcomes of direct relevance and use to the development of the child's IFSP/IEP. The assessment information can be used to assist in developing the child's IFSP/IEP and to formulate subsequent programming content to be targeted by the intervention team.

The comprehensive coverage of Section 2 is a third feature that makes it valuable both as an initial assessment tool and in monitoring the child's subsequent progress. The major developmental areas of fine motor, gross motor, adaptive, cognitive, social-communication, and social behavior are included in the Family Report. This scope of information provides a comprehensive view of the child's repertoire.

Fourth, completing this section of the Family Report encourages caregivers to observe their child's behaviors during daily activities. Although caregivers may complete this section of the Family Report from their knowledge of and experience with the child, they are encouraged to verify their recollections through observations of the child in familiar environments. Observing their child's behavior may help families select IFSP/IEP goals or outcomes of greatest potential impact and may also assist caregivers in choosing intervention strategies that best fit their child's characteristics and that are compatible with family activities.

A final feature of this section is its positive orientation. The Family Report does not use a problem, weakness, or need orientation but, rather, permits

Family Report I	Family Report II
Fine Motor—focuses on grasping, reaching, and manipulation	*Fine Motor*—focuses on manipulating objects and prewriting skills
Gross Motor—focuses on coordination of movement, balance, and mobility	*Gross Motor*—focuses on balance and mobility in standing and walking and on play skills
Adaptive—focuses on feeding, hygiene, and undressing	*Adaptive*—focuses on feeding, hygiene, and dressing
Cognitive—focuses on responses to environmental stimulation, problem solving, and indexing concepts such as causality, object permanence, imitation, and object differentiation	*Cognitive*—focuses on understanding of concepts, categorizing, sequencing, recalling events, problem solving, play, premath, and prereading skills
Social-Communication—focuses on social-communication interactions, comprehension, and word production skills	*Social-Communication*—focuses on social-communication interactions and the production of words, phrases, and sentences
Social—focuses on adult and peer interactions and responses to social conventions	*Social*—focuses on interactions with others and the environment and knowledge of self and others

Figure 23. The six areas of the Family Report I: Birth to Three Years and II: Three to Six Years.

caregivers to indicate a child's current behavioral repertoire and what behaviors to target for the future.

Content and Organization of Section 2 of the Family Report   As in the AEPS Test, Section 2 of the Family Report is divided into six developmental areas, as shown in Figure 23. At the beginning of each area is a brief sentence explaining the developmental focus of the questions as well as providing a few examples. Each item in Section 2 of the Family Report is numbered consecutively by developmental area. As shown in Figure 22, some items have subitems that are noted with letters (e.g., a, b, c). Items in Section 2 of the Family Report correspond with goals/objectives found on the corresponding AEPS Test and can be matched by referring to the letter–number combination in parentheses at the end of each item; for example, if an item from the Cognitive Area of Section 2 of the Family Report I: Birth to Three Years is followed by (C1), then an interventionist would know that the item corresponds with Strand C Goal 1 within the Cognitive Area. Another example would be a Family Report II: Three to Six Years item in the Fine Motor Area followed by (A3.1). This code tells the interventionist that the item corresponds with Objective 3.1 in Strand A of the Fine Motor Area.

At the end of each area is a question that asks caregivers to identify the next skills that they want their child to learn. At the end of the entire Section 2, caregivers are asked to list their most important intervention priorities.

Items have been written in clear, simple language to assist caregivers in reading and understanding the content. The form is designed to accommodate the results from four separate administrations. Space is provided at the top of each page to enter the date of each administration. Boxes are located below the column headings for entering scores.

Use of Section 2 of the Family Report   Section 2 of the Family Report is an observation-based assessment/evaluation instrument developed specifically for caregivers. Caregivers are encouraged to complete this section of the Family Report independently or with minimal assistance from professionals. Before scoring an item in this section, caregivers should observe their child attempting or doing the target behavior. There may be items, however, that caregivers can score based on their knowledge of what their child can and cannot do (e.g., caregivers likely know if their child can walk up and down stairs). Items that are not observed may require that caregivers create a situation to directly elicit the target behavior.

Caregivers should observe or test a behavior several times before scoring an item to ensure that the child demonstrates the skill consistently and independently. If caregivers have questions about the intent of an item or are unable to interpret a behavior exhibited by their child, then they should seek assistance from a professional. If necessary, this section of the Family Report can be administered using an interview format; for example, if a parent has limited reading skills, then program staff may read each item and the response categories to the caregiver and record his or her response.

No specific sequence for administration of this section of the Family Report is required; however, caregivers should be strongly encouraged to score all items plus the sub-items at the first administration. If the Family Report is used to monitor child progress over time, then subsequent administrations can be focused on intervention targets only. Before using this section of the Family Report, it is important that program staff tell caregivers that they should not expect their child to be able to successfully perform all items. This point should be emphasized for caregivers of children with severe disabilities.

Scoring Items in Section 2 of the Family Report   Caregivers may rate each of the items in this section of the Family Report by selecting one of the three response options that most accurately reflects their child's current level of functioning: "Yes," "Sometimes," and "Not Yet." When the child performs the skill or behavior consistently and independently across settings, materials, and people, a Y is entered in the appropriate box. Y is also used when the child previously performed the skill but now uses a more advanced skill (e.g., the item that asks if the child can copy shapes would be scored Y if the child NOW draws them independently). If caregivers are unable to observe an item, then a question mark can be inserted in the box.

When the child's performance of a specific skill or behavior may be questionable, such as an emerging skill, an S is entered in the appropriate box; for example, the child may demonstrate a skill only with certain materials (e.g., drinks from a special cup) or in specific situations (e.g., uses words with caregivers but not with others). The S response should also be used if the child needs several verbal or physical prompts to produce the behavior. When a child clearly does not demonstrate a skill, an N is entered in the appropriate box. At the end of each area, caregivers are asked to indicate what skill (in that area) they would like their child to learn.

Some items in Section 2 of the Family Report contain one or more subitems denoted with letters that ask caregivers to provide additional or clarifying information; for example, item three in the Cognitive Area of the Family Report II: Three to Six Years asks: "Does your child use spatial position and time words correctly?" This item has two sub-items. One sub-item asks caregivers to circle the words that their child knows to designate time (e.g., yesterday, tomorrow), and the other sub-item asks caregivers to circle the words that the child uses to indicate the position of objects or people (e.g., behind, first). Other sub-items allow caregivers to identify the parts of a skill that their child is able to do; for example, item two in the Adaptive Area of the Family Report II: Three to Six Years asks, "Does your child help prepare and serve food?" and gives the examples of removing peels and wrappers, using a knife to spread soft foods, pouring liquid, and using a fork or spoon to serve food from one container to another. If the caregiver has observed the child only serving food from one container to another with a fork or spoon, then he or she would score the item as S.

Outcomes Summary of Section 2 of the Family Report   If desired, program staff may convert Section 2 letter scores to numerical scores by assigning a 2 to the Y responses, a 1 to the S responses, and a 0 to the N responses; however, in most cases, the information provided by the Family Report is best used to assist program staff in scoring the Child Observation Data Recording Form. If discrepancies are found between team member observations, then the caregivers and the professional should attempt to observe the targeted behavior again and work to understand and resolve the discrepancy; for example, caregivers and professionals may find behaviors that the child uses at home but not at school or the reverse.

Section 2 of the Family Report allows families the opportunity to observe their child in various settings, to provide critical information for IFSP/IEP development, and to participate fully in the decision-making process regarding the assessment, intervention, and evaluation of their child's growth and development.

JUAN

Juan's parents were worried about attending the scheduled IFSP meeting with his teacher, physical therapist, and speech-language pathologist. Before the meeting,

Juan's teacher asked his parents if they would like to complete a Family Report and IFSP/IEP Planning Guide. Juan's parents asked for clarification as to the purpose and intended use of the information. Ms. Campbell explained the process for completing the Family Report and the IFSP/IEP Planning Guide and how the information would be used. Juan's parents agreed to fill out the Family Report and the IFSP/IEP Planning Guide before the scheduled meeting. Mr. Gonzales spoke up at the beginning of the meeting. "We—my wife and I—really liked doing this form," he said pointing to the Family Report. "Doing this helped us see what Juan can do and what the teacher wants to know." Mrs. Gonzales added, "We were surprised that Juan can do some things that we didn't know. Filling out the other pages [IFSP/IEP Planning Guide] helped us think about what we want Juan to learn this year."

IFSP/IEP Planning Guide

The IFSP/IEP Planning Guide is a simple one-page form developed to assist families in preparing for their IFSP/IEP meeting. Parents or caregivers may or may not find completing this form to be useful, and, therefore, completing the IFSP/IEP Planning Guide should be the family's choice.

As shown in Figure 20, the IFSP/IEP Planning Guide is divided into four sections for recording information: 1) identifying information, 2) strengths and resources of the child and family, 3) goals and priorities for the child and family, and 4) comments. The child's name and birth date, the family's name, the date of the IFSP/IEP meeting, the time, the location, and the names of people attending are entered in the first section. The strengths and resources section includes one column for listing the child's strengths and resources and a second column for indicating the family's strengths and resources. The third section provides space for writing the child's goals and family priorities. Information in the IFSP/IEP Planning Guide can assist teams in identifying appropriate outcomes for the child and family on the IFSP/IEP. The final section, Comments, provides space for additional remarks to be recorded.

Child Progress Record

In addition to involving parents in the initial assessment of their child, it is useful to have caregivers and other family members participate in the ongoing monitoring of their child's progress. The Child Progress Record I: Birth to Three Years and Child Progress Record II: Three to Six Years were developed for this purpose. In order to be sensitive to families whose children may not be tested at their appropriate chronological age level because of the severity of their developmental delays, the Child Progress Record is labeled with a I (for birth to three years) and a II (for three to six years).

As with the Family Report, the Child Progress Record parallels the AEPS Test. Each of the goals/objectives from the respective AEPS Test is listed hierarchically on the appropriate level of the Child Progress Record by area and by strand. As children meet the stated criteria for a goal/objective, striking or

FINE MOTOR AREA

Strand A: Reach, Grasp, and Release

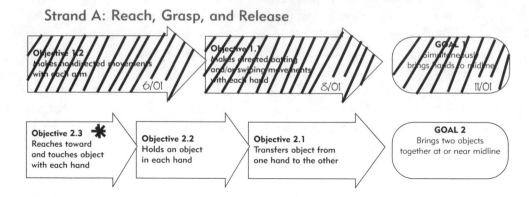

Figure 24.   Strand A from the Fine Motor Area of the Child Progress Record I: Birth to Three Years on which progress data are noted.

shading through the particular goal/objective can indicate their progress. This form provides parents and caregivers with a visual record of their child's accomplishments, current targets, and future goals/objectives. Figure 24 contains a partial strand from the Fine Motor Area of the Child Progress Record I: Birth to Three Years. Goals/objectives that have been met were noted with slash marks, whereas current targeted goals/objectives are noted with an *.

The Child Progress Record was designed to be updated quarterly in conjunction with re-administrations of the AEPS Test. Children progress at different rates; for example, children with severe disabilities may acquire new skills very slowly, appearing to make little progress. Interventionists may wish to add items to some children's Child Progress Record by scaling back the objectives to smaller, more discrete targets. The Child Progress Record is contained in Appendix E of this volume.

SUMMARY

The purpose of this chapter was to describe a process for including caregivers in assessment, goal development, intervention, and evaluation activities to the extent that they choose to be involved. A second purpose was to describe the set of AEPS materials specifically designed for use by caregivers. These materials were developed to be caregiver friendly and to be used in a variety of ways in order to accommodate variations in family values and needs.

The family participation process is offered as a set of guidelines that will most likely require at least some tailoring to meet specific family and program configurations. Indeed, the need to individualize processes as well as materials cannot be overemphasized.

A Team Approach to Using the AEPS

Many young children eligible for early intervention or early childhood special education (EI/ECSE) require a variety of specialists to assess and deliver therapeutic and educational services. The Individuals with Disabilities Education Act (IDEA) as well as recommended practice (e.g., Odom & McLean, 1996; Sandall, McLean, & Smith, 2000) indicate that children be offered a multidisciplinary evaluation to ensure that all of their needs are addressed. Subsequently, intervention efforts must address all areas of children's needs, which may require a team of professionals to be available to consult and deliver services. The concept of team is firmly established in the field of EI/ECSE from the standpoint of both legal and recommended practice requirements. This chapter provides information on how teams can use the AEPS Test in a collaborative fashion to identify children's strengths and needs and deliver quality services. It is important to note here, as we have emphasized elsewhere, that parents and other caregivers are *always* considered an essential part of the team.

THE IMPORTANCE OF COLLABORATION

The importance of team collaboration in the assessment process has been stressed throughout the early intervention literature (e.g., Dinnebeil, Hale, & Rule, 1999). To complete an accurate and comprehensive assessment, team members must develop partnerships and understand the importance of ongoing cooperation and collaboration among professionals and families. For our purposes, *collaboration* is defined as an ongoing interactive and integrative process between team members focused on reaching mutually agreed upon goals (Straka & Bricker, 1996). Collaboration between team members brings a depth and richness to assessment information that is necessary for identifying outcomes and/or developing quality goals/objectives for intervention purposes.

The AEPS Test can be used by a wide variety of professionals and caregivers. The organization of the AEPS Test promotes collaboration by organizing team members' observations. The AEPS Test format also permits observation of children while they are engaged in daily activities. Finally, the AEPS Test allows team members to observe children as they demonstrate what they can do, how they learn new skills, how they interact with familiar people and activities, and how they organize their experiences in a familiar environment.

The AEPS's flexibility permits the use of diverse assessment strategies and various team models. An early interventionist may complete the AEPS Test, with caregiver input, to obtain initial information on a child's developmental strengths and needs. If the child has been identified as needing comprehensive and/or specialized services (e.g., physical therapy, occupational therapy, communication therapy), then the interventionist will also need to work together with a variety of professionals to complete the AEPS Test.

Many specialists have training and experience in conducting traditional assessments using instruments that are relevant to their own discipline—usually involving the examiner and the child in a one-to-one interaction. Given their discipline-specific training, specialists may not be familiar or experienced with curriculum-based measures such as the AEPS Test. Therefore, it may be the responsibility of the early interventionist to encourage team members to participate in the administration of a curriculum-based measure. Start encouraging the team members by explaining to specialists that completion of the AEPS Test through collaborative team efforts is useful because the accuracy and quality of the test results are enhanced when specialists participate in the assessment process; for example, if a child has a communication delay, then it is important to include a communication specialist to complete and score the Social-Communication and Social Areas of the AEPS Test; likewise, if the child has a motor impairment, then it is important for a physical therapist to assist in completing the Gross Motor section of the AEPS Test.

There are multiple advantages for team members to complete a single curriculum-based instrument such as the AEPS Test. First, the AEPS Test can eliminate the redundancy and inconsistency that often occur when professionals complete separate assessments. When team members organize assessment efforts around the administration of the AEPS Test, they can confidently obtain a coordinated and comprehensive developmental profile of a child.

Second, the coordination of comprehensive assessment services by using the AEPS Test may also reduce confusion for families. When all team members use the AEPS Test as a reference point to record and discuss assessment data, families may begin to participate actively in the assessment process.

Third, professionals' observations stimulate cross-disciplinary discussions around "why" they scored a particular behavior as 1 (meets criterion inconsistently) as opposed to 2 (meets criterion consistently). These cross-disciplinary discussions may result in mutual learning by team members during and after assessment activities. These interactions can produce excellent professional development opportunities as team members acquire new knowledge during ongoing assessment activities.

Fourth, using the AEPS Test encourages *ongoing team collaboration* during subsequent intervention and evaluation activities. One of the historical barriers to collaborative service delivery is getting all team members on the "same page." The AEPS Test eliminates this barrier by providing an assessment format whereby team members can combine their assessment information and collaboratively discuss their findings. A next logical step after completing a team assessment is to develop and deliver collaborative intervention services and to coordinate evaluation efforts over time.

TEAM APPROACHES FOR COMPLETING THE AEPS TEST

Providing collaborative services is largely dependent on team members' understanding each other and working together as they design and complete comprehensive assessment activities. Team members should remain flexible as the structure (i.e., number and type of team members) and interactions (i.e., roles, responsibilities, communication) of a team change in response to the multi-dimensional developmental needs of children who require early intervention assessment services.

Team composition directly affects how professionals interact in response to the individualized assessment needs of a child and family. The unique developmental concerns of each child must drive the composition of the cross-disciplinary team, which directly affects team interactions (i.e., possible assessment approach); for example, if the concerns include cognitive and language development, then the team composition would most likely include a developmental and communication specialist. Furthermore, location of assessment activities may alter team composition and interaction during assessment procedures; for example, if the child is currently enrolled in child care, then team members might discuss appropriate collaborative assessment activities in relationship to the typical routines within the child care setting and/or necessary observations during a planned assessment activity that would be directed by the child care worker.

The identified assessment team members are responsible for determining how to interact most productively (i.e., take on roles and responsibilities) as they address the assessment needs of the child and family. Given that the assessment needs of the child often vary, team members will find that a variety of team approaches can exist while using the AEPS Test. Using a collaborative *multiple observer approach* (i.e., multiple team members) to complete the AEPS Test is preferred. It may be appropriate, however, to employ other approaches such as a *collaborative single observer approach*. These two approaches are the most frequently used collaborative strategies when completing the AEPS Test and are described next.

Multiple Observers

When possible, the child should be observed during daily activities by all team members who work together to complete the AEPS Test. Use of the AEPS Test by teams may involve multiple observations of children in familiar environments during play and daily routines. Familiar environments might be child care, center-based, or home settings. The team must obtain information to understand the environment(s) where a child lives, plays, and learns because this is how the team determines "where" and "when" it might be best to complete assessment activities; for example, the physical therapist may want to observe a child outdoors on the play equipment at the park, whereas the occupational therapist may want to conduct his or her observations of the child during tabletop activities to examine fine motor skills or during snack time at the child care setting to observe skills in the adaptive area.

After the necessary information is gathered regarding the child's environment, specific team responsibilities in relationship to the administration of the AEPS Test should be discussed. Team completion of the AEPS Test typically results in professionals collaboratively determining responsibilities to collect information in different areas of the instrument (e.g., the occupational therapist completes the Adaptive Area, the speech-language pathologist completes the Social-Communication Area).

Although the test may be "pulled apart" in order for team members to administer different areas, it is essential that team members appreciate the need to subsequently share and combine the developmental information that has been collected. To produce a comprehensive and valid picture of a child's behavioral repertoire, team members must combine their assessment data into a holistic view of the child.

Family members should be encouraged to complete the Family Report or at least those parts that appear relevant to them. Doing so will likely assist caregivers in becoming contributing members to the team and not passive recipients of information gathered by the professionals. Professional team members are responsible for gathering information for their assigned areas of development (e.g., Fine Motor, Gross Motor, Adaptive, Social-Communication) with the understanding that after completion of their specific area responsibilities, they will contribute to a cross-disciplinary discussion. Cross-disciplinary discussion is important because children's behavior may vary across settings or time; for example, when the physical therapist completes the Gross Motor Area of the AEPS Test, he or she may notice that the child's social interactions consist mostly of pushing other children rather than using words to communicate. This will be important information to share with the communication specialist. The team discussion should also address the consistency of performance across activities. One specialist may see the child exhibit a skill during a more structured activity (e.g., small group time), whereas the therapist responsible for scoring that skill may *not* see the child exhibit the behavior in less structured activities (e.g., free play). In addition, parents may report variations on a child's behavior at home that specialists may not have observed in a center-based setting; for example, an older sibling can get the child to use more language at home than peers can elicit in the child care setting.

Another scenario for using the AEPS Test with multiple observers is for the center-based interventionist to arrange a variety of interesting and fun activities for children. A set of Assessment Activities is contained in Appendix A of Volume 2 and can be used to facilitate data collection. As groups of children participate in these assessment activities, team members can observe the target children for the occurrence of specific test items. Each observing team member can then score portions of the AEPS Test. After areas are scored, team members, including caregivers, discuss results and combine their information into a developmental profile for the child. This approach can also be used in the home setting where a caregiver may be asked to engage the child in a specific activity while the team members observe.

Single Observer in Collaboration with Team Members

A second common approach for using the AEPS Test is to select one team member to complete the test; for example, Younghee is in a center-based program where she has been identified as needing assistance in the Social-Communication and Social Areas of development. Younghee's team includes her mother, the classroom early interventionist, and a communication specialist, Ms. Tanbeck. The communication specialist might take the lead in administering the AEPS Test because the focus of intervention may be in the Social-Communication Area; however, it is essential that Ms. Tanbeck seek validating information from Younghee's teacher and mother.

TEAM ASSESSMENT OF YOUNGHEE

Based on a previous discussion with Mr. Allen, Younghee's teacher, Ms. Tanbeck arrives in the classroom on Monday at 10 A.M. to observe and score the AEPS Test for Younghee, as well as two other children. Each child has been identified as having social-communication delays. Ms. Tanbeck has chosen to facilitate two brief AEPS assessment activities within the classroom. She chose assessment activities that would quickly and naturally elicit the behaviors she needed to observe for scoring the social-communication area of the AEPS Test. At the conclusion of these activities, Ms. Tanbeck shares her observations with Mr. Allen and reports that although Younghee was not observed using any verbal skills during the activities, she did note that Younghee often uses gestures to communicate. Mr. Allen and Ms. Tanbeck determine that a follow-up observation is necessary. Mr. Allen suggests that Ms. Tanbeck return for further observation during snack time because Younghee sometimes talks more during this activity. Ms. Tanbeck returns to the classroom and observes Younghee as she participates in the snack activity. She notes that Younghee uses one-word utterances to indicate desired needs but does not use words for social communication with peers or the staff. Ms. Tanbeck further observes the large group activity that follows snack time and she notes similar behavior from Younghee. Ms. Tanbeck also consults with Younghee's mother and she learns that Younghee's communicative behavior at home is consistent with what she has observed in the classroom. The assessment findings are compiled and transferred into a written summary; Ms. Tanbeck, Mr. Allen, and Younghee's mother meet to discuss these find- ings. Based on their discussion, they agree that the results provide an accurate pic-

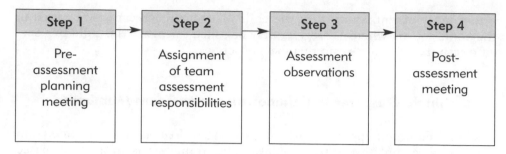

Figure 25.   Four steps in team use of the AEPS Test.

ture of Younghee's communication strengths and needs. Consequently, they utilize the AEPS Test results to select appropriate language goals/objectives for Younghee.

AEPS TEST TEAM ASSESSMENT: A FOUR-STEP PROCESS

As indicated previously, the AEPS Team is designed to accommodate different team compositions and approaches. All team members are encouraged, however, to organize themselves around the four basic team assessment steps shown in Figure 25.

If the steps shown in Figure 25 are to be effective, then the team must 1) have administrative support as they form, develop, and maintain collaborative efforts; 2) be committed to a philosophy that emphasizes interdependence and a holistic view of a child during assessment and intervention; 3) work on joint communication that produces positive team interactions; and 4) have effective strategies for solving conflicts and making decisions.

Step 1: Pre-Assessment Planning Meeting

The first step in team assessment is the *pre-assessment planning meeting.* The meeting is conducted prior to using the AEPS Test. The pre-assessment planning meeting will allow team members to discuss *who* will be responsible for observing each area. Although team members may be assigned to conduct the assessment in their area of expertise, they should have a shared philosophy to gather all pertinent information that they observe (e.g., the communication specialist notes a behavior problem).

Furthermore, during the pre-assessment planning meeting, team members should discuss the best setting(s) to observe the child and *when* it is likely to see the behaviors in each area. If the child is in a child care setting, then the child care worker should inform the team members of the daily schedule and activities that may naturally elicit behaviors that they want to observe. If the assessment is to occur in the home setting, then family members can share information about the home schedule. Given knowledge of the child's daily activities, a specialist can schedule him- or herself in a classroom or home setting at appropriate times to observe. Another option for a center-based setting is to ask the teacher to arrange a series of Assessment Activities. These activities would occur when the professionals are available for systematic observation and scoring of the AEPS Test.

Step 2: Assignment of Team Assessment Responsibilities

This step involves team members discussing the *responsibilities* involved in regard to the assessment decisions that were made; for example, the interventionist may be responsible for having specific snack items available on a particular day when the occupational therapist is scheduled to observe (e.g., items that encourage use of hands and fingers). The communication specialist may be responsible for running a circle activity. During circle time, the classroom interventionist would record assessment data as the specialist provided opportunities for a child to demonstrate the behaviors of interest. The caregiver may be asked to engage the child in a specific activity while the home visitor observes.

Step 3: Assessment Observation

This step involves team members following through on plans agreed to at Steps 1 and 2. Team members record the child's behaviors on a Child Observation Data Recording Form during planned, child-initiated, and routine activities that occur in familiar settings. If children do not perform all behaviors within planned, child-initiated, or routine activities, then it may be necessary for the specialists to conduct direct test procedures, return to the setting/ activity at another time, or try another setting/activity.

Unless parents or other caregivers indicate an unwillingness or inability, they should be encouraged to complete a Family Report on their child. It is likely that completion of the AEPS family materials will assist family members in understanding their child's developmental status, will improve their ability to contribute to the assessment outcomes, and, finally, will enhance their ability to develop IFSP/IEP content that matches their family values and needs.

Step 4: Post-Assessment Meeting

This step involves all team members (e.g., early interventionist, caregiver, specialists) convening for a post-assessment meeting to engage in a cross-disciplinary discussion regarding observed behaviors. The post-assessment meeting should be held shortly after the observations are completed. As part of the team, caregivers are expected to participate. The results noted in the AEPS data collection forms (i.e., Family Report, Child Observation Data Recording Form) are discussed and then compiled and organized for the IFSP/ IEP meeting. The team should indicate potential priority IFSP/IEP outcomes by placing checkmarks beside priority items in the IFSP/IEP box on the Child

Observation Data Recording Form. Caregivers can also indicate priorities on the Family Report.

Following these four steps will help ensure that the team works collaboratively to collect the necessary information to develop a comprehensive and valid picture of the child's repertoire. Following these steps will also help ensure that the team is well prepared to develop IFSPs/IEPs that target outcomes or goals/objectives that are appropriate and important for the child and that are consistent with family desires and values.

SUMMARY

Recommended practice suggests that team members collaborate in the assessment of young children to identify their strengths and developmental needs. The AEPS Test lends itself to collaborative assessment by permitting specialists to focus on their particular area of expertise and by also providing a structure for combining data from a variety of team members.

The AEPS is a curriculum-based assessment/evaluation measure that can be used to introduce specialized disciplines to an educational model that guides team members into collaborative practice. The AEPS Test is especially useful for children who have diverse and multiple needs. For collaboration to work, service providers must see themselves as part of a team and practice behaviors that foster exchange and sharing. Using the AEPS and the four-step process outlined in this chapter can help professionals build collaborative team assessment skills.

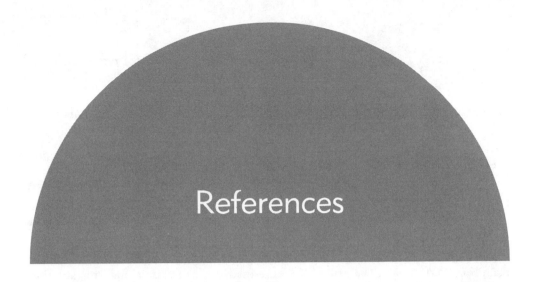

References

Anderson, S., Boigon, S., & Davis, K. (1991). *Oregon Project Curriculum for Visually Impaired and Blind Preschool Children (OPC)*. Medford, OR: Jackson Co. Education Service District.

Bagnato, S.J., & Neisworth, J.T. (1991). *Assessment for early intervention: Best practices for professionals.* New York: The Guilford Press.

Bagnato, S.J., Neisworth, J.T., & Munson, S.M. (1997). *LINKing assessment and early intervention: An authentic curriculum-based approach.* Baltimore: Paul H. Brookes Publishing Co.

Bailey, E., & Bricker, D. (1986). A psychometric study of a criterion-referenced assessment instrument designed for infants and young children. *Journal of the Division for Early Childhood, 10*(2), 124–134.

Bayley, N. (1969). *Bayley Scales of Infant Development.* New York: Psychological Corporation.

Baylcy, N. (1993). *Bayley Scales of Infant Development–II.* San Antonio, TX: Psychological Corporation.

Benner, S. (1992). *Assessing young children with special needs.* New York: Longman Publishing.

Bricker, D. (1981). *Adaptive assessment for evaluating the progress of severely/profoundly handicapped children functioning between birth and two years.* Final report submitted to the U.S. Department of Education, Office of Special Education Program, Washington, DC.

Bricker, D. (1989a). *Early intervention for at-risk and handicapped infants, toddlers, and preschool children.* Palo Alto, CA: VORT Corp.

Bricker, D. (1989b). *Psychometric and utility study of a comprehensive early assessment instrument for handicapped infants and children.* Final Report submitted to the U.S. Office of Education, Office of Special Education Programs, Washington, DC.

Bricker, D., Ayers, E.J., Slentz, K., & Kaminski, R. (1992). *Assessment, evaluation, and programming system test for three to six years.* Eugene: University of Oregon, Center on Human Development.

Bricker, D., Bailey, E., & Slentz, K. (1990). Reliability, validity, and utility of the Evaluation and Programming System: For infants and young children (EPS-I). *Journal of Early Intervention, 14*(2), 147–160.

Bricker, D., Janko, S., Cripe, J., Bailey, E.J., & Kaminski, R (1989). *Evaluation and programming system: For infants and young children.* Eugene: University of Oregon, Center on Human Development.

Bricker, D., & Pretti-Frontczak, K. (Eds.). (1996). *Assessment, Evaluation, and Programming System for Infants and Children: Volume 3: AEPS measurement for three to six years.* Baltimore: Paul H. Brookes Publishing Co.

Bricker, D., & Pretti-Frontczak, K. (1997). *A study of the psychometric properties of the Assessment, Evaluation, and Programming Test for Three to Six Years.* Unpublished report, University of Oregon, Center on Human Development, Early Intervention Program.

Bricker, D., Pretti-Frontczak, K., & McComas, N. (1998). *An activity-based approach to early intervention* (2nd ed.). Baltimore: Paul H. Brookes Publishing Co.

Bricker, D., & Waddell, M. (Eds.). (1996). *Assessment, Evaluation, and Programming System for Infants and Children: Volume 4: AEPS curriculum for three to six years.* Baltimore: Paul H. Brookes Publishing Co.

CAPE—The Consortium on Adaptive Performance Evaluation. (1978). *Adaptive performance instrument (API).* Seattle: Author.

Cripe, J.J.W. (1990). *Evaluating the effectiveness of training procedures in a linked system approach to individual family service plan development.* Unpublished doctoral dissertation, University of Oregon, Eugene.

Dinnebeil, L., Hale, L., & Rule, S. (1999). Early intervention program practices that support collaboration. *Topics in Early Childhood Special Education, 19*(4), 225–235.

Hamilton, D.A. (1995). The utility of the Assessment, Evaluation, and Programming System in the development of quality IEP goals and objectives for young children, birth to three, with visual impairments. *Dissertation Abstracts International, 56*(08), 2994A. (University Microfilms No. AAI95-41906).

Haring, N., White, O., Edgar, E., Affleck, J., & Hayden, A. (1981). *Uniform performance assessment system (UPAS).* Columbus, OH: Charles E. Merrill.

Hsia, T. (1993). *Evaluating the psychometric properties of the Assessment, Evaluation, and Programming System for Three to Six Years: AEPS Test.* Unpublished doctoral dissertation, University of Oregon, Eugene.

Huefner, D.S. (2000). The risks and opportunities of the IEP requirements under IDEA '97. *The Journal of Special Education, 33*(4), 195–204.

Individuals with Disabilities Education Act Amendments of 1997, PL 105-17, 20 U.S.C. §§ 1400 *et seq.*

Knobloch, H., Stevens, F., & Malone, A. (1980). *Manual of developmental diagnosis. The administration and interpretation of the Revised Gesell Armatruda Developmental and Neurologic Examination.* Hagerstown, MD: Harper & Row.

McCarthy, D. (1972). *McCarthy Scales of Children's Abilities.* New York: Psychological Corporation.

McLean, M., & McCormick, K. (1993). Assessment and evaluation in early intervention. In W. Brown, S.K. Thurman, & L.F. Pearl (Eds.), *Family-centered early intervention with infants and toddlers: Innovative cross-disciplinary approaches* (pp. 43–79). Baltimore: Paul H. Brookes Publishing Co.

Messick, S. (1989). Meaning and values in test validation: The science and ethics of assessment. *Educational Researcher, 18*(2), 5–11.

Newborg, J., Stock, J., & Wnek, L. (1988). *The Battelle Developmental Profile.* Allen, TX: Developmental Learning Materials.

Notari, A., & Bricker, D. (1990). The utility of a curriculum-based assessment instrument in the development of individualized education plans for infants and young children. *Journal of Early Intervention, 14*(2), 5–11; 117–32.

Notari, A., & Drinkwater, S.G. (1991). Best practice for writing child outcomes: An evaluation of two methods. *Topics in Early Childhood Special Education, 11*(3), 92–106.

Odom, S., & McLean, M. (Eds.). (1996). *Early intervention/early childhood special education recommended practices.* Austin, TX: PRO-ED.

Pretti-Frontczak, K., & Bricker, D. (2000). Enhancing the quality of Individualized Education Plan (IEP) goals and objectives. *Journal of Early Intervention, 23*(2), 92–105.

Pretti-Frontczak, K., & Bricker, D. (2001). Use of the embedding strategy during daily activities by early childhood education and early childhood special education teachers. *Infant and Toddler Intervention: The Transdisciplinary Journal, 11*(2), 29–46.

Sandall, S., McLean, M., & Smith, B. (2000). *DEC recommended practices in early intervention/early childhood special education.* Denver: Division for Early Childhood of the Council for Exceptional Children.

Slentz, K. (1986). *Evaluating the instructional needs of young children with handicaps: Psychometric adequacy of the Evaluation and Programming System—Assessment Level II (EPS-II).* Unpublished doctoral dissertation, University of Oregon, Eugene.

Straka, E. (1994). Assessment of young children for communication delays. *Dissertation Abstracts International, 56*(02), 456A. (University Microfilms No. AAT95-19689).

Straka, E., & Bricker, D. (1996). Building a collaborative team. In D. Bricker & A. Widerstrom (Eds.), *Preparing personnel to work with infants and young children and their families: A team approach* (pp. 321–345). Baltimore: Paul H. Brookes Publishing Co.

Wetherby, A.M., & Prizant, B. (1993). *Communication and Symbolic Behavior Scales— normed edition.* Baltimore: Paul H. Brookes Publishing Co.

APPENDIX

A

Psychometric Properties of the AEPS

INTRODUCTION

The forerunner to the AEPS Test was the Adaptive Performance Instrument (API). Work began on the API in the early 1970s by a group of investigators identified as the Consortium on Adaptive Performance Evaluation (CAPE, 1978). Although many individuals were associated with CAPE and participated in the early development and testing of the API, Dale Gentry, Owen White, Lizbeth Vincent, Evelyn Lynch, Jeff Seibert, Verna Hart, Katie McCarton, and Diane Bricker provided the sustaining leadership for this project from the mid-1970s to the early 1980s (Bricker, 1981).

Initially, the AEPS was created for the developmental age range of birth to 3 years and, therefore, the initial work beginning in the late 1970s was focused on the AEPS Birth to Three Test. Development began on the AEPS Three to Six Years in the mid-1980s and the first formal study of its psychometric properties was initiated in 1985. This appendix is composed of two sections: the first section reviews the work focused on describing findings pertinent to Birth to Three Years, whereas the second section addresses the research relevant to Three to Six Years.

BIRTH TO THREE YEARS

An extensive investigation of the AEPS Test for Birth to Three Years was conducted from 1984 to 1987 with support provided by the U.S. Department of Education. The goal of the research was to provide information on selected psychometric properties of the AEPS Test (then called the EPS). Results from this project can be found in Bailey and Bricker (1986) and Bricker, Bailey, and Slentz (1990).

The overall findings from Bailey and Bricker (1986) indicated that *interrater agreement* was adequate to good for all areas of the AEPS Test for Birth to Three Years except for the Cognitive Area. *Test–retest reliability* coefficients also ranged from adequate to good for all areas. *Concurrent validity* between children's performances on the Gesell Developmental Schedule (Knobloch, Stevens, & Malone, 1980) and the AEPS Test suggested that the AEPS Test was a valid measure of children's skills and abilities for this sample of 30 children. The relationships between area scores and between area scores and total test scores were also examined. All correlations indicated a relationship between the areas and whole test but not between the individual areas. Finally, data were collected from a small sample of interventionists regarding the *utility* of the AEPS Test. These findings indicated that the AEPS Test could be successfully administered in a reasonable amount of time. Findings from the Bailey and Bricker (1986) investigation were used to make modifications to AEPS Test items.

An investigation by Bricker et al. (1990) produced similar findings regarding the AEPS Test for Birth to Three Years. First, *interrater agreement* was again found to be adequate to good for all areas (i.e., the mean correlations across areas was $r = .87$, $p<.001$). Second, test-retest reliability coefficients ranged from $r = .77$ for the Social Area to $r = .95$ for the Gross Motor Area. The mean correlations across areas was $r = .88$ ($p<.001$). Third, concurrent validity between children's performances on the Gesell Developmental Schedule (Knobloch et al., 1980), the *Bayley Scales of Infant Development* (Bayley, 1969), and the AEPS Test suggested that the AEPS Test was a valid measure of children's skills and abilities for this sample of 155 children. Fourth, the relationship between area scores and total test scores was examined. All correlations were significant at $p<.001$.

An *item analysis* was completed by examining AEPS Test performance scores of 77 children who were typically developing and at risk ranging in age from 2 months to 4 years. The children were grouped into four categories by age: birth to 1 year, 1–2 years, 2–3 years, and 3–4 years. Items were analyzed for each age group by calculating the frequency and percent of children who scored "pass" (i.e., 2), "inconsistent" (i.e., 1), and "fail" (i.e., 0). For this sample of children, the results indicate that all items are hierarchically arranged by age. For all AEPS Test items, the percentage of items passed by older children exceeded that of younger children. When examining the hierarchical arrangement of objectives to goals, the results were also encouraging. In the birth to 1 year age group, data indicate that 81% of the item sequences are hierarchically arranged (i.e., more infants passed the easiest objectives than the more difficult ones). For the 1–2 year age group, 89% of item sequences are hierarchically arranged, whereas 90% of item sequences are hierarchically arranged for the 2–3 year age group. The 3–4 year age range was not included in the analysis because of the limited number of children who were at risk and who did not have disabilities in this group.

A similar analysis by area found only two Fine Motor, four Gross Motor, five Social-Communication, five Cognitive, three Adaptive, and six Social item sequences that were not hierarchically arranged. These data strongly suggest that for this population of children, most AEPS Test goals/objectives (80%–90%) are hierarchically arranged from simple to more complex.

Questionnaires were also completed by 23 field test sites providing feedback on the utility of the AEPS Test. The majority of sites responded favorably to the test content and the administration guide. Questions concerning test content (e.g., Do the results from the AEPS Test accurately reflect the performance of your children?) elicited "yes" responses from 76% of the field test sites—indicating that a majority of these users generally found the content of the AEPS Test appropriate and useful for developing intervention plans. Questions about the AEPS Test items (e.g., Were the item criteria clear?) were rated "yes" by 87% of the sites. Several sites commented on the usefulness of the AEPS Test in relation to the populations that they served. Questions concerning the administration guide (e.g., Did you understand how to use the scoring system?) were answered "yes" by 92% of the sites. Data indicate that the administration guide effectively defined the organizational structure and the procedures for administration of the AEPS. The amount of time it took AEPS Test users to administer the test to one child ranged from 45 minutes to 5 hours, with a mean of 2 hours and 29 minutes. Ninety-one percent of the field test sites used the AEPS Test IFSP/IEP Goal and Objective Examples. The majority of AEPS Test users (78%) indicated that the goals/objectives covered the most important behaviors to be targeted for the children that they served, as well as saved them time in writing individualized family service plans (IFSPs)/ individualized education programs (IEPs). The amount of time saved writing IFSPs/IEPs per child ranged from 30 minutes to 2 hours, with a mean of 57 minutes saved per child.

In 1990, Notari and Bricker conducted the first in a series of studies examining the *treatment validity* of the AEPS. *Treatment validity* is defined as " . . . the meaning, relevance, and utility of scores, the import or value implications of scores as a basis for action, and the functional worth of scores in terms of the social consequences of their use" (Messick, 1989, p. 5). Treatment validity studies are necessary to determine if measures such as the AEPS Test improve the quality of services delivered to children and that, in turn, produce measurable child performance outcomes that surpass expectations or benchmarks. The primary purpose of the Notari and Bricker study was to examine the quality IFSP/IEP goals/objectives written from AEPS Test Birth to Three results. This study involved 48 early interventionists from three states and British Columbia and examined the effectiveness of the AEPS Test to generate goals/objectives that were functional, generic, measurable, and easy to embed in daily activities. The study also investigated the hierarchical relationship between goals/objectives.

The experimental groups who used the AEPS Test wrote higher quality goals/objectives than a comparison group who used other assessment tools to develop goals/objectives. The AEPS Test presented particular advantages in generating quality goals and providing guidance in the identification of specific long-term expectations for children that were developmentally and educationally consistent with the objectives.

Notari and Drinkwater (1991) investigated the quality of IFSP/IEP goals/ objectives written using the AEPS Test for Birth to Three Years. Goals and objectives for 17 children ages 3–26 months with Down syndrome were examined. In all, a total of 376 goals and objectives were rated with 224 from the AEPS Test and 152 from a computerized list (i.e., a list compiled by educators and therapists). Sets of goals/objectives were randomly combined and rated. An independent sample t-test was performed to determine whether significant differences existed in the quality of child IFSP/IEP goals/objectives and the hierarchical relationship between them. Significant differences were found between the two groups' goals/objectives, suggesting that when teachers used the AEPS Test for Birth to Three Years, they wrote goals/objectives that were "more functional, generic, easy to integrate within the instruc-tional content, and measurable, as compared to those based on computerized list" (p. 101). Notari and Drinkwater also reported that "the AEPS enabled teachers to sequence goals/objectives according to a hierarchical teaching sequence" (p. 101).

A study conducted by Cripe (1990) examined the *effectiveness of the AEPS family measures* (e.g., Family Interest Survey and Family Report, then called the Parent Form) and specific training on how to use the AEPS linked assessment, intervention, and evaluation system. Thirty interventionists from three states were divided into three treatment groups. The pretest measure was an IFSP completed on a child and family by the interventionists within the previous 12 months. The posttest measure was a second IFSP written following treatment.

Group 1 received the AEPS family measures, Group 2 received the same materials plus a half-day of training, and Group 3 received the same materials plus 2 days of training. The results indicated that interventionists in all groups included significantly more family-related outcomes on the IFSP at posttest. In addition, the quality of ratings (e.g., measurability, specificity, functionality, generality) was higher for IFSP outcomes at posttest for all groups. Group three, who received the materials plus 2 days of training, demonstrated the greatest improvement.

Straka (1994) conducted an investigation that compared the utility of outcomes of the AEPS Test with the Communication Symbolic and Behavior Scales (CSBS; Wetherby & Prizant, 1993) in regards to intervention planning for young children with communication problems. Four American Speech-Language-Hearing Association certified communication specialists participated in the study. Straka (1994) reported that communication specialists found the AEPS Test to be more useful than the CSBS in developing IEP goals/objectives. Straka reported few differences, however, in functionality, generality, instructional context, and measurability of goals/objectives developed from the CSBS and AEPS. Findings also indicated that the AEPS Test provided an easier format for developing goals/objectives (more efficient and less time consuming) and more guidance in identifying specific long-term goals/objectives. Lastly, Straka reported that the communication specialists found the AEPS Test to be more helpful in developing functional and appropriate goals/objectives that corresponded to the individualized needs of each child.

In 1995, Hamilton continued the investigation of the *treatment validity* of the AEPS Test by examining the quality of educational goals/objectives for young children with visual impairments. Forty special education teachers served as subjects. All teachers received 1 day of training on using the AEPS Test to write goals/objectives. Hamilton (1995) found that goals/objectives written by teachers for children with visual impairments were of higher quality when they used the AEPS Test versus the Oregon Project Curriculum for Visually Impaired and Blind Preschool Children (Anderson, Boigon, & Davis, 1991). Test main effect was significant, $F(1, 37) = 20.66$, $p<.001$. Teacher-written goals/objectives for young children with visual impairments based on AEPS Test information ($M = 21.20$) were of significantly higher quality overall, than goals/objectives based on Oregon Project information ($M = 15.95$).

THREE TO SIX YEARS

As indicated in the previous section, psychometric investigations of the AEPS Test for Birth to Three Years began in the late 1970s, whereas psychometric investigations of the AEPS Test for Three to Six Years began in the mid-1980s. The first formal study was completed in 1986.

The 1986 Slentz study examined selected psychometric properties of the AEPS Test for Three to Six Years. Fifty-four children who ranged in age from 34 to 76 months participated in the study. Seventeen children showed no delays in development, 22 were at risk for delays, and 15 were identified as having disabilities: 7 mild and 8 with more moderate disabilities. *Interobserver agreement* was found to be adequate to good for all areas and significant at $p<.001$ (i.e., correlations ranged from $r = .60$ to $r = .94$). *Test–retest reliability* coefficients ranged from adequate to good for all areas except the Gross Motor and Adaptive Areas. *Concurrent validity* between children's performances on McCarthy Scales of Children's Abilities (McCarthy, 1972), the Uniform Performance Assessment System (Haring, White, Edgar, Affleck, & Hayden, 1981), and the AEPS Test suggested that the AEPS Test was a valid measure of children's skills and abilities for a sub-sample of 18 children. The relationship between area scores and total test scores were also examined. All correlations were significant and ranged from $r = .37$ ($p<.01$) for the Adaptive Area to .97 ($p<.0001$) for the Cognitive Area.

The mean rank order of AEPS Test total scores was calculated for 3-year-olds in comparison with 4-year-olds and for 4-year-olds in comparison with 5-year-olds. A Mann-Whitney U test found that 4-year-olds' total test scores were significantly higher than 3-year-olds' total test scores ($p<.001$). The difference between 4- and 5-year-olds' total test scores was not significant— likely because of the small sample and the children's location on the age continuum (i.e., many 4-year-olds were close to 48 months of age).

Psychometric properties of the AEPS Test for Three to Six Years were also studied by Hsia (1993). Eighty-two children who ranged in age from 3 to 6 years participated in this study. Fifty-one of these children were classified as having no disabilities, 20 were classified as having disabilities (i.e., had been determined eligible to receive early intervention services), and 11 were classified as at risk. An AEPS Test was completed on each child by a trained examiner. The test was scored primarily through observation of the children as they participated in planned and free play activities while attending a center-based program.

Interobserver reliability was examined by correlating the children's area scores and total test scores from the AEPS Test protocols of two independent coders. Data from all 82 children were included in this analysis, although not all children had the opportunity to participate in all gross motor and adaptive activities necessary for scoring a complete protocol. The percent agreement between two independent coders ranged from .86 to .95 for individual areas and .90 for the total test.

A high degree of internal consistency ($r = .99$) was found for the total group and for the two subgroups (children with or who are at risk for disabilities, $r = .97$; children without disabilities, $r = .93$). At the area level, the total group correlations were .75 for the Fine Motor Area, .82 for the Adaptive Area, .83 for the Gross Motor and Social Areas, .95 for the Cognitive Area, .96 for the Social-Communication Area, and .97 for the total area scores. All correlations were significant at the $p<.01$ level. Correlations tended to be lower for the subgroups, but all were significant except for the Social Area for the subgroup with disabilities.

Hsia (1993) also examined the *sensitivity* of the AEPS Test. The AEPS Test was designed to be sensitive to variations in the performance of children of different ages and with different levels of disability; therefore, children who are older and are more able should score higher on the test than children who are younger or less able.

In analyzing the test's accuracy at distinguishing children of different ages, Hsia (1993) included only children *without disabilities*. For this analysis, children were assigned to one of three age groups (3-, 4-, and 5-year-old groups) based on their date of birth. A one-way analysis of variance was used to examine subjects' scores in each of the six areas and for the total test score. A multiple comparison procedure, the Scheffe test, was performed when a significant F was obtained. With the exception of the Adaptive Area, a significant F ratio was obtained for the other five areas and for the total test scores. The 5-year-olds scored significantly higher than the 3- and 4-year-olds, but the 3- and 4-year-olds were not significantly different from each other.

Because a number of children with disabilities were not involved in activities that assessed their gross motor and adaptive abilities, total scores for the children with disabilities for this analysis were obtained by summing the other four area scores (i.e., Fine Motor, Cognitive, Social-Communication, and Social). A one-way analysis of variance was performed using three groups of children: those without disabilities, those at risk or with mild disabilities, and those with moderate/severe disabilities. A statistically significant difference was found for all groups for all areas and for the total test. The Scheffe test indicated that children in the group without disabilities had higher area and total test scores than the children in both of the other groups.

With the exception of the Fine Motor Area, significant score differences were found between the three groups. The Fine Motor Area scores of the group without disabilities were significantly higher than those of the group with moderate/severe disabilities but not those of the group at risk or with mild disabilities. The group at risk or with mild disabilities had significantly higher total test scores than the group with moderate/severe disabilities, but, at the area level, only Social-Communication Area scores were significantly different.

A series of studies funded by the U.S. Department of Education was conducted beginning in the mid-1990s and continued the focus on the *treatment validity* of the AEPS Test for Three to Six Years (Bricker & Pretti-Frontczak, 1997). To examine the treatment validity of the AEPS Test, a series of hypotheses were generated. First, it was hypothesized that administration and use of the AEPS Test would improve the quality of written IFSP/IEP goals/objectives. Second, it was hypothesized that better written IFSP/IEP goals/objectives would increase teachers' use of a specific intervention strategy referred to as *embedding*. Third, it was hypothesized that the embedding of quality goals/ objectives during a variety of daily activities would lead to improved outcomes for young children.

Pretti-Frontczak and Bricker (2000) conducted a *treatment validity* study based on the hypothesis that using AEPS Test results produced higher quality goals/objectives. In particular, they examined whether a 2-day training session on how to write IEP goals/objectives and the use of the AEPS Test results improved the quality of IEP goals/objectives written by early childhood special education personnel. Findings are based on a comparison of pretraining goal/ objective ratings with posttraining goal/objective ratings for 86 participants from five states. Participants (i.e., teachers, therapists, coordinators) for the study were somewhat geographically diverse representing the middle, southern, and western regions of the country. Using paired t-tests, aggregated mean percent scores for goals/objectives using the AEPS Test before and following training were compared. Statistically significant differences for aggregated mean percent scores for each of the 10 goal quality indicator comparisons were found. In addition, statistically significant differences for aggregated mean percent scores for 9 of the 11 objective quality comparisons were found. The results of this finding are clear: use of the AEPS Test Three to Six Years in combination with training on writing goals/objectives improved the quality of goals/objectives written by participants.

In order to examine the second hypothesis associated with treatment validity (i.e., better written IFSP/IEP goals/objectives would increase teachers' use of a specific intervention strategy referred to as *embedding*), two additional studies were conducted. In the first study, 16 early childhood educators and early childhood special educators from four states participated (Bricker & Pretti-Frontczak, 1997; Pretti-Frontczak & Bricker, 2001). The teachers attended a two-day training session on how to use the AEPS Test to assess children and to write goals/objectives from assessment results. The quality of written goals/objectives, as well as the teacher's use of the embedding strategy before and after training, was measured.

Findings from the study of 16 early childhood education (ECE)/early childhood special education (ECSE) teachers indicated a significant improvement in the quality of *goals* written after training on all 10 quality indicators, which is especially noteworthy give the small sample size. Findings also indicated a significant ($p<.001$ to $p<.05$) improvement in the quality of written *objectives* on 7 of 11 quality indicators following training. A second analysis revealed that overall, 13 of the 16 participants improved the quality of objectives targeted specifically for use with the embedding strategy. Despite the writing of higher quality goals/objectives and the targeting of higher quality objectives by 13 of the 16 teachers, the percentage of intervals that teachers used the embedding strategy decreased from the pretraining phase to the posttraining phase for 11 of the 16 participants. A relationship between the decrease in teachers' use of the embedding strategy and the quality of target objectives was not found.

A follow-up study was conducted in which a group of ECE/ECSE teachers were given training on writing quality goals/objectives from AEPS Test results **and** explicit training on use of the embedding strategy across daily classroom activities (Pretti-Frontczak & Bricker, 2001). Seven ECE/ECSE teachers were recruited to participate in the follow-up study.

Findings from the follow-up study indicate that all objectives written from the AEPS Test results met the quality criteria rating of 7 or higher (i.e., 7 out of 11). Findings also indicated that the seven teachers used the embedding strategy with their target child an average of 9.7% of intervals observed on one measure and 10.6% of intervals observed on a second measure. The teachers in the study tended to embed target objectives by asking questions and providing verbal models. Lastly, the teachers were most likely to utilize the embedding strategy when they worked individually with the target children and engaged in language and pre-academic activities. The teachers were least likely to embed children's objectives during large group activities or while addressing adaptive skills.

When conducting treatment validity studies, it is important to examine outcomes that have relevance for the ultimate target—in this case—children. Two single subject studies were designed and conducted to determine if higher quality objectives written from AEPS Test results and embedded into daily activities would improve child outcomes (Bricker & Pretti-Frontczak, 1997).

In Study One, four preschool teachers from the northwestern region of the United States participated in the study. The teachers selected one child from their classroom for whom they targeted two objectives written from AEPS Test results and embedded during daily activities. Visual analysis was used to examine the functional relationship between using the embedding strategy with quality objectives written from the AEPS Test results and children's performance on targeted objectives. Child performance data from Study One suggest that, in general, a functional relationship exists between embedding children's objectives into daily activities and progress made on targeted objectives for training group children. Measures of the children's progress revealed changes from the baseline phase to the intervention phase in both trend and slope. Although the results of Study One were promising, they were mixed—not all children responded to the same extent when compared with one another's progress or when compared with their two targeted objectives. Moreover, the results were based on two targeted objectives for only four children. To further examine the relationship between teachers' use of the embedding strategy and child performance, a replication study was conducted.

The replication study was conducted with four different teachers. Each teacher selected one child from her classroom for whom she targeted two intervention objectives developed from the AEPS Test results. Teachers then were asked to embed these selected objectives in daily classroom activities. As in the previous study, visual analysis was used to examine the relationship between the embedding of quality objectives and child performance on these objectives. Although measures of child performance revealed some change from baseline to intervention in both trend and slope, the results were not compelling. Although the children did make progress toward their objectives, the results did not demonstrate a functional relationship between the teachers' use of the embedding strategy and child performance.

Results from these two studies provide limited evidence that teachers' embedding of quality objectives is associated with positive change in child performance. Continued work is needed to determine if the rate and length of time that teachers embed children's quality objectives are critical variables in effecting child performance over time.

SUMMARY

Ascertaining adequate support to conduct well-designed investigations of the AEPS Test has been difficult. To gather data from a range of subjects and interventionists from a variety of geographic locations is a costly endeavor. Although the investigations that have been conducted fall short of what should be done, the outcomes do provide some assurance that the AEPS Test is generally reliable and valid for the samples involved. We are grateful for the support provided by the U.S. Department of Education to conduct the major investigations reported in this appendix.

Perhaps the more important outcomes are those that suggest that using the AEPS Test improves the quality of IFSP/IEP goals and objectives developed by interventionists. Also, the research that has examined the utility of the test has provided extremely useful feedback. Again, this work only touches the surface of what needs to be done to establish that the AEPS Test and accompanying materials are effective and useful across a range of interventionists and children.

The developers of the AEPS hope to continue studying the properties, effectiveness, and usefulness of the materials as time and resources permit.

APPENDIX

B

IFSP/IEP Goal and Objective Examples

INTRODUCTION

This appendix contains a list of individualized family service plan (IFSP)/individualized education program (IEP) Goal and Objective Examples that can serve as guides or models that parallel items from the AEPS Test Birth to Three Years and Three to Six Years. Following administration of the AEPS Test, priority skills should be selected by the interventionists and family. Once priority skills are chosen, the interventionist can refer to this appendix to obtain guidance in developing goals/objectives that directly corresponds to the AEPS Test items and assessment information. The prototype goals/objectives contained in this appendix were designed to serve as models or guides for developing goals/objectives for individual children; however, in most cases, the goals/objectives will need modification to meet individual child needs.

IFSP/IEP Goal and Objective Examples

FINE MOTOR AREA

Strand A: Reach, Grasp, and Release

G1 The child will simultaneously bring hands together at or near the middle of the body.

    1.1 When presented with a toy (e.g., mobile, rattle), the child will bat and/or swipe at or toward toy with each hand.

    1.2 When presented with a toy (e.g., mobile, rattle), the child will make nondirected movements with each arm.

G2 The child will bring two hand-size objects together at or near the middle of the body (e.g., bang two objects together).

    2.1 The child will move an object (e.g., stick, block) from the left hand to the right hand and from the right hand to the left hand (i.e., transfer objects).

    2.2 The child will hold one object (e.g., squeeze-toy, block) in each hand at the same time.

    2.3 When presented with an object (e.g., block, rattle), the child will reach toward and touch the object with each hand.

G3 The child will grasp hand-size object (e.g., bath toy, block, rattle) with either hand using the ends of thumb, index, and second fingers; object is held by the fingers and does not rest in palm.

    3.1 The child will grasp hand-size object (e.g., bath toy, rattle, ball) with either hand using the palm, with the object placed toward the thumb and index finger; fingers are closed around object with thumb rotated toward fingers.

    3.2 The child will grasp cylindrical object (e.g., rattle, wooden spoon, crayon, marker) with either hand by closing fingers around it.

    3.3 The child will grasp hand-size object (e.g., bath toy, block) with either hand using the whole hand and holding object in center of palm with fingers closed around it.

G4 The child will grasp pea-size object (e.g., dry cereal, bead, button) with either hand using tip of index finger and thumb, object not held against palm; arm or hand does not rest on a surface for support.

    4.1 The child will grasp pea-size object (e.g., dry cereal, bead, button) with either hand using tip of index finger and thumb, object not held against palm; arm or hand may rest on surface for support.

    4.2 The child will grasp pea-size object (e.g., dry cereal, bead, button) with either hand using the side of index finger and thumb; other fingers are held loosely.

    4.3 The child will grasp pea-size object (e.g., dry cereal, bead, button) with either hand using some or all fingers in a raking and/or scratching movement.

G5 When given at least three objects, the child will align and stack objects (e.g., cube, can, spool) on top of another object with either hand, balancing and releasing it without knocking it over (e.g., block on a block, can on a can).

    5.1 Child will align at least three objects in a line (e.g., cans, plates, small chairs).

    5.2 The child will place and release object balanced on top of another object with either hand without knocking them over (e.g., blocks, cans).

    5.3 The child will release a hand-held object onto and/or into a larger target with either hand (e.g., put a ball in a box, put a bead in a cup, put a block on a can).

    5.4 The child will voluntarily release hand-held object with each hand (e.g., let go of a rattle to pick up another object).

Strand B: Functional Use of Fine Motor Skills

G1 The child will rotate either wrist on horizontal plane to turn part of an object (e.g., turn lid on jar, turn music box knob).

    1.1 The child will turn an object over using wrist and arm rotation with each hand; the hand is brought from palm down position to palm up position and back again (e.g., turn the page of a book, bring food to mouth).

G2 The child will assemble toys and/or objects by putting pieces together (e.g., pop beads, Legos, string beads, three- or four-piece puzzle). (Adult may demonstrate or point to correct space.)

    2.1 The child will fit different shapes into corresponding spaces (e.g., fit square, triangle, and/or circle into simple shape box and/or form board). (Adult may demonstrate or point to correct space.)

    2.2 The child will fit small objects into defined spaces (e.g., put toy car into garage, put ball in bucket, put doll in toy bed). (Adult may demonstrate or point to correct space.)

G3 The child will use left and/or right extended index finger to activate objects (e.g., dial a telephone, push elevator button).

    3.1 The child will activate objects with either hand (e.g., honk horn, push button).

G4 The child will orient picture book correctly with pages right side up with the front cover facing upward and turn pages one by one from beginning of book to the end (a few pages may be missed).

    4.1 The child will turn pages of books grasping edges of pages and will turn without tearing or ripping.

    4.2 The child will hold a picture book right side up, turning it if necessary to orient the pictures upright.

G5 The child will copy simple written shapes (e.g., cross, circle, square) after demonstration. (Shape should resemble the demonstrated model.)

5.1 The child will draw circles and lines (e.g., make circular shapes and linear strokes). (Lines do not need to be perfectly straight.)

5.2 The child will scribble by making back-and-forth marks or strokes. Tapping (i.e., dotting motion) with writing implement on paper is not considered scribbling.

GROSS MOTOR AREA

Strand A:
Movement and Locomotion in Supine and Prone Position

G1 When on back, the child will turn head in both directions, move arms, and kick legs independently of each other (arms and legs are not stiff when they move).

    1.1 When on back, the child will turn head to the right and the left, at least 45° from midline position.

    1.2 When on back, the child will alternately kick legs.

    1.3 When on back, the child will wave arms freely in all directions.

G2 The child will roll from stomach to back and from back to stomach in both directions by shifting weight to one side of the body, leading with head, shoulder, or hip without arching back or crossing legs.

    2.1 When on back, the child will roll (in both directions) to stomach by shifting weight to one side of the body, leading with head, shoulder, or hip without arching back or crossing legs.

    2.2 When lying on stomach, the child will roll (in both directions) to back by shifting weight to one side of the body, leading with head, shoulder, or hip without arching back or crossing legs.

G3 When placed on flat surface, the child will creep forward at least 6 feet, bearing weight on hands and knees using alternating arm and leg movements (i.e., moving one arm and opposite leg, then other arm and opposite leg).

    3.1 The child will rock back and forth at least two consecutive times while on hands and knees in a creeping position.

    3.2 When placed on stomach, the child will assume a creeping position on hands and knees with stomach lifted off surface.

    3.3 When placed on stomach, the child will crawl forward at least 2 feet with stomach touching the surface, pulling with arms, and supporting weight on hands and/or arms; legs alternately bend and straighten but do not cross.

    3.4 When on stomach, the child will pivot 180° in each direction in a semi-circle.

    3.5 When on stomach, the child will reach with one hand by supporting weight on one hand and/or arm while reaching toward object with the opposite hand.

    3.6 When on stomach, the child will lift head and chest off surface with weight on bent or straight arms; head is in midline, knees and legs should not be crossed.

Strand B: Balance in Sitting

G1 The child will move to a sitting position on the floor from any position (e.g., creeping, lying down, standing).

    1.1 From a sitting position on a flat surface, the child will move to a hands and knees position by using rotation (i.e., reaching across the body with either arm and shifting weight to knees).

    1.2 When sitting, the child will move back to a balanced, upright sitting position after reaching across the body to the right and to the left.

    1.3 When sitting, the child will move back to a balanced, upright sitting position after leaning to the left, to the right, and forward.

    1.4 When placed in sitting position, the child will sit in an upright position with back straight and hands not touching the floor for balance for at least 30 seconds.

    1.5 When placed in sitting position, the child will use hands for balance and hold head in midline for at least 60 seconds.

    1.6 When sitting in a supported position (e.g., supported by adult's hands), the child will hold head in midline and back straight for at least 30 seconds.

G2 The child will sit down in and get out of child-size chair.

    2.1 On adult prompt or spontaneously, the child will sit down in child-size chair.

    2.2 When placed in chair, the child will maintain sitting position in child-size chair without support.

Strand C: Balance and Mobility

G1 When walking unsupported, the child will move to avoid obstacles (e.g., toys, furniture, people).

    1.1 When walking unsupported, the child will walk for at least 6 feet.

    1.2 When holding onto support with one hand, the child will walk with head erect and back straight for at least 15 feet.

    1.3 When holding onto support with two hands, the child will walk with head erect and back straight for at least 15 feet.

    1.4 When in standing position, the child will stand alone with back straight and head in midline for at least 30 seconds.

    1.5 The child will cruise (i.e., side step to the left and to the right) while holding onto a stable support (e.g., couch, coffee table, wall) for at least 3 feet.

G2 After stooping or squatting, the child will regain a balanced standing position without using support or sitting down.

    2.1 When placed in a sitting position on the floor, the child will stand up without support.

    2.2 From a sitting, kneeling, and/or creeping position, the child will pull to a standing position using a support (e.g., low table, chair).

    2.3 From a sitting and/or creeping position, the child will pull to a kneeling position using a support (e.g., low table, chair).

G3 The child will avoid obstacles (e.g., toys, furniture, people) when running.

    3.1 The child will run smoothly with knees flexed, arms alternated, and balance maintained.

    3.2 The child will walk fast. (Motion differs from a run in that the body appears stiff and knees do not bend.)

G4 The child will walk up and down stairs. (The child may use one-hand support and need not alternate feet.)

    4.1 The child will walk up and down stairs using two-hand support (e.g., railings, adult's hands). (Child need not alternate feet.)

    4.2 The child will move up and down stairs by creeping, crawling, and/or scooting on buttocks.

    4.3 The child will climb onto and off of a low, stable structure (e.g., low step, raised platform).

Strand D: Play Skills

G1 When prompted and/or provided a model, the child will jump forward with feet together for at least one jump

    1.1 When prompted, the child will jump up with feet together (e.g., over rope, stick, chalk line).

    1.2 The child will jump from a low, stable structure (e.g., low step, raised platform, curb).

G2 The child will pedal and steer tricycle forward for at least 5 feet when sitting on riding toy.

    2.1 When sitting on riding toy with feet on surface, the child will push riding toy with feet while steering for at least 5 feet.

    2.2 The child will sit on riding toy and/or wagon while adult steers and pushes riding toy and/or pulls wagon for at least 5 feet.

G3 The child will catch ball (or similar object) with two hands, kick ball with one foot without falling, throw ball underhand or overhand within 18 inches of target, and roll ball within 18 inches of target.

    3.1 When a ball (or similar object) is tossed, the child will catch it using two hands.

    3.2 When given a ball (or similar object) on the floor, the child will kick it forward using one foot while maintaining balance.

    3.3 When given a ball (or similar object), the child will throw it forward (underhand/overhand) with one or two hands within 18 inches of target.

    3.4 When prompted, the child will roll ball with one or two hands within 18 inches of target.

G4 The child will climb up and down play equipment; move up and down inclines (e.g., slide, ramp); and move under, over, and through obstacles (e.g., tunnel, barrel).

    4.1 The child will move up and down inclines (e.g., climb up and slide down slide, creep or walk up ramp). Child may hold handrail or wall with one hand and need not alternate feet.

    4.2 When presented with obstacles, the child will move under, over, and through obstacles (e.g., crawl under jungle gym bars, move through barrel, climb into and out of sand box).

ADAPTIVE AREA

Strand A: Feeding

G1 When given a variety of foods and liquids, the child will use tongue and lips to take in and swallow without choking or gagging.

    1.1 When drinking liquid from a cup and/or glass, the child will use lips to seal the cup rim, draw in liquid, and retain liquid in mouth when swallowing.

    1.2 When presented with food on a spoon and/or fork, the child will use upper lip movement to take food off a spoon and/or fork. (The spoon and/or fork are not scraped on child's upper or lower lip.)

    1.3 When given solid/semi-solid food, the child will swallow solid (e.g., noodles, apples, meats, crackers) and semi-solid (e.g., applesauce, yogurt) bites of food without gagging, choking, or swallowing pieces whole.

    1.4 When in a semi-reclining or upright position, the child will swallow liquids from a bottle, breast, or cup without choking or gagging with minimal loss of liquid from mouth.

G2 When given hard and chewy food, the child will use teeth to bite through foods with tongue moving side to side and jaw moving side to side and diagonally to break up food.

    2.1 When given crisp and/or soft food, the child will use teeth or gums to bite through and chew with tongue moving side to side and jaw moving side to side and diagonally to break up food.

    2.2 When presented soft and/or crisp food, the child will munch (i.e., smack and/or suck food while opening and closing mouth with up and down movement of jaw) to break up soft and crisp foods.

G3 When given a drink from a cup and/or glass, the child will drink by bringing cup and/or glass to mouth and returning cup and/or glass to surface without spilling.

    3.1 When given a cup and/or glass, the child will bring cup and/or glass to mouth and drink with minimal spilling. (Child may release cup before returning to surface.)

    3.2 While adult holds cup and/or glass, the child will use lip closure to drink. (Some loss of liquid may occur.)

G4 The child will eat with a fork and/or spoon by spearing or scooping food and bringing it to mouth with minimal spilling.

    4.1 When given food and fork and/or spoon, the child will eat by bringing filled utensil to mouth. (Child may have assistance filling fork and/or spoon; some spilling may occur.)

    4.2 When presented with large and/or small pieces of food, the child will use fingers to grasp and bring food to mouth.

    4.3 While adult holds spoon, the child will eat food from spoon by opening mouth and closing jaw and lips around utensil.

G5 When presented with food, utensils, and liquid that will not overflow containers, the child will scoop food and pour liquids from one container to another without spilling (e.g., liquid from pitcher to glass, food from large bowl to plates).

    5.1   When presented with an amount of liquid that will not overfill the container, the child will pour liquid from one container to another without spilling.

    5.2   When presented with utensils and food in containers, the child will use utensils to transfer food from one container to another.

Strand B: Personal Hygiene

G1 The child will initiate going to the toilet and will demonstrate bowel and bladder control. (Child may need help completing routine; occasional reminders are acceptable.)

    1.1   The child will demonstrate bowel and bladder control when taken to toilet on a regular basis. (Occasional accidents are acceptable.)

    1.2   When pants or diapers are soiled or wet, the child will indicate awareness of soiled and wet pants and/or diapers by verbalizing, gesturing, and/or signing.

G2 After toileting or before eating, the child will wash and dry hands by turning faucet on and off, washing with soap, drying hands, and returning towel to rack or throwing towel away. (Child may request assistance in turning faucet on and off.)

    2.1   With adult assistance in turning the faucet on and off, the child will wash hands with soap and rinse with water.

G3 The child will brush teeth after another person puts toothpaste on toothbrush. (Another person may provide assistance for effective cleaning.)

    3.1   When the adult brushes the child's teeth, child will allow teeth to be brushed long enough to effectively clean teeth.

Strand C: Undressing

G1 With assistance in unfastening, the child will undress self by taking off coat and/or jacket, pants, shirt, socks, shoes, and hat.

    1.1   The child will take off pullover shirt and/or sweater

    1.2   The child will take off front-fastened coat, jacket, or shirt with the assistance of another person.

    1.3   The child will take off long pants from both feet when given another person's assistance in unfastening.

    1.4   The child will take off socks.

    1.5   With assistance in unfastening, the child will take off shoes.

    1.6   With assistance in unfastening, the child will take off hat.

COGNITIVE AREA

Strand A: Sensory Stimuli

G1 When presented with auditory, visual, and tactile event, the child will look at, turn to, reach for, and/or move toward the auditory, visual, and tactile event (e.g., doorbell, mobile, person's touch).

1.1 When presented with a sound, the child will look at, turn to, reach for, and/or move in the direction of the sound.

1.2 When given a visual event, the child will look at, turn to, reach for, and/or move toward an object and/or person presented within the child's sight.

1.3 When given tactile stimulation, (e.g., a touch) the child will look at, turn to, reach for, and/or move toward an object and/or person who touches child.

1.4 When given an auditory, visual, and tactile event, the child will respond to event (e.g., doorbell, mobile, person's touch) by momentarily ceasing or increasing activity.

Strand B: Object Permanence

G1 When presented with a moving object and/or person, the child will watch object and/or person until it disappears.

1.1 When objects are moved horizontally, vertically, and in circular directions, the child will visually follow objects.

1.2 When presented with a nonmoving object and/or person, the child will focus on it for at least 4 seconds.

G2 When an object is hidden first in one place and then in another place while the child is watching, the child will immediately find the object in the last hiding place.

2.1 When an object and/or person is hidden while the child is watching, the child will immediately find the object and/or person (e.g. people hiding as part of hide-and-seek game, ball rolling under table, crayon hidden under paper).

2.2 When an object and/or person is partially hidden while the child is watching, the child will immediately find the object and/or person (e.g., child retrieves toy that has been partially hidden under blanket by another person).

2.3 When an object and/or person is hidden while the child is watching, the child will react to its disappearance (e.g., cry, turn head to look around, become startled).

G3 When a familiar object is not in its usual place, the child will look for the object in more than one other place (e.g. when coat is not on coat rack, child will look in several likely places).

3.1 The child will spontaneously look for desired object in its usual place (e.g., child looks for toys in toy box, coat in coat closet).

Strand C: Causality

G1 Spontaneously or when adult demonstrates action, the child will correctly activate a mechanical toy (e.g., wind the dial, turn the handle).

1.1 When presented with a simple toy, the child will activate a simple toy spontaneously or after demonstration (e.g., squeeze a squeeze-toy, shake a rattle).

Strand E: Problem Solving

G1 Spontaneously or on request, the child will indicate (e.g., tell, demonstrate) why particular solutions to problems that occur within context would or would not work (e.g., child stands on a chair to reach toys on shelf and says to an adult, "This chair is too small. I can't reach," and goes to find a taller chair).

1.1 Spontaneously or on request, the child will indicate (e.g., tell, demonstrate) acceptable solutions to problems (e.g., child is having difficulty cutting and points to a different pair of scissors when asked, "What can you try?"). Adult may provide general cues (e.g., "What can we do?" "What can you try?").

1.2 Spontaneously or on request, the child will name or select appropriate/functional means to a goal when problems and their solutions have been identified (e.g., child brings a large, empty container in response to an adult's request, "Find something for carrying the blocks").

G2 The child will make statements and appropriately answer questions that require the child to
- Give reasons for inferences
- Make predictions about future or hypothetical events
- Determine possible causes for events

2.1 Spontaneously or on request, the child will give plausible reasons for making inferences (e.g., child says, "She is sad"; an adult asks, "How do you know that the girl is sad?"; Child answers, "Because she is crying").

2.2 Spontaneously or on request, the child will make plausible predictions about future or hypothetical events that take place within context (e.g., an adult who is reading an unfamiliar story pauses and asks the child, "What do you think will happen?" The child makes a plausible prediction).

2.3 Spontaneously or on request, the child will tell possible causes for observed events (e.g., in response to an adult's question, "Why do you think she is crying?" the child tells a possible cause, "Maybe somebody broke her doll").

Strand F: Play

G1 The child will engage in the following play behaviors with peers:
- Enacts roles or identities
- Plans and acts out recognizable events, themes, or storylines
- Uses imaginary and representational props

1.1 The child will assume recognizable roles or identities when playing with peers by announcing the roles or changing voice, manner, or behaviors to indicate indentities (e.g., child says, "I'll be the bus driver," sits in the front seat of the pretend bus, and tells the other children in an adult voice, "Please sit down and be quiet while I'm driving").

  1.2   The child will use words and actions to plan and enact recognizable events, themes, or storylines, alone or with peers (e.g., child says, "I'll be the mommy and I'm going to the store." Child puts on a hat and takes a purse, pretends to go to the store, comes home, and cooks dinner).

  1.3   The child will play using imaginary props, alone or with peers (e.g., child gallops around the room pretending to hold reins and says, "Giddy up, horsie. Go fast").

G2   The child will engage in games with rules maintaining participation and conforming to game rules.

  2.1   The child will continue to participate in organized games until completion of game (e.g., child rolls a ball back and forth to adult until adult says, "It's time for snack"). An adult may provide group directions.

  2.2   The child will follow the rules in organized games (e.g., child waits for a turn, follows an appropriate sequence of steps in a game, and knows the beginning and end of the game). An adult may provide group directions.

Strand G: Premath

G1   The child will count 20 or more items, assigning numbers to objects in the correct order, and counting each one only once. The child will touch, point to, or move each item while counting (e.g., child correctly counts 22 of 25 crayons, moving each one to a pile on the side of the table as it is counted).

  1.1   The child will count between 10 and 20 items, assigning numbers to objects in the correct order and counting each item only once. The child will touch, point to, or move each item while counting (e.g., child correctly counts 13 of 15 chairs, pointing to each one in turn while counting). The child may make mistakes above 10.

  1.2   The child will count at least three and up to nine items, assigning numbers to objects in the correct order and counting each item only once. The child will touch, point to, or move each item while counting (e.g., child counts four of six puppies, touching each one in turn while counting).

G2   The child will correctly discriminate numerals from letters, using number symbols to represent quantity and as identifiers for daily events, objects, and personal information (e.g., child correctly uses the term "number" only when identifying numerals in print and never for letters and correctly associates printed numerals with other quantity concepts).

  2.1   The child will associate number words with the correct printed numerals up to 10 (e.g., child says "one" when presented with the numeral 1, "two" when presented with the numeral 2, and so forth up to 10).

2.2 The child will discriminate numbers from letters and other symbols by matching and sorting printed numerals from letters and will find numbers when asked (e.g., when asked to find something with numbers, the child identifies a calendar, the room number over the door, or the house number).

Strand H: Phonological Awareness and Emergent Reading

G1 The child will demonstrate awareness of the component sounds of his or her primary language by rhyming words, segmenting words into sounds (e.g., given the word "snake," the child can say words that start with the /s/ sound, end with the /s/ sound, and rhyme with snake), blending sounds into words, and identifying same and different sounds at the beginning and end of words.

    1.1 The child will use rhyming skills by recognizing words that do and do not rhyme and filling in missing words in rhymes. (The word produced can be a nonsense word if it rhymes.)

    1.2 The child will identify each word in multiple four- to six-word utterances by saying each word separately and in the correct sequence and identify each separate sound or syllable of words (e.g., child says, "We-want-to-go-outside" when an adult says the sentence and asks the child, "Can you say each word by itself?"; adult says, "Tell me the sounds in the word *hop*." The child says, "h-o-p," with each sound identifiable and in the correct sequence).

    1.3 When the sounds and syllables are produced slowly and in the correct order, the child will blend two to three syllables into a word and three to four separate sounds into words (e.g., adult says, "Tell me what word these sounds make: b-a-t," and the child says, "Bat.")

    1.4 The child will identify same and different sounds in words by recognizing words with the same/different initial and ending sounds and by producing words with the same initial sounds.

G2 The child will use at least 20 individual letter sounds to sound out words and write words (e.g., the child sounds out and writes the word "map" by blending the sounds m-a-p). The child's attempts to sound out words do not need to be completely accurate, and invented spellings are acceptable.

    2.1 The child will assign appropriate sounds to letters as he or she attempts to write words. Invented spellings are acceptable, as are any sounds that can reasonably be associated with letters (e.g., a child might spell "house" as h-o-w-s).

    2.2 The child will produce correct sounds in sequence as he or she attempts to sound out words. The child does not actually need to decode the word correctly as long as plausible sounds are assigned to each letter (e.g., child might sound out "boat" as "bow-at").

    2.3 Given books, letter puzzles, alphabet cards, or similar materials, the child will match sounds to printed letters by producing correct sounds for at least 15 letters.

G3 Spontaneously or on request, the child will read at least five common words by sight. One of the words may be the child's first name.

3.1 Spontaneously or on request, the child will name at least 20 letters of the alphabet.

SOCIAL-COMMUNICATION AREA

Strand A: Social-Communicative Interactions

G1 The child will use words, phrases, or sentences to do the following:
- Express anticipated outcomes
- Describe imaginary objects, events, or people
- Label own or others' affect/emotions
- Describe past events
- Make commands to and requests of others
- Obtain information
- Inform

Errors in syntax are acceptable.

1.1 The child will use words, phrases, or sentences to express anticipated outcomes (e.g., the adult asks, "What will happen if I strike this match?" and the child says, "It will burn"). Errors in syntax are acceptable.

1.2 The child will use words, phrases, or sentences to tell about pretend objects, events, or people (e.g., the child says, "Let's build a campfire. You go get some wood," and acts out a camping scene). Errors in syntax are acceptable.

1.3 The child will use words, phrases, or sentences to label own or others' affect/emotions (e.g., the child sees a peer frowning and says, "Terry's mad"). Errors in syntax are acceptable.

1.4 The child will use words, phrases, or sentences to describe actions and events that occurred in the immediate and distant past (e.g., the child says, "I made a hat," when telling a parent about what he or she made earlier during an art activity). Errors in syntax are acceptable.

1.5 The child will use words, phrases, or sentences to make commands to and requests of others (e.g., the child says, "Give me the red one"). Errors in syntax are acceptable.

1.6 The child will use words, phrases, or sentences to obtain information (e.g., the child asks classroom teachers, "Mommy come back?"; "Tell me the time"). Errors in syntax are acceptable.

1.7 The child will use words, phrases, or sentences to describe objects, actions, and events and to inform others about plans, intentions, and experiences (e.g., the child calls to a parent, "I'm going outside"). Errors in syntax are acceptable.

G2 The child will use conversational rules to initiate and maintain communicative exchanges for two or more consecutive exchanges. An exchange includes a response from both the child and another person. Conversational rules include the following:
- Alternating between speaker/listener role
- Responding to topic changes

- Asking questions for clarification
- Responding to contingent questions
- Initiating context-relevant topics
- Responding to others' topic initiations

2.1   The child will use appropriate responses in conversation to alternate between speaker and listener roles (e.g., the child pauses after making a comment or asking a question and looks toward communicative partner).

2.2   The child will respond to conversational topic changes initiated by others with comments, answers, or questions related to the new topic (e.g., the child says, "I want to play outside some more," and the adult says, "We need to go inside now to fix a snack," and the child responds, "What is it?").

2.3   The child will indicate a need for clarification (i.e., repetition, elaboration, confirmation) by commenting or questioning during communicative exchanges (e.g., the child says, "What?" when the child does not understand what another person has said).

2.4   The child will supply relevant information following another person's request for clarification, repetition, elaboration, or confirmation of the child's previous statement (e.g., the child says, "She threw it," and an adult asks, "Who threw it?" and the child answers, "Rachel. Rachel threw it").

2.5   The child will initiate topics relevant to situations or communicative partners (e.g., the child sees a peer with crayons and says, "I want the red one").

2.6   The child will respond to another's conversation with a related response, including acknowledgment of another's statement, an answer to a question, a request for clarification, or a related comment (e.g., an adult comments, "You have new shoes on today," and the child says, "My mommy got them at the store").

G3   The child will change the form, length, and grammatical complexity of phrases and sentences according to listeners' needs and social roles (e.g., the child uses shorter and less complex sentences to ask a younger child, "Want a cookie?").

3.1   The child will use voice pitch (i.e., high, low) and voice intensity (i.e., loud, soft) that is appropriate to the situation, listener, and communicative meaning (e.g., the child shouts when playing but begins to whisper after noticing that father is sleeping).

3.2   The child will look toward the speaker's face and establish an appropriate physical proximity and body posture in relation to others during communicative exchanges (e.g., when the child's name is called, the child turns and looks to locate the speaker).

Strand B: Production of Words, Phrases, and Sentences

G1   The child will use the following verb forms:
- Auxiliary
- The copula verb "to be"

- Third person singular
- Irregular past tense
- Regular past tense
- Present progressive "ing"

1.1 The child will use appropriate forms of auxiliary (helping) verbs in combination with other verbs (e.g., "He is running," "He will do it," "She should not fall," "They have been bad"). The number of forms that the child uses is less important than the child's ability to use a form appropriate to the grammatical and semantic context of the sentence.

1.2 The child will use appropriate forms of the verb "to be" to link subject nouns to the predicates (e.g., the child says, "I'm happy").

1.3 The child will use appropriate regular and irregular third person singular verb forms (e.g., regular: "It jumps"; irregular: "She has a bike").

1.4 The child will use appropriate irregular forms of past tense verbs such as *came, ran, fell, broke, sat, went, told, heard, did, ate, woke, made, drank,* and *wrote* (e.g., the child says, "Mommy went to work").

1.5 The child will use appropriate regular past tense verbs such as a verb plus "ed" ending (e.g., the child says, "We walked home").

1.6 The child will use appropriate present progressive verb forms (i.e., verb plus "ing" ending; e.g., the child says, "I'm going outside").

G2 The child will use the following noun inflections:

- Possessive "s" (e.g., Susan's)
- Irregular plural (e.g., mice)
- Regular plural (e.g., toys)

2.1 The child will use nouns with an apostrophe "s" to express possession (e.g., the child says, "Mom's hat fell off").

2.2 The child will use irregular plural noun forms (e.g., the child says, "Those mice are in the cage").

2.3 The child will use regular plural noun forms (i.e., noun plus "s" or "es" ending; e.g., the child says, "I see the dogs").

G3 The child will use the following forms to ask questions:

- Yes/no questions
- Questions with inverted auxiliary
- "When" questions
- "Why," "who," and "how" questions
- "What" and "where" questions
- Rising inflection

3.1 The child will ask questions that require a yes or no response from the listener (e.g., the child asks, "Can't I go?").

3.2 The child will ask questions by reversing the order of the subject and the auxiliary (helping) verb (i.e., verb precedes the noun; e.g., the child asks, "Is he hiding?").

3.3 The child will ask questions beginning with the word "when" (e.g., the child asks, "When will we eat?").

3.4   The child will ask questions beginning with the words "why," "who," and "how" (e.g., the child asks, "Why did he do that?" "Who is it?" "How do you do that?").

3.5   The child will ask questions beginning with the words "what" and "where" (e.g., the child asks, "Where is she going?" "What is that?").

3.6   The child will ask questions by using raised pitch at the end of utterances so that the utterances sound like questions (e.g., the child asks, "See that airplane?").

G4   The child will use appropriate pronouns to serve the following functions:
- As subjects in phrases or sentences
- As objects in phrases or sentences
- To show possession
- To represent indefinite people and objects
- To identify or point out objects

4.1   The child will use subject pronouns (i.e., she, he, they, I, you, it, we) appropriately as subjects in phrases or sentences (e.g., child says, "They went home," "I did it," "You have ice cream?")

4.2   The child will use object pronouns (i.e., me, you, her, him, it, us, them) appropriately as objects (i.e., receives an object or relation) in phrases or sentences (e.g., the child says, "John hurt me," "I want you to go," "I gave it to her").

4.3   The child will use possessive pronouns (i.e., my/mine, your/yours, his, her/hers, its, our/ours, their/theirs) appropriately to express possession in phrases or sentences (e.g., the child says, "Those are her shoes," "I like his toy better").

4.4   The child will use indefinite pronouns (i.e., any, some, none, anything, something, nothing, all, lots, many, everything, every, more) appropriately to refer to unspecified people or objects (e.g., the child says, "Can't I have any?" "Do you want some?" "No one wants more").

4.5   The child will use demonstrative pronouns (i.e., this, that, these, those) appropriately to single out or identify objects (e.g., the child says, "I want those," "That's not my coat," "Can I have this cookie?")

G5   The child will use descriptive, relational, and functional words as
- Adjectives
- Adverbs
- Prepositions
- Conjunctions
- Articles

5.1   The child will use adjectives to modify nouns and pronouns (e.g., the child says, "My hands are cold").

5.2   The child will use adjectives to compare degrees of quality or quantity (e.g., the child says, "My truck is best," "I have the most ice cream").

5.3   The child will use adverbs to modify verbs (e.g., the child says, "That tastes bad").

5.4 The child will use prepositions or prepositional phrases (i.e., in, with, to, up, for, down, off, over, of, like, at, by, in front of, in back of, through, near, on, under, out) appropriately (e.g., the child says, "The person goes in the car"). The number of different prepositions that the child uses is less important than the child's ability to use prepositions and prepositional phrases appropriate to the grammatical and semantic context of the sentence.

5.5 The child will use conjunctions (i.e., and, but, or, because, so, if, only, except) to connect words, phrases, and sentences (e.g., the child says, "I want juice and a cookie").

5.6 The child will use articles (i.e., the, a, an) to precede nouns (e.g., the child says, "I can't find the ball").

SOCIAL AREA

Strand A: Interaction with Others

G1 The child will interact with others as play partners during daily activities by doing the following:
- Responding to others in distress or need
- Establishing and maintaining proximity to others
- Taking turns with others
- Initiating greeting to others who are familiar
- Responding to affective initiations from others

1.1 The child will respond appropriately to others in distress or need (e.g., the child pats or hugs a peer who is crying).

1.2 The child will establish and maintain proximity to others during unstructured, child-directed activities (e.g., the child walks over to a peer playing with dolls and begins playing beside the peer).

1.3 The child will take turns with others during daily activities (e.g., the child hands a watering can to a peer at the water table).

1.4 The child will greet others with whom they are familiar by vocalizing, verbalizing, hugging, patting, touching, or smiling.

1.5 The child will respond with socially appropriate responses to other's affective initiations (e.g., the child smiles in response to a peer's smile).

G2 The child will use verbal or nonverbal strategies to initiate cooperative activities and encourage peer(s) to participate (e.g., the child says, "Come on, let's build a house" to a group of peers).

2.1 The child will use socially appropriate verbal or nonverbal strategies to join others engaged in cooperative activities (e.g., the child approaches a group of peers building a sand castle, sits next to them for a while, then begins to help peer who is digging a tunnel).

2.2 The child will maintain jobs, roles, or identities that supplement other children's jobs, roles, or identities during cooperative activities (e.g., the child holds two blocks together while a peer puts a third block on top to build a house).

2.3 During daily activities, the child will share or exchange objects with others engaged in the same activity (e.g., the child shares a glue bottle with a peer when both are gluing leaves and flowers onto paper).

G3 The child will select appropriate strategies to resolve conflicts. Strategies include the following:
- Negotiating
- Using simple strategies
- Claiming and defending possessions

3.1 The child will initiate solutions to bring about agreement when in conflict with a peer or an adult (e.g., when both the child and a peer want to play in a corner of the sandbox, the child says, "I'll dig here and you dig there").

3.2 The child will use a variety of simple strategies (e.g., makes demand, walks/runs away, reports to adult) to resolve conflicts with other people (e.g., when a peer hits the child, the child turns to an adult and says, "Susan hit me").

3.3 The child will use verbal or nonverbal strategies to claim and defend possessions (e.g., the child says, "That coat is mine," and takes the coat from peer).

Strand B: Participation

G1 The child will initiate and complete age-appropriate activities without adult prompting (e.g., during free play, child gets out puzzle, puts it together, then puts it away).

1.1 The child will respond to the first request to finish activities (e.g., child carries out adult's request to pick up all of the blocks or to finish putting together a puzzle).

1.2 The child will respond to the first request to begin activities (e.g., child sits at table watching peers draw with crayons; child begins to draw with paper and crayons in response to adult's first request to do so).

G2 The child will engage in the following behaviors during structured small group activities (i.e., groups of five or fewer children):
- Interact appropriately with materials
- Respond appropriately to directions
- Look at appropriate object, person, or event
- Remain with the group

An adult may provide group directions to help the child.

2.1 The child will interact with materials in a functional or demonstrated fashion during structured small group activities (i.e., groups of five or fewer children). An adult may provide group directions.

2.2 The child will respond with appropriate verbal or motor actions to group directions provided by an adult (e.g., during painting activity, child follows directions to dip paintbrush in paint and brush it across paper) during structured small group activities (i.e., groups of five or fewer children).

    2.3   The child will look at object, person, or event that is the focus of activity (e.g., the child looks at a person while that person is talking) during small group activities (i.e., groups of five or fewer children). An adult may provide group directions.

    2.4   The child will stay seated or in an indicated area (e.g., the child remains in seat at table during table activities) for the duration of an activity during structured small group activities (i.e., groups of five or fewer children). An adult may provide group directions.

G3   The child will engage in the following behaviors during large group activities (i.e., groups of six or more children):
- Interact appropriately with materials
- Respond appropriately to directions
- Look at appropriate object, person, or event
- Remain with the group

An adult may provide group directions to help the child.

    3.1   The child will interact with materials in a functional or demonstrated fashion (e.g., the child passes a ball to the next child during a group game) during structured large group activities (i.e., groups of six or more children). An adult may provide group directions.

    3.2   The child will respond with appropriate verbal or motor actions to group directions provided by an adult (e.g., during a music activity, the child selects a musical instrument and follows directions to play instrument while marching) during structured large group activities (i.e., groups of six or more children).

    3.3   The child will look at object, person, or event that is the focus of activity (e.g., during show-and-tell activity, the child looks at a person who is talking and showing a toy boat) during structured large group activities (i.e., groups of six or more children). An adult may provide group directions.

    3.4   The child will stay seated or in an indicated area (e.g., the child remains in seat at the table for snack time) for the duration of an activity during large group activities (i.e., groups of six or more children). An adult may provide group directions.

Strand C: Interaction with Environment

G1   The child will use socially appropriate strategies to meet physical needs such as the following:
- Physical needs when uncomfortable, sick, hurt, or tired
- Observable physical needs
- Physical needs of hunger and thirst

    1.1   The child will use socially appropriate ways to meet physical needs when uncomfortable, sick, hurt, or tired (e.g., the child requests an adult's help when injured or sick).

    1.2   The child will use socially appropriate ways to meet observable physical needs (e.g., the child removes wet or soiled clothing).

1.3 The child will use socially appropriate ways to express or meet physical needs of hunger and thirst (e.g., the child requests food or drink).

G2 The child will follow context-specific rules outside of the home and classroom (e.g., store, park, doctor's office, restaurant, bus).

2.1 The child will ask adult's permission as required to engage in established routines at home, at school, and in the community (e.g., the child asks a parent for permission to go to a neighbor's house).

2.2 The child will follow established rules at home and within the classroom. Adult may provide group directions/cues (e.g., "It is storytime").

Strand D: Knowledge of Self and Others

G1 The child will use verbal and/or nonverbal strategies (including initiating preferred activities and selecting activities and/or objects) to communicate personal likes and dislikes about people, objects, and activities (e.g., the child says, "Mmm, I love chocolate cake," while eating cake).

1.1 The child will use verbal and/or nonverbal communication to initiate preferred purposeful activities during free time (e.g., the child goes to the shelf and selects books to look at during play). General cues may be provided by an adult (e.g., "Find something to do").

1.2 The child will select activities or objects when given a choice (e.g., the child selects crackers from a plate of crackers and cheese).

G2 The child will demonstrate understanding of how his or her own behaviors, thoughts, and feelings relate to consequences for others (e.g., after grabbing a peer's favorite toy, the child will return the toy as the peer starts to cry).

2.1 The child will identify affect/emotions of others that are consistent with behaviors being displayed (e.g., the child says, "She likes it," in response to a peer smiling at getting a favorite cookie during snack time).

2.2 The child will identify own affect/emotions that are consistent with displayed behaviors (e.g., the child cries after losing a doll and says, "I'm sad").

G3 The child will correctly communicate the following information about self and others:
- Address (number, street, and town)
- Telephone numbers
- Birthday (month and day)
- Name(s) of sibling(s) and full name of self
- Gender (self and others)
- First name and age

3.1 The child will correctly state own address, including the number, street, and town.

3.2 The child will correctly state at least two telephone numbers (e.g., own telephone number, parent's work number, an emergency number, grandma's number).

3.3 The child will correctly state month and day of own birthday.

3.4 The child will correctly state the first name(s) of sibling(s) and first and last names of self.

3.5 The child will correctly identify self and others as being either a girl or a boy.

3.6 The child will correctly state own first name and age in years.

Child Observation
Data Recording Form I
Birth to Three Years

2.2 The child will discriminate numbers from letters and other symbols by matching and sorting printed numerals from letters and will find numbers when asked (e.g., when asked to find something with numbers, the child identifies a calendar, the room number over the door, or the house number).

Strand H: Phonological Awareness and Emergent Reading

G1 The child will demonstrate awareness of the component sounds of his or her primary language by rhyming words, segmenting words into sounds (e.g., given the word "snake," the child can say words that start with the /s/ sound, end with the /s/ sound, and rhyme with snake), blending sounds into words, and identifying same and different sounds at the beginning and end of words.

1.1 The child will use rhyming skills by recognizing words that do and do not rhyme and filling in missing words in rhymes. (The word produced can be a nonsense word if it rhymes.)

1.2 The child will identify each word in multiple four- to six-word utterances by saying each word separately and in the correct sequence and identify each separate sound or syllable of words (e.g., child says, "We-want-to-go-outside" when an adult says the sentence and asks the child, "Can you say each word by itself?"; adult says, "Tell me the sounds in the word *hop*." The child says, "h-o-p," with each sound identifiable and in the correct sequence).

1.3 When the sounds and syllables are produced slowly and in the correct order, the child will blend two to three syllables into a word and three to four separate sounds into words (e.g., adult says, "Tell me what word these sounds make: b-a-t," and the child says, "Bat.")

1.4 The child will identify same and different sounds in words by recognizing words with the same/different initial and ending sounds and by producing words with the same initial sounds.

G2 The child will use at least 20 individual letter sounds to sound out words and write words (e.g., the child sounds out and writes the word "map" by blending the sounds m-a-p). The child's attempts to sound out words do not need to be completely accurate, and invented spellings are acceptable.

2.1 The child will assign appropriate sounds to letters as he or she attempts to write words. Invented spellings are acceptable, as are any sounds that can reasonably be associated with letters (e.g., a child might spell "house" as h-o-w-s).

2.2 The child will produce correct sounds in sequence as he or she attempts to sound out words. The child does not actually need to decode the word correctly as long as plausible sounds are assigned to each letter (e.g., child might sound out "boat" as "bow-at").

2.3 Given books, letter puzzles, alphabet cards, or similar materials, the child will match sounds to printed letters by producing correct sounds for at least 15 letters.

G3 Spontaneously or on request, the child will read at least five common words by sight. One of the words may be the child's first name.

    3.1 Spontaneously or on request, the child will name at least 20 letters of the alphabet.

SOCIAL-COMMUNICATION AREA

Strand A: Social-Communicative Interactions

G1 The child will use words, phrases, or sentences to do the following:
- Express anticipated outcomes
- Describe imaginary objects, events, or people
- Label own or others' affect/emotions
- Describe past events
- Make commands to and requests of others
- Obtain information
- Inform

Errors in syntax are acceptable.

    1.1 The child will use words, phrases, or sentences to express anticipated outcomes (e.g., the adult asks, "What will happen if I strike this match?" and the child says, "It will burn"). Errors in syntax are acceptable.

    1.2 The child will use words, phrases, or sentences to tell about pretend objects, events, or people (e.g., the child says, "Let's build a campfire. You go get some wood," and acts out a camping scene). Errors in syntax are acceptable.

    1.3 The child will use words, phrases, or sentences to label own or others' affect/emotions (e.g., the child sees a peer frowning and says, "Terry's mad"). Errors in syntax are acceptable.

    1.4 The child will use words, phrases, or sentences to describe actions and events that occurred in the immediate and distant past (e.g., the child says, "I made a hat," when telling a parent about what he or she made earlier during an art activity). Errors in syntax are acceptable.

    1.5 The child will use words, phrases, or sentences to make commands to and requests of others (e.g., the child says, "Give me the red one"). Errors in syntax are acceptable.

    1.6 The child will use words, phrases, or sentences to obtain information (e.g., the child asks classroom teachers, "Mommy come back?"; "Tell me the time"). Errors in syntax are acceptable.

    1.7 The child will use words, phrases, or sentences to describe objects, actions, and events and to inform others about plans, intentions, and experiences (e.g., the child calls to a parent, "I'm going outside"). Errors in syntax are acceptable.

G2 The child will use conversational rules to initiate and maintain communicative exchanges for two or more consecutive exchanges. An exchange includes a response from both the child and another person. Conversational rules include the following:
- Alternating between speaker/listener role
- Responding to topic changes

- Asking questions for clarification
- Responding to contingent questions
- Initiating context-relevant topics
- Responding to others' topic initiations

2.1 The child will use appropriate responses in conversation to alternate between speaker and listener roles (e.g., the child pauses after making a comment or asking a question and looks toward communicative partner).

2.2 The child will respond to conversational topic changes initiated by others with comments, answers, or questions related to the new topic (e.g., the child says, "I want to play outside some more," and the adult says, "We need to go inside now to fix a snack," and the child responds, "What is it?").

2.3 The child will indicate a need for clarification (i.e., repetition, elaboration, confirmation) by commenting or questioning during communicative exchanges (e.g., the child says, "What?" when the child does not understand what another person has said).

2.4 The child will supply relevant information following another person's request for clarification, repetition, elaboration, or confirmation of the child's previous statement (e.g., the child says, "She threw it," and an adult asks, "Who threw it?" and the child answers, "Rachel. Rachel threw it").

2.5 The child will initiate topics relevant to situations or communicative partners (e.g., the child sees a peer with crayons and says, "I want the red one").

2.6 The child will respond to another's conversation with a related response, including acknowledgment of another's statement, an answer to a question, a request for clarification, or a related comment (e.g., an adult comments, "You have new shoes on today," and the child says, "My mommy got them at the store").

G3 The child will change the form, length, and grammatical complexity of phrases and sentences according to listeners' needs and social roles (e.g., the child uses shorter and less complex sentences to ask a younger child, "Want a cookie?").

3.1 The child will use voice pitch (i.e., high, low) and voice intensity (i.e., loud, soft) that is appropriate to the situation, listener, and communicative meaning (e.g., the child shouts when playing but begins to whisper after noticing that father is sleeping).

3.2 The child will look toward the speaker's face and establish an appropriate physical proximity and body posture in relation to others during communicative exchanges (e.g., when the child's name is called, the child turns and looks to locate the speaker).

Strand B: Production of Words, Phrases, and Sentences

G1 The child will use the following verb forms:
- Auxiliary
- The copula verb "to be"

- Third person singular
- Irregular past tense
- Regular past tense
- Present progressive "ing"

1.1 The child will use appropriate forms of auxiliary (helping) verbs in combination with other verbs (e.g., "He is running," "He will do it," "She should not fall," "They have been bad"). The number of forms that the child uses is less important than the child's ability to use a form appropriate to the grammatical and semantic context of the sentence.

1.2 The child will use appropriate forms of the verb "to be" to link subject nouns to the predicates (e.g., the child says, "I'm happy").

1.3 The child will use appropriate regular and irregular third person singular verb forms (e.g., regular: "It jumps"; irregular: "She has a bike").

1.4 The child will use appropriate irregular forms of past tense verbs such as *came, ran, fell, broke, sat, went, told, heard, did, ate, woke, made, drank,* and *wrote* (e.g., the child says, "Mommy went to work").

1.5 The child will use appropriate regular past tense verbs such as a verb plus "ed" ending (e.g., the child says, "We walked home").

1.6 The child will use appropriate present progressive verb forms (i.e., verb plus "ing" ending; e.g., the child says, "I'm going outside").

G2 The child will use the following noun inflections:
- Possessive "s" (e.g., Susan's)
- Irregular plural (e.g., mice)
- Regular plural (e.g., toys)

2.1 The child will use nouns with an apostrophe "s" to express possession (e.g., the child says, "Mom's hat fell off").

2.2 The child will use irregular plural noun forms (e.g., the child says, "Those mice are in the cage").

2.3 The child will use regular plural noun forms (i.e., noun plus "s" or "es" ending; e.g., the child says, "I see the dogs").

G3 The child will use the following forms to ask questions:
- Yes/no questions
- Questions with inverted auxiliary
- "When" questions
- "Why," "who," and "how" questions
- "What" and "where" questions
- Rising inflection

3.1 The child will ask questions that require a yes or no response from the listener (e.g., the child asks, "Can't I go?").

3.2 The child will ask questions by reversing the order of the subject and the auxiliary (helping) verb (i.e., verb precedes the noun; e.g., the child asks, "Is he hiding?").

3.3 The child will ask questions beginning with the word "when" (e.g., the child asks, "When will we eat?").

3.4   The child will ask questions beginning with the words "why," "who," and "how" (e.g., the child asks, "Why did he do that?" "Who is it?" "How do you do that?").

3.5   The child will ask questions beginning with the words "what" and "where" (e.g., the child asks, "Where is she going?" "What is that?").

3.6   The child will ask questions by using raised pitch at the end of utterances so that the utterances sound like questions (e.g., the child asks, "See that airplane?").

G4   The child will use appropriate pronouns to serve the following functions:
- As subjects in phrases or sentences
- As objects in phrases or sentences
- To show possession
- To represent indefinite people and objects
- To identify or point out objects

4.1   The child will use subject pronouns (i.e., she, he, they, I, you, it, we) appropriately as subjects in phrases or sentences (e.g., child says, "They went home," "I did it," "You have ice cream?")

4.2   The child will use object pronouns (i.e., me, you, her, him, it, us, them) appropriately as objects (i.e., receives an object or relation) in phrases or sentences (e.g., the child says, "John hurt me," "I want you to go," "I gave it to her").

4.3   The child will use possessive pronouns (i.e., my/mine, your/yours, his, her/hers, its, our/ours, their/theirs) appropriately to express possession in phrases or sentences (e.g., the child says, "Those are her shoes," "I like his toy better").

4.4   The child will use indefinite pronouns (i.e., any, some, none, anything, something, nothing, all, lots, many, everything, every, more) appropriately to refer to unspecified people or objects (e.g., the child says, "Can't I have any?" "Do you want some?" "No one wants more").

4.5   The child will use demonstrative pronouns (i.e., this, that, these, those) appropriately to single out or identify objects (e.g., the child says, "I want those," "That's not my coat," "Can I have this cookie?")

G5   The child will use descriptive, relational, and functional words as
- Adjectives
- Adverbs
- Prepositions
- Conjunctions
- Articles

5.1   The child will use adjectives to modify nouns and pronouns (e.g., the child says, "My hands are cold").

5.2   The child will use adjectives to compare degrees of quality or quantity (e.g., the child says, "My truck is best," "I have the most ice cream").

5.3   The child will use adverbs to modify verbs (e.g., the child says, "That tastes bad").

5.4 The child will use prepositions or prepositional phrases (i.e., in, with, to, up, for, down, off, over, of, like, at, by, in front of, in back of, through, near, on, under, out) appropriately (e.g., the child says, "The person goes in the car"). The number of different prepositions that the child uses is less important than the child's ability to use prepositions and prepositional phrases appropriate to the grammatical and semantic context of the sentence.

5.5 The child will use conjunctions (i.e., and, but, or, because, so, if, only, except) to connect words, phrases, and sentences (e.g., the child says, "I want juice and a cookie").

5.6 The child will use articles (i.e., the, a, an) to precede nouns (e.g., the child says, "I can't find the ball").

SOCIAL AREA

Strand A: Interaction with Others

G1 The child will interact with others as play partners during daily activities by doing the following:
- Responding to others in distress or need
- Establishing and maintaining proximity to others
- Taking turns with others
- Initiating greeting to others who are familiar
- Responding to affective initiations from others

1.1 The child will respond appropriately to others in distress or need (e.g., the child pats or hugs a peer who is crying).

1.2 The child will establish and maintain proximity to others during unstructured, child-directed activities (e.g., the child walks over to a peer playing with dolls and begins playing beside the peer).

1.3 The child will take turns with others during daily activities (e.g., the child hands a watering can to a peer at the water table).

1.4 The child will greet others with whom they are familiar by vocalizing, verbalizing, hugging, patting, touching, or smiling.

1.5 The child will respond with socially appropriate responses to other's affective initiations (e.g., the child smiles in response to a peer's smile).

G2 The child will use verbal or nonverbal strategies to initiate cooperative activities and encourage peer(s) to participate (e.g., the child says, "Come on, let's build a house" to a group of peers).

2.1 The child will use socially appropriate verbal or nonverbal strategies to join others engaged in cooperative activities (e.g., the child approaches a group of peers building a sand castle, sits next to them for a while, then begins to help peer who is digging a tunnel).

2.2 The child will maintain jobs, roles, or identities that supplement other children's jobs, roles, or identities during cooperative activities (e.g., the child holds two blocks together while a peer puts a third block on top to build a house).

2.3 During daily activities, the child will share or exchange objects with others engaged in the same activity (e.g., the child shares a glue bottle with a peer when both are gluing leaves and flowers onto paper).

G3 The child will select appropriate strategies to resolve conflicts. Strategies include the following:
- Negotiating
- Using simple strategies
- Claiming and defending possessions

3.1 The child will initiate solutions to bring about agreement when in conflict with a peer or an adult (e.g., when both the child and a peer want to play in a corner of the sandbox, the child says, "I'll dig here and you dig there").

3.2 The child will use a variety of simple strategies (e.g., makes demand, walks/runs away, reports to adult) to resolve conflicts with other people (e.g., when a peer hits the child, the child turns to an adult and says, "Susan hit me").

3.3 The child will use verbal or nonverbal strategies to claim and defend possessions (e.g., the child says, "That coat is mine," and takes the coat from peer).

Strand B: Participation

G1 The child will initiate and complete age-appropriate activities without adult prompting (e.g., during free play, child gets out puzzle, puts it together, then puts it away).

1.1 The child will respond to the first request to finish activities (e.g., child carries out adult's request to pick up all of the blocks or to finish putting together a puzzle).

1.2 The child will respond to the first request to begin activities (e.g., child sits at table watching peers draw with crayons; child begins to draw with paper and crayons in response to adult's first request to do so).

G2 The child will engage in the following behaviors during structured small group activities (i.e., groups of five or fewer children):
- Interact appropriately with materials
- Respond appropriately to directions
- Look at appropriate object, person, or event
- Remain with the group

An adult may provide group directions to help the child.

2.1 The child will interact with materials in a functional or demonstrated fashion during structured small group activities (i.e., groups of five or fewer children). An adult may provide group directions.

2.2 The child will respond with appropriate verbal or motor actions to group directions provided by an adult (e.g., during painting activity, child follows directions to dip paintbrush in paint and brush it across paper) during structured small group activities (i.e., groups of five or fewer children).

2.3 The child will look at object, person, or event that is the focus of activity (e.g., the child looks at a person while that person is talking) during small group activities (i.e., groups of five or fewer children). An adult may provide group directions.

2.4 The child will stay seated or in an indicated area (e.g., the child remains in seat at table during table activities) for the duration of an activity during structured small group activities (i.e., groups of five or fewer children). An adult may provide group directions.

G3 The child will engage in the following behaviors during large group activities (i.e., groups of six or more children):
- Interact appropriately with materials
- Respond appropriately to directions
- Look at appropriate object, person, or event
- Remain with the group

An adult may provide group directions to help the child.

3.1 The child will interact with materials in a functional or demonstrated fashion (e.g., the child passes a ball to the next child during a group game) during structured large group activities (i.e., groups of six or more children). An adult may provide group directions.

3.2 The child will respond with appropriate verbal or motor actions to group directions provided by an adult (e.g., during a music activity, the child selects a musical instrument and follows directions to play instrument while marching) during structured large group activities (i.e., groups of six or more children).

3.3 The child will look at object, person, or event that is the focus of activity (e.g., during show-and-tell activity, the child looks at a person who is talking and showing a toy boat) during structured large group activities (i.e., groups of six or more children). An adult may provide group directions.

3.4 The child will stay seated or in an indicated area (e.g., the child remains in seat at the table for snack time) for the duration of an activity during large group activities (i.e., groups of six or more children). An adult may provide group directions.

Strand C: Interaction with Environment

G1 The child will use socially appropriate strategies to meet physical needs such as the following:
- Physical needs when uncomfortable, sick, hurt, or tired
- Observable physical needs
- Physical needs of hunger and thirst

1.1 The child will use socially appropriate ways to meet physical needs when uncomfortable, sick, hurt, or tired (e.g., the child requests an adult's help when injured or sick).

1.2 The child will use socially appropriate ways to meet observable physical needs (e.g., the child removes wet or soiled clothing).

1.3 The child will use socially appropriate ways to express or meet physical needs of hunger and thirst (e.g., the child requests food or drink).

G2 The child will follow context-specific rules outside of the home and classroom (e.g., store, park, doctor's office, restaurant, bus).

2.1 The child will ask adult's permission as required to engage in established routines at home, at school, and in the community (e.g., the child asks a parent for permission to go to a neighbor's house).

2.2 The child will follow established rules at home and within the classroom. Adult may provide group directions/cues (e.g., "It is storytime").

Strand D: Knowledge of Self and Others

G1 The child will use verbal and/or nonverbal strategies (including initiating preferred activities and selecting activities and/or objects) to communicate personal likes and dislikes about people, objects, and activities (e.g., the child says, "Mmm, I love chocolate cake," while eating cake).

1.1 The child will use verbal and/or nonverbal communication to initiate preferred purposeful activities during free time (e.g., the child goes to the shelf and selects books to look at during play). General cues may be provided by an adult (e.g., "Find something to do").

1.2 The child will select activities or objects when given a choice (e.g., the child selects crackers from a plate of crackers and cheese).

G2 The child will demonstrate understanding of how his or her own behaviors, thoughts, and feelings relate to consequences for others (e.g., after grabbing a peer's favorite toy, the child will return the toy as the peer starts to cry).

2.1 The child will identify affect/emotions of others that are consistent with behaviors being displayed (e.g., the child says, "She likes it," in response to a peer smiling at getting a favorite cookie during snack time).

2.2 The child will identify own affect/emotions that are consistent with displayed behaviors (e.g., the child cries after losing a doll and says, "I'm sad").

G3 The child will correctly communicate the following information about self and others:
- Address (number, street, and town)
- Telephone numbers
- Birthday (month and day)
- Name(s) of sibling(s) and full name of self
- Gender (self and others)
- First name and age

3.1 The child will correctly state own address, including the number, street, and town.

3.2 The child will correctly state at least two telephone numbers (e.g., own telephone number, parent's work number, an emergency number, grandma's number).

3.3 The child will correctly state month and day of own birthday.

3.4 The child will correctly state the first name(s) of sibling(s) and first and last names of self.

3.5 The child will correctly identify self and others as being either a girl or a boy.

3.6 The child will correctly state own first name and age in years.

APPENDIX

C

Child Observation
Data Recording Form I
Birth to Three Years

    1.2   When presented with a simple and/or mechanical toy, the child will play with it in some way to try to make it move and/or make a noise (e.g., shake a squeeze-toy, push dial on a wind-up radio).

    1.3   When action of a simple and/or mechanical toy is demonstrated (e.g., shake rattle, wind-up toy radio), the child will respond by increasing or ceasing activity (e.g., wave arms, vocalize, laugh, smile, kick legs).

G2   When a game is played (e.g., Peekaboo, Pat-a-cake), the child will produce some action from the game to show desire to continue to play the game (e.g., clap hands, cover eyes).

    2.1   When a game is played (e.g., Peekaboo, Pat-a-cake), the child will respond in some way (e.g., smile, laugh, wave arms, kick legs) to show desire to continue to play the game.

Strand D: Imitation

G1   After demonstration of a new motor action that is not part of a familiar game and/or activity (e.g., pat knee, tap foot), the child will repeat the action (e.g., pat knee, tap foot).

    1.1   After demonstration of a familiar action (e.g., clap hands, cover eyes), the child will repeat the action (e.g., clap hands, cover eyes).

G2   After saying words that the child is not familiar with, the child will imitate these words.

    2.1   The child will imitate speech sounds that the child is not familiar with after demonstration of the speech sound.

    2.2   Upon demonstration of a word familiar to the child, the child will imitate the word.

Strand E: Problem Solving

G1   The child will use any means to retain objects that the child is using when new object is acquired (e.g., hold several blocks in one hand and pick up a block with the other).

    1.1   The child will hold onto one object when given a second object (e.g., put one object in each hand).

    1.2   The child will hold an object when presented with an object (e.g., hold ball in hands).

G2   The child will use an object to obtain another object (e.g., use stool to get cookie on high shelf, use stick to get object under cabinet).

    2.1   Child will use part of object and/or support to obtain another object (e.g., pulls on string attached to object, pulls on blanket on which object is resting).

G3   When presented with a barrier, the child will move large objects (e.g., grocery cart, doll carriage, riding toy) around barrier (e.g., toys, furniture, people).

    3.1   When presented with a barrier, the child will move barrier (e.g., tables, chairs, large toys) out of the way and/or will move around barrier to obtain objects.

3.2   The child will move around barriers (e.g., tables, chairs, large toys) in order to get to a different place.

G4   When presented with a common problem (e.g., an object that is out of reach), the child will use different strategies to solve the problem (e.g., attempt to reach a toy, climb on a chair to reach it, then ask an adult to reach it).

4.1   When presented with a common problem, the child will attempt to solve common problems by using more than one strategy (e.g., fit a puzzle piece by turning it or selecting a different puzzle piece).

Strand F: Interaction with Objects

G1   The child will use imaginary objects when playing (e.g., pretend to brush hair with imaginary brush, pretend to fly in an airplane).

1.1   When playing, the child will use representational actions with objects (e.g., pretend to write with stick, feed doll with crayon, pretend to drink out of a block).

1.2   When playing, the child will use functionally appropriate actions with objects (e.g., hold a telephone to ear, comb hair with comb).

1.3   During play, the child will use simple motor actions on different objects (e.g., shaking, banging, patting, pushing).

1.4   When playing with objects, the child will use sensory examination of objects (e.g., look, listen, touch, taste, smell).

Strand G: Early Concepts

G1   The child will categorize similar objects by putting at least three objects in a group according to conceptual category (e.g. food, clothing, animals) without adult assistance.

1.1   The child will put together at least three objects that are conventionally or functionally related (e.g., during pretend play, child collects doll, bottle, and blanket together).

1.2   When presented with a visual cue, the child will group objects according to size, shape, and/or color.

1.3   When given three to four different objects and/or pictures, the child will match the object with the picture.

G2   Upon request, the child will demonstrate functional use of one-to-one correspondence by assigning one object to each of two or more people and/or objects (e.g., place one fork next to each plate, give one paintbrush to each child).

2.1   When presented with several similar objects and asked to indicate one, the child will show, give, and/or assign one and only one object (e.g., when offered a plate of crackers, child will take one and only one when asked).

G3   Child will recognize environmental symbols (signs, logos, labels) by assigning correct meaning to words or symbols and/or producing associated word or action (e.g. child says, "I want hamburger" at sight of fast-food logo).

3.1 The child will use the words or word approximation in any language (including sign language) to correctly label familiar objects, actions, people, and events in pictures.

G4 When given reading material, the child will demonstrate functional use of reading material by using reading behaviors with book (e.g., use narration based on pictures, look at menu and choose to eat spaghetti).

4.1 While adult reads out loud, the child will orally fill in or complete familiar text while looking at picture books.

4.2 While looking at picture books with adult, the child will make comments and ask questions.

4.3 During shared reading time, the child will sit and attend to entire short story during shared reading time.

G5 On request, the child will demonstrate use of common opposite concepts by showing, sorting, labeling, or selecting objects with the appropriate quality from at least six pairs (e.g., when adult asks child, "Are your pants wet or dry?" child will respond correctly).

5.1 On request, the child will demonstrate use of at least four pairs of common opposite concepts by showing, sorting, labeling, or selecting the appropriate qualities (examples may include, but are not limited to, the following: big/little, hot/cold, wet/dry, up/down, fast/slow, top/bottom, stop/go).

5.2 On request, the child will demonstrate use of at least two common pairs of opposite concepts by showing, sorting, labeling, or selecting the appropriate qualities (examples may include, but are not limited to, the following: big/little, hot/cold, wet/dry, up/down, fast/slow, top/bottom, stop/go).

G6 Without prompts, the child will repeat at least two lines of familiar and simple nursery rhymes.

6.1 When adult recites the entire nursery rhyme except one rhyming word, the child will fill in the appropriate word.

6.2 While familiar adult recites nursery rhyme, the child will show recognition of sound game by joining in with adult, keep pace and intonation of the rhyme, and emphasize main ideas, nouns, and rhyming words (e.g., while the adult sings "Itsy, bitsy spider," the child clearly says key words such as "spider," "spout," "rain," and "out" with special emphasis).

SOCIAL-COMMUNICATION AREA

Strand A: Prelinguistic Communicative Interactions

G1 When a person is speaking within 3 feet of the child, the child will turn and look for at least 5 seconds toward the face of the person speaking.

1.1 When a person who is within 3 feet of the child presents and comments on an object, the child will turn and look toward the object and person speaking for at least 5 seconds.

1.2 When a noise-producing object is within 3 feet of the child, the child will turn and look toward the object for at least 5 seconds.

G2 When a person is looking at an object, person, or event, the child will look in the direction of the person's gaze for longer than 1 second.

2.1 When a person points to and comments on an object, the child will look in the same direction that the person is pointing for longer than 1 second.

2.2 When a person presents an object within the child's reach, the child will look in the direction of the object for longer than 1 second.

G3 Spontaneously or after adult initiation, the child will engage in two or more consecutive vocal exchanges by babbling. An exchange includes a response from both the child and the other person (e.g., child babbles, person imitates, child babbles again, and person imitates).

3.1 Spontaneously or after adult initiation, the child will engage in two or more consecutive vocal exchanges by cooing. An exchange includes a response from both the child and the other person (e.g., child coos, person imitates, child coos again, and person imitates).

Strand B: Transition to Words

G1 The child will gain a person's attention (e.g., look at, reach for, touch, vocalize) and then point to an object, person, and/or event (e.g., pull on a person's arm, then point out the window).

1.1 When adult poses a simple question, the child will respond with a vocalization and gesture (e.g., person asks, "Where's Mommy?" and child points to mother and says, "Ma-ma").

1.2 The child will point to an object, person, and/or event when engaged in activity or observation (e.g. child points to picture or points to other children playing).

1.3 The child will gesture and/or vocalize when greeting and leaving others.

1.4 When presented with undesired object/person/or action, the child will use gestures and/or vocalizations to protest actions and/or reject objects or people.

G2 Without adult cues, the child will use 10 consistent word approximations to refer to objects, people, and/or events.

2.1 The child will use consistent consonant–vowel combinations to refer to objects, people, and/or events. Sounds may be unrelated to the actual label but consistently refer to same object, person, and/or event.

2.2 When using verbal communication, the child will use nonspecific consonant–vowel combinations and/or jargon.

2.3 When expressing affective states, the child will vocalize (e.g. the child may coo when content, whine when wants attention, or scream when upset).

2.4 When vocalizing, the child will use at least two different vowel sounds (e.g., ah, eh, oh).

Strand C: Comprehension of Words and Sentences

G1 Without contextual cues, the child will locate (e.g., look at, reach for, touch, point to) at least 20 familiar objects, people, and/or events when named by another person.

    1.1 The child will locate (e.g., look at, reach for, touch, point to) at least 20 common objects, people, and/or events in unfamiliar pictures when named by another person.

    1.2 The child will locate (e.g., look at, reach for, touch, point to) at least 10 common objects, people, and/or events in familiar pictures when named by another person.

    1.3 With contextual cues, the child will locate (e.g., look at, reach for, touch, point to) at least five common objects, people, and/or events when named by another person.

    1.4 When called, the child will indicate recognition of own name (e.g., brighten, increase activity level, smile, turn toward a person, vocalize).

    1.5 The child will quiet when hearing a familiar voice.

G2 The child will respond with appropriate motor action when given two-step directions that do not relate to the immediate context (e.g., when doll is not present in the immediate context, person prompts child to "Go get your doll and put it on the table").

    2.1 The child will respond with appropriate motor action when given two-step directions that relate to the immediate context (e.g., when playing with dolls and dishes, person prompts child to "Get the cup and give baby a drink").

    2.2 The child will respond with appropriate motor action when given one-step directions that do not relate to the immediate context (e.g., when ball is not present in immediate context, person prompts child to "Get the ball").

    2.3 The child will respond with appropriate motor action when given one-step directions that relate to the immediate context (e.g., when standing in front of the coat rack, person prompts child to "Get your coat").

Strand D: Production of Social-Communicative Signals, Words, and Sentences

G1 The child will use 50 single words appropriately that include at least five descriptive words, five action words, two pronouns, 15 labeling words, and three proper names.

    1.1 The child will use five different descriptive words appropriately (e.g., big, little, hot, red).

    1.2 The child will use five different action words appropriately (e.g., open, go, eat, sit).

    1.3 The child will use two different pronouns appropriately (e.g., me, mine, it, my, I, you, this).

    1.4   The child will use 15 different object and/or event labels appropriately (e.g., ball, cup, hat, bubbles).

    1.5   The child will use three different proper names appropriately (e.g., Mama, James, Daddy, Spot).

G2 The child will use a variety of two-word utterances to express agent–action, action–object, and agent–object; possession; location; description; recurrence; and negation.

    2.1   The child will use 10 different two-word utterances to express agent–action (e.g., "Mama go"), action–object (e.g., "Roll ball"), and agent–object (e.g., "Daddy truck").

    2.2   The child will use five different two-word utterances to express possession (e.g., "My book," "Mommy car").

    2.3   The child will use five different two-word utterances to indicate location (e.g., "There Mommy," "In wagon").

    2.4   The child will use five different two-word utterances to describe objects, people, and/or events (e.g., "Pan hot," "Red block").

    2.5   The child will use five different two-word utterances to indicate recurrence (e.g., "More juice," "Go again").

    2.6   The child will use five different two-word utterances to express rejection, disappearance, and/or denial (e.g., "Not go," "Juice gone").

G3 The child will use a variety of three-word utterances to express negation; questions; action–object–location; agent–action–object.

    3.1   The child will use five different three-word utterances that include a negative term (e.g., "Not baby's coat," "No do that").

    3.2   The child will ask five different two- and three-word questions using "Wh-" words or using rising intonation (e.g., "Where my coat?" "We eat lunch?").

    3.3   The child will use five different three-word utterances to express action–object–location (e.g., "Put baby in," "Roll ball here").

    3.4   The child will use five different three-word utterances to express agent–action–object (e.g., "I blow bubble," "He throw ball").

SOCIAL AREA

Strand A: Interaction with Familiar Adults

G1 The child will respond appropriately toward familiar adult's affect including gesturing, requesting, hugging, kissing, patting, touching, and/or reaching toward adult.

    1.1   The child will spontaneously display affection toward familiar adult.

    1.2   When familiar adult initiates affective tones (e.g., smiles, laughs, frowns, uses sharp voice), child will respond with similar socially appropriate affect (e.g., smile in response to adult's laughter, cry in response to adult's sharp voice).

1.3 The child will smile in response to an approach, vocalization, smile, and/or appearance of a familiar adult.

G2 The child will initiate and maintain interactions with familiar adult for two or more consecutive exchanges (e.g., child claps hands, adult says, "Pat-a-cake"; child claps hands again, and adult says, "Pat-a-cake").

2.1 The child will initiate simple social games with familiar adult (e.g., child crawls under the table then peeks out at adult, and adult says, "Boo").

2.2 When familiar adult initiates social interaction, the child will respond (e.g., wave "bye-bye" in response to adult's goodbye; laugh or cover eyes after adult says "Peekaboo"; sign, vocalize, and/or verbalize in response to adult's verbalization).

2.3 The child will use familiar adult for comfort, closeness, or physical contact by directing position, proximity, gestures, expression, gaze, or vocalization toward adult across a variety of situations.

G3 The child will initiate and maintain a communicative exchange with a familiar adult by directing gestures, signs, vocalizations, and/or verbalizations for two or more consecutive exchanges. An exchange is a response from the child and from the adult.

3.1 The child will initiate communication toward familiar adult by using gestures, signs, vocalizations, and/or verbalizations.

3.2 The child will respond to communication from familiar adults by gesturing, signing, vocalizing, verbalizing, following requests, and/or attending.

Strand B: Interaction with Environment

G1 The child will take care of observable physical needs in socially appropriate ways (e.g., wash hands or request help when hands are dirty, try to take off wet clothing, ask for help when hurt).

1.1 The child will take care of hunger, thirst, and rest needs in socially appropriate ways (e.g., go to cupboard and get cracker when hungry, indicate thirst by holding up cup).

1.2 The child will use appropriate strategies for self-soothing by maintaining or regaining composure. This may include a change from the high emotional response of crying, anger, fear, or frustration to more relaxed or low emotional self-expressions.

G2 When given several verbal and/or contextual cues, the child will participate in a series of behaviors associated with established social routines such as mealtime, toileting, dressing, bathing (e.g., as adult sets table, child washes hands, gets bib, goes to table).

2.1 When given general verbal and/or contextual cues, the child will perform one behavior associated with established social routine such as mealtime, toileting, dressing, bathing (e.g., adult says, "It's time to take a nap," and child gets blanket).

Strand C: Interaction with Peers

G1 The child will initiate and maintain interaction with peer for two or more consecutive exchanges (e.g., child builds tower, peer knocks it down, then child stacks one block, and peer stacks the next one).

    1.1 The child will initiate social behavior toward peer (e.g., give toy to peer, smile at peer, direct communication toward peer).

    1.2 When peers initiate social behavior toward child, the child will respond with appropriate affect (e.g., peer says, "Hi," child says, "Hi"; peer hits child, child says, "Don't").

    1.3 During free play activities, the child will play close to peers.

    1.4 The child will observe peers at play.

    1.5 The child will play appropriately with toys without adult assistance. Child may or may not be close to adult or peers.

G2 The child will initiate and maintain a communicative exchange with peer by using gestures, signs, vocalizations, and/or verbalizations for two or more consecutive exchanges. An exchange is a response from the child and from the peer.

    2.1 The child will initiate communication with peer by using gestures, signs, vocalizations, and/or verbalizations.

    2.2 The child will respond to communication from peer by gesturing, signing, vocalizing, and/or verbalizing.

IFSP/IEP Goal and Objective Examples

FINE MOTOR AREA

Strand A: Bilateral Motor Coordination

G1 The child will use two hands to manipulate objects, each hand performing different movements (e.g., string objects, build with small Lego toys, tie shoes, button coat).

    1.1 The child will perform any two-handed task holding an object with one hand while the other hand manipulates (e.g., holds paper while drawing, steadies container while removing playdough).

G2 The child will cut out shapes (at least 3 inches in diameter) with curved lines, cutting close to the line. Child holds scissors between thumb and first two fingers of one hand and holds paper with other hand (e.g., circles, ovals).

    2.1 The child will cut out shapes (at least 3 inches in diameter) with straight lines, cutting close to the line. Child holds scissors between thumb and first two fingers of one hand and holds paper with other hand (e.g., squares, rectangles, triangles).

    2.2 The child will cut paper in two using at least three consecutive cuts; edges may be jagged. Child holds scissors between thumb and first two fingers of one hand and holds paper with other hand.

Strand B: Emergent Writing

G1 The child will write using a three-finger grasp, moving implement with fingers while wrist and forearm remain stable on writing surface.

    1.1 The child will use a three-finger grasp—thumb and first two fingers—to hold a writing implement.

G2 The child will print pseudo-letters using a writing instrument, moving downward from left to right on each line. The shapes produced do not need to be actual letters or words but may be invented spellings and/or pseudo letters.

    2.1 The child will draw using representational figures. Drawing is either recognizable to others or the child is able to describe or label features of the drawings.

    2.2 The child will copy complex shapes (i.e., shapes with angles such as rectangle, square, triangle) from a drawn model.

    2.3 The child will copy simple shapes (i.e., shapes with circular contours or lines such as circle, cross, T) from a drawn model.

G3   The child will print own first name without a model. Letters must be in correct order, but errors are permissible (e.g., letter printed backwards). Name should be recognizable.

    3.1   The child will print any three upper- or lowercase letters without a model; verbal cues may be provided. Errors are permissible (e.g., letter printed backward); however, individual letters should be recognizable.

    3.2   The child will copy own first name from a model (e.g., paper on which child's own first name is printed). Letters should be in correct order and recognizable. Errors are permissible (e.g., letter printed backward).

    3.3   The child will copy three upper- or lowercase letters from a model (e.g., single letters printed on paper or cards). Printing errors are permissible (e.g., letter printed backward); however, individual letters should be recognizable.

GROSS MOTOR AREA

Strand A: Balance and Mobility

G1   The child will avoid obstacles while running by controlling starts, stops, and sudden changes in direction.

    1.1   The child will run. Trunk is inclined slightly forward, arms swing freely, legs alternately flex and extend, and there is a period of no support by either leg.

G2   The child will walk up and down stairs, alternating feet, without holding a handrail or the wall or another person.

    2.1   The child will walk up and down stairs without alternating feet. The child may hold a handrail or the wall with one hand for support.

Strand B: Play Skills

G1   The child will jump forward with feet together; hips, knees, and ankles are flexed; and body is crouched on takeoff and landing. Arms lead with a vigorous forward and upward thrust and body is fully extended as it becomes airborne. Child lands on two feet without falling. (e.g., child jumps over a rope, tape, chalk line).

    1.1   The child will jump up and down in place with hips, knees, and ankles flexed on takeoff and landing. Arms lead with a vigorous forward and upward thrust and body extends as it becomes airborne. Child lands on two feet without falling. An adult may model the action.

    1.2   The child will jump from a low platform (e.g., curb, low step, raised platform) of at least 10 inches to the supporting surface. Child lands on two feet without falling. An adult may model the action.

    1.3   The child will balance on one foot for at least 3 seconds. An adult may model the action.

G2   The child will perform the following ball activities: bounces, catches, kicks, and throws.

    2.1   The child will bounce a large ball (at least 8 inches in diameter) at least twice, using the palm of one hand.

    2.2   The child will catch a ball (at least 6 inches in diameter) using palms of two hands. Ball is thrown underhand from a distance of 6–10 feet.

    2.3   The child will kick a stationary large ball (at least 8 inches in diameter) with one foot while maintaining balance. Ideally, support leg is flexed while kicking leg swings backward and forward and follows through in direction of kick.

    2.4   The child will throw a hand-size ball forward with one hand, using overhand throw. Throwing arm is moved backward in preparation, and child uses shoulder and elbow to throw.

G3   The child will skip at least 15 feet using an alternating step–hop pattern.

    3.1   The child will hop forward with five or more consecutive hops on one foot.

G4   While sitting on a two-wheel bicycle, the child will pedal forward and steer the bicycle at least 20 feet.

    4.1   While sitting on a two-wheel bicycle with training wheels, with both feet on the pedals, the child will pedal the bicycle forward and steer for at least 10 feet.

ADAPTIVE AREA

Strand A: Mealtime

G1   The child will eat and drink a variety of foods using appropriate utensils with little or no spilling. The child will exhibit culturally appropriate social dining skills by performing all of the following activities:

- Puts proper amount of food in mouth, chews with mouth closed, swallows before taking another bite
- Takes in proper amount of liquid and returns cup to surface
- Eats a variety of food textures
- Selects and eats a variety of food types
- Eats with utensil

    1.1   While eating, the child will put an appropriate amount of food in mouth, chew with mouth closed, and swallow before taking another bite.

    1.2   While drinking, the child will take in an appropriate amount of liquid from a child-size cup without spilling and return the cup to the table at least once before emptying the cup.

    1.3   The child will eat a variety of food textures including semi-solid foods (e.g., applesauce, yogurt), chewy foods (e.g., meats, dried fruits), hard foods (e.g., apples, raw vegetables), and soft foods (e.g., bananas, macaroni).

1.4 The child will select and eat a variety of foods from different food groups (e.g., dairy, meat, fruit, vegetables, bread).

1.5 The child will use appropriate utensil (e.g., spear meat with fork, scoop soup with spoon) to bring food to mouth with minimal spilling.

G2 The child will perform the following activities prior to eating:
- Prepare food for eating
- Use a knife to spread food
- Pour liquids into a variety of containers
- Serve food with utensils

2.1 The child will prepare food for eating by removing inedible parts (e.g., peels skin or shell from food, removes paper wrapping, pulls tab on juice can).

2.2 The child will use a blunt-edged knife to spread soft, spreadable foods (e.g., margarine, cream cheese, jam) on bread or cracker. The bread or cracker should be covered by the food and be intact after the child spreads the food. The food does not have to be spread smoothly.

2.3 The child will pour liquid from one container (e.g., pitcher, bottle) into another container (e.g., cup, bowl, glass). The child should not spill the liquid and should stop pouring at an appropriate time to avoid overfilling the receiving container.

2.4 The child will use a utensil to transfer food from one container to another.

Strand B: Personal Hygiene

G1 The child will initiate trips to the bathroom, pull down pants, use toilet paper, pull up pants, flush the toilet, wash hands, and remain dry and un-soiled between trips to the bathroom. Reminders are acceptable.

1.1 The child will complete the following toileting routine: pull down pants, use toilet paper after using the toilet, pull up pants, flush toilet, and wash hands.

1.2 The child will initiate a trip to the bathroom and use the toilet or potty chair for urination or bowel movements, remaining dry and unsoiled between trips to the bathroom. Occasional reminders are acceptable. The child may have assistance with other toileting skills (e.g., pulling pants down and up, washing hands).

1.3 The child will accurately indicate (e.g., tell, sign, gesture) to an adult the need to use a toilet or potty chair for urination and bowel movement.

G2 The child will perform the following washing and grooming activities:
- Use a tissue to clean nose
- Brush teeth
- Bathe and dry self

- Brush or comb hair
- Wash and dry face

2.1 The child will use a tissue to blow or wipe nose. The child may be given assistance to thoroughly clean nose.

2.2 The child will put toothpaste on a toothbrush, brush teeth, and rinse mouth. Reminders are acceptable (e.g., "What should you do next?").

2.3 The child will perform the following bathing routine: remove clothing, get into a bathtub or shower, use soap to clean body, rinse off, obtain a towel, dry body, and return the towel to towel rack. Reminders are acceptable, and the child may be given assistance to thoroughly clean and dry self.

2.4 The child will use a brush to brush hair or a comb to comb hair.

2.5 The child will complete face washing and drying routine by turning on the faucet, washing face with soap, rinsing face, turning off faucet, drying face with a towel, and returning the towel to a towel rack.

Strand C: Dressing and Undressing

G1 The child will use any functional means to perform all of the following unfastening activities:
- Unfasten buttons/snaps/Velcro fasteners on garments
- Untie string-type fasteners
- Unzip zippers

1.1 The child will unfasten buttons/snaps/Velcro fasteners on garments (e.g., shirt, dress, pants) when undressing, using any functional means that does not damage the clothing or fastener.

1.2 The child will untie string-type fasteners (e.g., shoelace, hood string) when undressing, using any functional means that does not damage the clothing or fastener.

1.3 The child will unzip and detach zipper on coat, jacket, or sweater when undressing, using any functional means that does not damage the clothing or zipper.

G2 The child will select appropriate clothing (i.e., shorts in summer, sweater in winter, nightgown at bedtime) and dress self at designated time (e.g., after breakfast). Reminders are acceptable.

2.1 The child will use any functional means to put long pants over both feet and pull them up to the waist. Adult may fasten any fasteners.

2.2 The child will use any functional means to put on front-opening garments (e.g., blouse, shirt, coat). An adult may fasten any fasteners.

2.3 The child will use any functional means to put on pullover garments (e.g., T-shirt, dress, sweater).

2.4 The child will use any functional means to put shoes on both feet. An adult may tie shoes.

2.5 The child will use any functional means to pull garments (e.g., underpants, shorts, skirt) over feet and up to waist. Adult may fasten any fasteners.

G3   The child will use any functional means to perform the following activities:
- Tie string-type fastener
- Fasten buttons/snaps/Velcro fastener
- Thread and zip zipper

  3.1   The child will use any functional means to tie string-type fastener (e.g., shoelace) on own clothing or shoes.

  3.2   The child will use any functional means to fasten buttons/snaps/ Velcro fasteners on own clothing or shoes.

  3.3   The child will use any functional means to thread and zip zippers on own clothing or shoes.

COGNITIVE AREA

Strand A: Concepts

G1   The child will follow directions, answer questions, or identify objects, people, or events that describe color, shape, and size.

  1.1   The child will follow directions; answer questions; or identify objects, people, or events using at least eight different terms that describe color (e.g., child selects the red paint in response to direction, "Get the red paint"). Terms may include, but are not limited to, the following: *red, blue, orange, pink, yellow, black, purple, gray, green, white,* and *brown.*

  1.2   The child will follow directions, answer questions, or identify objects using at least five different terms that describe shape (e.g., while playing with form boards, the child finds a square and gives it to an adult in response to the adult's request, "Find a square"). Terms may include, but are not limited to, the following: *circle, triangle, diamond, square, rectangle,* and *star.*

  1.3   The child will follow directions, answer questions, or identify objects or people using at least six different terms that describe size (e.g., while building with blocks of various sizes, child hands adult a small block in response to adult's request, "Give me a small one"). Terms may include, but are not limited to, the following: *big, tall, little, thick, thin, fat, small, short, large, skinny, tiny, gigantic, chubby, itsy bitsy,* and *long.*

G2   The child will follow directions; answer questions; or identify objects, people, or events using different terms that describe quality and quantity. Examples of terms for these concepts are described in the underlying objectives.

  2.1   The child will follow directions; answer questions; or identify objects, people, or events using at least 10 different terms that describe quality (e.g., while carrying a full basket of toys, the child says, "This is heavy"). Terms may include, but are not limited to, the following: *hot, soft, good, bad, hard, same, rough, smooth, light, loud, heavy, dry, cold, sour, wet, sweet, different, quiet, slow, fast, clean,* and *dirty.*

2.2 The child will follow directions, answer questions, or identify objects or events using at least eight different terms that describe quantity (e.g., at snack time, the child takes several raisins and says, "I have a lot of raisins"). Terms may include, but are not limited to, the following: *all, less, many, empty, none, lots, full, some, more, any, few,* and *each.*

G3 The child will follow directions, answer questions, or identify objects or events using different terms that describe spatial and temporal relations. Examples of terms for these concepts are described in the underlying objectives.

3.1 The child will follow directions, answer questions, or identify objects, people, or events using at least 12 different terms that describe spatial relations (e.g., child puts crayons in the box in response to the adult's direction, "Put crayons into the box"). Terms may include, but are not limited to, the following: *into, here, beside, next to, back, middle, down, between, front, last, up, there, behind, in back of, in front of, first, under, bottom,* and *on.*

3.2 The child will follow directions, answer questions, or identify events using at least seven different terms that describe temporal relations (e.g., the child says, "we get snack after we play"). Terms may include, but are not limited to, the following: *yesterday, later, early, after, before, tomorrow, if–then, last, today,* and *first.*

Strand B: Categorizing

G1 The child specifies a criterion (e.g., category, function, physical attribute) and sorts objects, people, or events into groups according to that criterion (e.g., child separates miniature toys into the following groups: people, animals, and vehicles). An adult may provide a general cue (e.g., "Put all of the ones together that go together").

1.1 The child will place objects into groups according to some categorical criterion (e.g., food, animals, clothing). An adult may provide the categories (e.g., "Put the food on the table and the clothing in the box").

1.2 The child will place objects into a group according to their function (e.g., things to eat with, things that go in the water).

1.3 The child will place objects into a group according to some physical attribute (e.g., color, shape, size, texture).

Strand C: Sequencing

G1 In response to three-step directions that are not routinely given, the child will correctly perform the sequence as directed; for example, during a gross motor activity, an adult gestures and tells the child, "Run to the bench, pick up the ball, then run to the slide"; the child then follows these directions in the correct sequence. Contextual cues such as gestures may be given.

    1.1 In response to three-step directions that are routinely given, the child will correctly perform the sequence as directed; for example, after being outside, an adult gestures and tells the child, "Take off your coat, hang it up, then wash your hands"; the child follows the directions in the correct sequence. Contextual cues such as gestures may be given.

G2 The child will place three or more objects in series according to length or size (e.g., child puts books on a shelf in order of height). The child may self-correct.

    2.1 The child will match two related sets of two or more objects by assigning each object from one set to its matching object from the other set (e.g., child fits a set of different-size lids to correct bowls). The child may self-correct.

G3 The child will retell a sequence of at least three events verbally, through gestures and demonstration or by arranging pictures into correct sequence (e.g., an adult tells a three-part story and asks the child to retell the story; the child gestures, tells the story verbally, or arranges the story pictures in correct sequence to retell the story).

    3.1 The child will respond appropriately to questions about the sequence of familiar stories or events verbally, through gestures and demonstration, or by arranging pictures in the correct sequence (e.g., when telling a story, the child responds appropriately to an adult's question, "Then what happened?").

Strand D: Recalling Events

G1 Without contextual cues, the child will spontaneously and accurately relate (e.g., tell, demonstrate) events that occurred on the same day at least 30 minutes after the occurrence of the event (e.g., at the end of the school day, an adult asks, "What did you make in art today?" when art project and materials are not present in the environment. The child responds by accurately telling what was made during the art activity).

    1.1 With contextual cues (e.g., being in the same setting or with the same object), the child will spontaneously and accurately relate (e.g., tell, demonstrate) events that occurred on the same day at least 30 minutes after the occurrence of the events (e.g., during circle time with the toys present, an adult asks, "What did you do to have fun today?" The child responds by saying, "I played with the dolls," which had occurred prior to circle time).

    1.2 Spontaneously or on request, the child will accurately relate (e.g., tell, demonstrate) events that occurred immediately before (e.g., child washes hands, walks out of the bathroom, and tells an adult, "I washed my hands").

AEPS™

Child Observation
Data Recording Form I
Birth to Three Years

Child's name: _____

_____

Child's date of birth: _____

Today's date: _____

Family's name and address: _____

_____

Name of person completing form: _____

Directions: Before using the Child Observation Data Recording Form, it is necessary to review the material beginning on page 45 in this volume and the material beginning on page 21 of Volume 2. Methods of collecting child performance data as well as scoring procedures and guidelines are described. Child Observation Data Recording Form items should only be scored by comparing a child's performance on each item with each item's stated associated criterion. To score items without comparing a child's performance with stated criteria will invalidate the test results. The test items with their associated criteria can be found in Volume 2.

FINE MOTOR AREA

S = Scoring key	N = Notes
2 = Consistently meets criterion	A = Assistance provided
1 = Inconsistently meets criterion	B = Behavior interfered
0 = Does not meet criterion	D = Direct test
	M = Modification/adaptation
	Q = Quality of performance
	R = Report

Name:_____

Test period: _____
Test date: _____
Examiner: _____

	IFSP/IEP	S	N	S	N	S	N	S	N
A. Reach, Grasp, and Release									
1. Simultaneously brings hands to midline (p. 36)									
1.1 Makes directed batting and/or swiping movements with each hand									
1.2 Makes nondirected movements with each arm									
2. Brings two objects together at or near midline (p. 36)									
2.1 Transfers object from one hand to the other									
2.2 Holds an object in each hand									
2.3 Reaches toward and touches object with each hand									
3. Grasps hand-size object with either hand using ends of thumb, index, and second fingers (p. 37)									
3.1 Grasps hand-size object with either hand using the palm, with object placed toward the thumb and index finger									
3.2 Grasps cylindrical object with either hand by closing fingers around it									
3.3 Grasps hand-size object with either hand using whole hand									
4. Grasps pea-size object with either hand using tip of the index finger and thumb with hand and/or arm not resting on surface for support (p. 39)									
4.1 Grasps pea-size object with either hand using tip of the index finger and thumb with hand and/or arm resting on surface for support									
4.2 Grasps pea-size object with either hand using side of the index finger and thumb									

Name: _____

	Test period:							
	Test date:							
	Examiner:							

	IFSP/ IEP	S	N	S	N	S	N	S	N
4.3 Grasps pea-size object with either hand using fingers in a raking and/or scratching movement									
5. Aligns and stacks objects (p. 41)									
5.1 Aligns objects									
5.2 Places and releases object balanced on top of another object with either hand									
5.3 Releases hand-held object onto and/or into a larger target with either hand									
5.4 Releases hand-held object with each hand									
B. Functional Use of Fine Motor Skills									
1. Rotates either wrist on horizontal plane (p. 42)									
1.1 Turns object over using wrist and arm rotation with each hand									
2. Assembles toy and/or object that require(s) putting pieces together (p. 42)									
2.1 Fits variety of shapes into corresponding spaces									
2.2 Fits object into defined space									
3. Uses either index finger to activate objects (p. 43)									
3.1 Uses either hand to activate objects									
4. Orients picture book correctly and turns pages one by one (p. 44)									
4.1 Turns pages of books									
4.2 Turns/holds picture book right side up									
5. Copies simple written shapes after demonstration (p. 44)									
5.1 Draws circles and lines									
5.2 Scribbles									

An Area Raw Score can be computed by adding all of the 2 and 1 scores entered in the S column for a specific test period. To compute the Area Percent Score: divide the Area Raw Score by the Area Raw Score Possible, then multiply by 100.

RESULTS				
Test date	_____	_____	_____	_____
Area Raw Score	_____	_____	_____	_____
Area Raw Score Possible	66	66	66	66
Area Percent Score	_____	_____	_____	_____

FINE MOTOR AREA

EXAMINER: _____ DATE: _____

COMMENTS: _____

_____

_____

_____

_____

EXAMINER: _____ DATE: _____

COMMENTS: _____

_____

_____

_____

_____

EXAMINER: _____ DATE: _____

COMMENTS: _____

_____

_____

_____

_____

EXAMINER: _____ DATE: _____

COMMENTS: _____

_____

_____

_____

_____

GROSS MOTOR AREA

S = Scoring key	N = Notes
2 = Consistently meets criterion	A = Assistance provided
1 = Inconsistently meets criterion	B = Behavior interfered
0 = Does not meet criterion	D = Direct test
	M = Modification/adaptation
	Q = Quality of performance
	R = Report

Name: _____

Test period: _____

Test date: _____

Examiner: _____

	IFSP/IEP	S	N	S	N	S	N	S	N
A. Movement and Locomotion in Supine and Prone Position									
1. Turns head, moves arms, and kicks legs independently of each other (p. 49)									
1.1 Turns head past 45° to the right and left from midline position									
1.2 Kicks legs									
1.3 Waves arms									
2. Rolls by turning segmentally from stomach to back and from back to stomach (p. 50)									
2.1 Rolls from back to stomach									
2.2 Rolls from stomach to back									
3. Creeps forward using alternating arm and leg movements (p. 52)									
3.1 Rocks while in a creeping position									
3.2 Assumes creeping position									
3.3 Crawls forward on stomach									
3.4 Pivots on stomach									
3.5 Bears weight on one hand and/or arm while reaching with opposite hand									
3.6 Lifts head and chest off surface with weight on arms									
B. Balance in Sitting									
1. Assumes balanced sitting position (p. 55)									
1.1 Assumes hands and knees position from sitting									

Child Observation Data Recording Form I: Gross Motor Area

Name: _____

Test period: ____ ____ ____ ____
Test date: ____ ____ ____ ____
Examiner: ____ ____ ____ ____

	IFSP/ IEP	S	N	S	N	S	N	S	N
1.2 Regains balanced, upright sitting position after reaching across the body to the right and to the left									
1.3 Regains balanced, upright sitting position after leaning to the left, to the right, and forward									
1.4 Sits balanced without support									
1.5 Sits balanced using hands for support									
1.6 Holds head in midline when in supported sitting position									
2. Sits down in and gets out of chair (p. 57)									
2.1 Sits down in chair									
2.2 Maintains a sitting position in chair									
C. Balance and Mobility									
1. Walks avoiding obstacles (p. 58)									
1.1 Walks without support									
1.2 Walks with one-hand support									
1.3 Walks with two-hand support									
1.4 Stands unsupported									
1.5 Cruises									
2. Stoops and regains balanced standing position without support (p. 59)									
2.1 Rises from sitting position to standing position									
2.2 Pulls to standing position									
2.3 Pulls to kneeling position									
3. Runs avoiding obstacles (p. 60)									
3.1 Runs									
3.2 Walks fast									
4. Walks up and down stairs (p. 60)									
4.1 Walks up and down stairs using two-hand support									

Name: _____

	Test period:							
	Test date:							
	Examiner:							

	IFSP/IEP	S	N	S	N	S	N	S	N
4.2 Moves up and down stairs									
4.3 Gets up and down from low structure									
D. Play Skills									
1. Jumps forward (p. 62)									
1.1 Jumps up									
1.2 Jumps from low structure									
2. Pedals and steers tricycle (p. 63)									
2.1 Pushes riding toy with feet while steering									
2.2 Sits on riding toy or in wagon while adult pushes									
3. Catches, kicks, throws, and rolls ball or similar object (p. 64)									
3.1 Catches ball or similar object									
3.2 Kicks ball or similar object									
3.3 Throws ball or similar object at target									
3.4 Rolls ball at target									
4. Climbs up and down play equipment (p. 64)									
4.1 Moves up and down inclines									
4.2 Moves under, over, and through obstacles									

An Area Raw Score can be computed by adding all of the 2 and 1 scores entered in the S column for a specific test period. To compute the Area Percent Score: divide the Area Raw Score by the Area Raw Score Possible, then multiply by 100.

RESULTS					
	Test date	_____	_____	_____	_____
	Area Raw Score	_____	_____	_____	_____
	Area Raw Score Possible	110	110	110	110
	Area Percent Score	_____	_____	_____	_____

GROSS MOTOR AREA

EXAMINER: _____ DATE: _____

COMMENTS: _____

_____

_____

_____

_____

EXAMINER: _____ DATE: _____

COMMENTS: _____

_____

_____

_____

_____

EXAMINER: _____ DATE: _____

COMMENTS: _____

_____

_____

_____

_____

EXAMINER: _____ DATE: _____

COMMENTS: _____

_____

_____

_____

_____

ADAPTIVE AREA

S = Scoring key	N = Notes
2 = Consistently meets criterion	A = Assistance provided
1 = Inconsistently meets criterion	B = Behavior interfered
0 = Does not meet criterion	D = Direct test
	M = Modification/adaptation
	Q = Quality of performance
	R = Report

Name: _____

Test period: _____
Test date: _____
Examiner: _____

	IFSP/IEP	S	N	S	N	S	N	S	N
A. Feeding									
1. Uses tongue and lips to take in and swallow solid foods and liquids (p. 71)									
1.1 Uses lips to take in liquids from a cup and/or glass									
1.2 Uses lips to take food off spoon and/or fork									
1.3 Swallows solid and semi-solid foods									
1.4 Swallows liquids									
2. Bites and chews hard and chewy foods (p. 72)									
2.1 Bites and chews soft and crisp foods									
2.2 Munches soft and crisp foods									
3. Drinks from cup and/or glass (p. 72)									
3.1 Drinks from cup and/or glass with some spilling									
3.2 Drinks from cup and/or glass held by adult									
4. Eats with fork and/or spoon (p. 73)									
4.1 Brings food to mouth using utensil									
4.2 Eats with fingers									
4.3 Accepts food presented on spoon									
5. Transfers food and liquid between containers (p. 73)									
5.1 Pours liquid between containers									
5.2 Transfers food between containers									

Child Observation Data Recording Form I: Adaptive Area

	Test period: Test date: Examiner:								
Name:_____	IFSP/ IEP	S	N	S	N	S	N	S	N
B. Personal Hygiene									
1. Initiates toileting (p. 74)									
1.1 Demonstrates bowel and bladder control									
1.2 Indicates awareness of soiled and wet pants and/or diapers									
2. Washes and dries hands (p. 74)									
2.1 Washes hands									
3. Brushes teeth (p. 74)									
3.1 Cooperates with teeth brushing									
C. Undressing									
1. Undresses self (p. 75)									
1.1 Takes off pullover shirt/sweater									
1.2 Takes off front-fastened coat, jacket, or shirt									
1.3 Takes off pants									
1.4 Takes off socks									
1.5 Takes off shoes									
1.6 Takes off hat									

An Area Raw Score can be computed by adding all of the 2 and 1 scores entered in the S column for a specific test period. To compute the Area Percent Score: divide the Area Raw Score by the Area Raw Score Possible, then multiply by 100.

RESULTS					
	Test date	_____	_____	_____	_____
	Area Raw Score	_____	_____	_____	_____
	Area Raw Score Possible	64	64	64	64
	Area Percent Score	_____	_____	_____	_____

ADAPTIVE AREA

EXAMINER: _____ DATE: _____

COMMENTS: _____

_____

_____

_____

_____

EXAMINER: _____ DATE: _____

COMMENTS: _____

_____

_____

_____

_____

EXAMINER: _____ DATE: _____

COMMENTS: _____

_____

_____

_____

_____

EXAMINER: _____ DATE: _____

COMMENTS: _____

_____

_____

_____

_____

COGNITIVE AREA

S = Scoring key	N = Notes
2 = Consistently meets criterion	A = Assistance provided
1 = Inconsistently meets criterion	B = Behavior interfered
0 = Does not meet criterion	D = Direct test
	M = Modification/adaptation
	Q = Quality of performance
	R = Report

Name: _____

Test period: _____
Test date: _____
Examiner: _____

	IFSP/ IEP	S	N	S	N	S	N	S	N
A. Sensory Stimuli									
1. Orients to auditory, visual, and tactile events (p. 82)									
1.1 Orients to auditory events									
1.2 Orients to visual events									
1.3 Orients to tactile stimulation									
1.4 Responds to auditory, visual, and tactile events									
B. Object Permanence									
1. Visually follows object and/or person to point of disappearance (p. 83)									
1.1 Visually follows object moving in horizontal, vertical, and circular directions									
1.2 Focuses on object and/or person									
2. Locates object in latter of two successive hiding places (p. 83)									
2.1 Locates object and/or person hidden while child is watching									
2.2 Locates object and/or person who is partially hidden while child is watching									
2.3 Reacts when object and/or person hides from view									
3. Maintains search for object that is not in its usual location (p. 84)									
3.1 Looks for object in usual location									
C. Causality									
1. Correctly activates mechanical toy (p. 85)									
1.1 Correctly activates simple toy									

	IFSP/IEP	S	N	S	N	S	N	S	N
Test period:									
Test date:									
Examiner:									

Name:_____

	IFSP/IEP	S	N	S	N	S	N	S	N
1.2 Acts on mechanical and/or simple toy in some way									
1.3 Indicates interest in simple and/or mechanical toy									
2. Reproduces part of interactive game and/or action in order to continue game and/or action (p. 85)									
2.1 Indicates desire to continue familiar game and/or action									
D. Imitation									
1. Imitates motor action that is not commonly used (p. 86)									
1.1 Imitates motor action that is commonly used									
2. Imitates words that are not frequently used (p. 86)									
2.1 Imitates speech sounds that are not frequently used									
2.2 Imitates words that are frequently used									
E. Problem Solving									
1. Retains objects when new object is obtained (p. 87)									
1.1 Retains one object when second object is obtained									
1.2 Retains object									
2. Uses an object to obtain another object (p. 87)									
2.1 Uses part of object and/or support to obtain another object									
3. Navigates large object around barriers (p. 87)									
3.1 Moves barrier or goes around barrier to obtain object									
3.2 Moves around barrier to change location									
4. Solves common problems (p. 88)									
4.1 Uses more than one strategy in attempt to solve common problem									
F. Interaction with Objects									
1. Uses imaginary objects in play (p. 89)									
1.1 Uses representational actions with objects									

Child Observation Data Recording Form I: Cognitive Area

	IFSP/IEP	S	N	S	N	S	N	S	N
Test period: Test date: Examiner:									
1.2 Uses functionally appropriate actions with objects									
1.3 Uses simple motor actions on different objects									
1.4 Uses sensory examination with objects									
G. Early Concepts									
1. Categorizes like objects (p. 90)									
1.1 Groups functionally related objects									
1.2 Groups objects according to size, shape, and/or color									
1.3 Matches pictures and/or objects									
2. Demonstrates functional use of one-to-one correspondence (p. 90)									
2.1 Demonstrates concept of one									
3. Recognizes environmental symbols (signs, logos, labels) (p. 91)									
3.1 Labels familiar people, actions, objects, and events in pictures									
4. Demonstrates functional use of reading materials (p. 91)									
4.1 Orally fills in or completes familiar text while looking at picture books									
4.2 Makes comments and asks questions while looking at picture books									
4.3 Sits and attends to entire story during shared reading time									
5. Demonstrates use of common opposite concepts (p. 92)									
5.1 Demonstrates use of at least four pairs of common opposite concepts									
5.2 Demonstrates use of at least two pairs of common opposite concepts									
6. Repeats simple nursery rhymes (p. 93)									
6.1 Fills in rhyming words in familiar rhymes									
6.2 Says nursery rhymes along with familiar adult									

Name:_____

An Area Raw Score can be computed by adding all of the 2 and 1 scores entered in the S column for a specific test period. To compute the Area Percent Score: divide the Area Raw Score by the Area Raw Score Possible, then multiply by 100.

RESULTS	Test date	_____	_____	_____	_____
	Area Raw Score	_____	_____	_____	_____
	Area Raw Score Possible	116	116	116	116
	Area Percent Score	_____	_____	_____	_____

COGNITIVE AREA

EXAMINER: _____ DATE: _____

COMMENTS: _____

_____

_____

_____

EXAMINER: _____ DATE: _____

COMMENTS: _____

_____

_____

_____

EXAMINER: _____ DATE: _____

COMMENTS: _____

_____

_____

_____

EXAMINER: _____ DATE: _____

COMMENTS: _____

_____

_____

SOCIAL-COMMUNICATION AREA

S = Scoring key	N = Notes
2 = Consistently meets criterion	A = Assistance provided
1 = Inconsistently meets criterion	B = Behavior interfered
0 = Does not meet criterion	D = Direct test
	M = Modification/adaptation
	Q = Quality of performance
	R = Report

Name: _____

Test period: _____
Test date: _____
Examiner: _____

	IFSP/IEP	S	N	S	N	S	N	S	N
A. Prelinguistic Communicative Interactions									
1. Turns and looks toward person speaking (p. 99)									
1.1 Turns and looks toward object and person speaking									
1.2 Turns and looks toward noise-producing object									
2. Follows person's gaze to establish joint attention (p. 99)									
2.1 Follows person's pointing gesture to establish joint attention									
2.2 Looks toward an object									
3. Engages in vocal exchanges by babbling (p. 100)									
3.1 Engages in vocal exchanges by cooing									
B. Transition to Words									
1. Gains person's attention and refers to an object, person, and/or event (p. 101)									
1.1 Responds with a vocalization and gesture to simple questions									
1.2 Points to an object, person, and/or event									
1.3 Gestures and/or vocalizes to greet others									
1.4 Uses gestures and/or vocalizations to protest actions and/or reject objects or people									
2. Uses consistent word approximations (p. 102)									
2.1 Uses consistent consonant–vowel combinations									
2.2 Uses nonspecific consonant–vowel combinations and/or jargon									
2.3 Vocalizes to express affective states									

	IFSP/ IEP	S	N	S	N	S	N	S	N
Test period:									
Name: _____ Test date:									
Examiner:									
2.4 Vocalizes open syllables									
C. Comprehension of Words and Sentences									
1. Locates objects, people, and/or events without contextual cues (p. 103)									
1.1 Locates common objects, people, and/or events in unfamiliar pictures									
1.2 Locates common objects, people, and/or events in familiar pictures									
1.3 Locates common objects, people, and/or events with contextual cues									
1.4 Recognizes own name									
1.5 Quiets to familiar voice									
2. Carries out two-step direction without contextual cues (p. 104)									
2.1 Carries out two-step direction with contextual cues									
2.2 Carries out one-step direction without contextual cues									
2.3 Carries out one-step direction with contextual cues									
D. Production of Social-Communicative Signals, Words, and Sentences									
1. Uses 50 single words (p. 105)									
1.1 Uses five descriptive words									
1.2 Uses five action words									
1.3 Uses two pronouns									
1.4 Uses 15 object and/or event labels									
1.5 Uses three proper names									
2. Uses two-word utterances (p. 106)									
2.1 Uses two-word utterances to express agent–action, action–object, and agent–object									
2.2 Uses two-word utterances to express possession									
2.3 Uses two-word utterances to express location									

Child Observation Data Recording Form I: Social-Communication Area

Name: _____

Test period: _____
Test date: _____
Examiner: _____

	IFSP/IEP	S	N	S	N	S	N	S	N
2.4 Uses two-word utterances to describe objects, people, and/or events									
2.5 Uses two-word utterances to express recurrence									
2.6 Uses two-word utterances to express negation									
3. Uses three-word utterances (p. 107)									
3.1 Uses three-word negative utterances									
3.2 Asks questions									
3.3 Uses three-word action–object–location utterances									
3.4 Uses three-word agent–action–object utterances									

An Area Raw Score can be computed by adding all of the 2 and 1 scores entered in the S column for a specific test period. To compute the Area Percent Score: divide the Area Raw Score by the Area Raw Score Possible, then multiply by 100.

RESULTS

Test date	_____	_____	_____	_____
Area Raw Score	_____	_____	_____	_____
Area Raw Score Possible	92	92	92	92
Area Percent Score	_____	_____	_____	_____

SOCIAL-COMMUNICATION AREA

EXAMINER: _____ DATE: _____

COMMENTS: _____

_____

_____

_____

_____

EXAMINER: _____ DATE: _____

COMMENTS: _____

_____

_____

_____

_____

EXAMINER: _____ DATE: _____

COMMENTS: _____

_____

_____

_____

_____

EXAMINER: _____ DATE: _____

COMMENTS: _____

_____

_____

_____

_____

SOCIAL-COMMUNICATION OBSERVATION FORM (SCOF)[1]

Activity: _____   Total time: _____

I. Transition to Words (Strand B)

	Communicative Signal			Communicative Function				
	Interpretable	Partially interpretable	Not interpretable	Gains attention	Responds to questions	Refers to objects/ people	Greets	Protests/ Refuses
Gesture								
Vocalization								
Vocalizes/Gestures								

II. Production of Social-Communicative Signals, Words, and Sentences (Strand D)

Word approximations, words, and word combinations	Context	Functions				
		Initiation	Response to comment	Response to question	Imitation	Inappropriate
1.						
2.						
3.						
4.						
5.						
6.						
7.						
8.						
9.						
10.						
11.						
12.						

[1] Users may need to make multiple copies of this form to accommodate an adequate sample of a child's communicative behavior.

SOCIAL-COMMUNICATION SUMMARY FORM (SCSF)

I. Transition to Words (Strand B)

⬭ Interpretable gestures + ⬭ Partially interpretable gestures + ⬭ Not interpretable gestures = ⬭ Total gestures

Divide ⬭ Interpretable gestures ÷ ⬭ Total gestures × 100 = ⬭ % of all gestures are interpretable

⬭ Interpretable vocalizations + ⬭ Partially interpretable vocalizations + ⬭ Not interpretable vocalizations = ⬭ Total vocalizations

Divide ⬭ Interpretable vocalizations ÷ ⬭ Total vocalizations × 100 = ⬭ % of all vocalizations are interpretable

⬭ Interpretable vocalizations/ gestures + ⬭ Partially interpretable vocalizations/ gestures + ⬭ Not interpretable vocalizations/ gestures = ⬭ Total vocalizations/ gestures

Divide ⬭ Interpretable vocalizations/ gestures ÷ ⬭ Total vocalizations/ gestures × 100 = ⬭ % of all vocalizations/ gestures are interpretable

Social-Communication Summary Form

II. Production of Social-Communicative Signals, Words, and Sentences (Strand D)

Word approximations, words, and word combinations		2.1 Agent–action		2.5 Two-word recurrence	
1.1 Descriptive words		2.1 Action–object		2.6 Two-word negation	
1.2 Action words		2.1 Agent–object		3.1 Three-word negative	
1.3 Pronouns		2.2 Two-word possession		3.2 Asks questions	
1.4 Object/event labels		2.3 Two-word location		3.3 Action–object–location	
1.5 Proper names		2.4 Two-word description		3.4 Agent–action–object	

SOCIAL AREA

S = Scoring key	N = Notes
2 = Consistently meets criterion	A = Assistance provided
1 = Inconsistently meets criterion	B = Behavior interfered
0 = Does not meet criterion	D = Direct test
	M = Modification/adaptation
	Q = Quality of performance
	R = Report

Name: _____

Test period: _____ _____ _____ _____
Test date: _____ _____ _____ _____
Examiner: _____ _____ _____ _____

	IFSP/IEP	S	N	S	N	S	N	S	N
A. Interaction with Familiar Adults									
1. Responds appropriately to familiar adult's affect (p. 111)									
1.1 Displays affection toward familiar adult									
1.2 Responds appropriately to familiar adult's affective tone									
1.3 Smiles in response to familiar adult									
2. Initiates and maintains interaction with familiar adult (p. 111)									
2.1 Initiates simple social game with familiar adult									
2.2 Responds to familiar adult's social behavior									
2.3 Uses familiar adults for comfort, closeness, or physical contact									
3. Initiates and maintains communicative exchange with familiar adult (p. 112)									
3.1 Initiates communication with familiar adult									
3.2 Responds to communication from familiar adult									
B. Interaction with Environment									
1. Meets observable physical needs in socially appropriate ways (p. 114)									
1.1 Meets internal physical needs of hunger, thirst, and rest									
1.2 Uses appropriate strategies to self-soothe									
2. Participates in established social routines (p. 115)									
2.1 Responds to established social routines									
C. Interaction with Peers									
1. Initiates and maintains interaction with peer (p. 116)									

Child Observation Data Recording Form I: Social Area

Name: _____

Test period:

Test date:

Examiner:

	IFSP/IEP	S	N	S	N	S	N	S	N
1.1 Initiates social behavior toward peer									
1.2 Responds appropriately to peer's social behavior									
1.3 Plays near one or two peers									
1.4 Observes peers									
1.5 Entertains self by playing appropriately with toys									
2. Initiates and maintains communicative exchange with peer (p. 117)									
2.1 Initiates communication with peer									
2.2 Responds to communication from peer									

An Area Raw Score can be computed by adding all of the 2 and 1 scores entered in the S column for a specific test period. To compute the Area Percent Score: divide the Area Raw Score by the Area Raw Score Possible, then multiply by 100.

RESULTS				
Test date				
Area Raw Score				
Area Raw Score Possible	50	50	50	50
Area Percent Score				

SOCIAL AREA

EXAMINER: _____ DATE: _____

COMMENTS: _____

_____

_____

_____

_____

EXAMINER: _____ DATE: _____

COMMENTS: _____

_____

_____

_____

_____

EXAMINER: _____ DATE: _____

COMMENTS: _____

_____

_____

_____

_____

EXAMINER: _____ DATE: _____

COMMENTS: _____

_____

_____

_____

_____

Summary of AEPS Results

For each domain, plot the percent correct for each test period (1–4) to determine if the child's performance is improving over time.

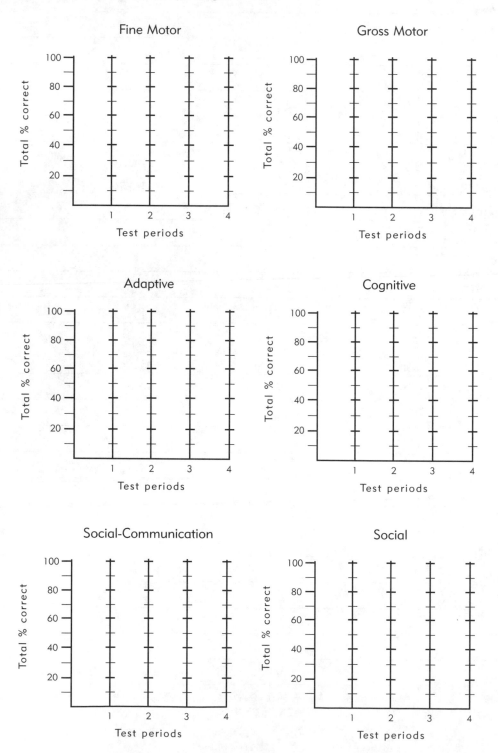

APPENDIX
C

Child Observation
Data Recording Form II
Three to Six Years

Child Observation
Data Recording Form II
Three to Six Years

Child's name: _____

_____

Child's date of birth: _____

Today's date: _____

Family's name and address: _____

_____

Name of person completing form: _____

Directions: Before using the Child Observation Data Recording Form, it is necessary to review the material beginning on page 45 in this volume and the material beginning on page 21 of Volume 2. Methods of collecting child performance data as well as scoring procedures and guidelines are described. Child Observation Data Recording Form items should only be scored by comparing a child's performance on each item with each item's stated associated criterion. To score items without comparing a child's performance with stated criteria will invalidate the test results. The test items with their associated criteria can be found in Volume 2.

Assessment, Evaluation, and Programming System for Infants and Children (AEPS)™, Second Edition, edited by Diane Bricker
© 2002 Paul H. Brookes Publishing Co., Inc. All rights reserved.

FINE MOTOR AREA

S = Scoring key	N = Notes
2 = Consistently meets criterion	A = Assistance provided
1 = Inconsistently meets criterion	B = Behavior interfered
0 = Does not meet criterion	D = Direct test
	M = Modification/adaptation
	Q = Quality of performance
	R = Report

Name: _____

	IFSP/IEP	Test period: _____		Test date: _____		Examiner: _____		_____	
		S	N	S	N	S	N	S	N
A. Bilateral Motor Coordination									
1. Uses two hands to manipulate objects, each hand performing different movements (p. 129)									
1.1 Holds object with one hand while the other hand manipulates									
2. Cuts out shapes with curved lines (p. 129)									
2.1 Cuts out shapes with straight lines									
2.2 Cuts paper in two									
B. Emergent Writing									
1. Writes using three-finger grasp (p. 130)									
1.1 Uses three-finger grasp to hold writing implement									
2. Prints pseudo-letters (p. 130)									
2.1 Draws using representational figures									
2.2 Copies complex shapes									
2.3 Copies simple shapes									
3. Prints first name (p. 131)									
3.1 Prints three letters									
3.2 Copies first name									
3.3 Copies three letters									

An Area Raw Score can be computed by adding all of the 2 and 1 scores entered in the S column for a specific test period. To compute the Area Percent Score: divide the Area Raw Score by the Area Raw Score Possible, then multiply by 100.

RESULTS					
Test date	_____	_____	_____	_____
Area Raw Score	_____	_____	_____	_____
Area Raw Score Possible	30	30	30	30
Area Percent Score	_____	_____	_____	_____

FINE MOTOR AREA

EXAMINER: _____ DATE: _____

COMMENTS: _____

_____

_____

_____

EXAMINER: _____ DATE: _____

COMMENTS: _____

_____

_____

_____

EXAMINER: _____ DATE: _____

COMMENTS: _____

_____

_____

_____

EXAMINER: _____ DATE: _____

COMMENTS: _____

_____

_____

_____

GROSS MOTOR AREA

S = Scoring key	N = Notes
2 = Consistently meets criterion	A = Assistance provided
1 = Inconsistently meets criterion	B = Behavior interfered
0 = Does not meet criterion	D = Direct test
	M = Modification/adaptation
	Q = Quality of performance
	R = Report

Name:_____

Test period: _____

Test date: _____

Examiner: _____

	IFSP/IEP	S	N	S	N	S	N	S	N
A. Balance and Mobility									
1. Runs avoiding obstacles (p. 136)									
1.1 Runs									
2. Alternates feet walking up and down stairs (p. 136)									
2.1 Walks up and down stairs									
B. Play Skills									
1. Jumps forward (p. 137)									
1.1 Jumps in place									
1.2 Jumps from platform									
1.3 Balances on one foot									
2. Bounces, catches, kicks, and throws ball (p. 137)									
2.1 Bounces ball									
2.2 Catches ball									
2.3 Kicks ball									
2.4 Throws ball									
3. Skips (p. 138)									
3.1 Hops									
4. Rides and steers two-wheel bicycle (p. 138)									
4.1 Pedals and steers two-wheel bicycle with training wheels									

An Area Raw Score can be computed by adding all of the 2 and 1 scores entered in the S column for a specific test period.
To compute the Area Percent Score: divide the Area Raw Score by the Area Raw Score Possible, then multiply by 100.

RESULTS					
	Test date	_____	_____	_____	_____
	Area Raw Score	_____	_____	_____	_____
	Area Raw Score Possible	34	34	34	34
	Area Percent Score	_____	_____	_____	_____

GROSS MOTOR AREA

EXAMINER: _____ DATE: _____

COMMENTS: _____

_____

_____

_____

EXAMINER: _____ DATE: _____

COMMENTS: _____

_____

_____

_____

EXAMINER: _____ DATE: _____

COMMENTS: _____

_____

_____

_____

EXAMINER: _____ DATE: _____

COMMENTS: _____

_____

_____

_____

ADAPTIVE AREA

S = Scoring key	N = Notes
2 = Consistently meets criterion	A = Assistance provided
1 = Inconsistently meets criterion	B = Behavior interfered
0 = Does not meet criterion	D = Direct test
	M = Modification/adaptation
	Q = Quality of performance
	R = Report

Name: _____

	Test period:								
	Test date:								
	Examiner:								
	IFSP/IEP	S	N	S	N	S	N	S	N
A. Mealtime									
1. Eats and drinks a variety of foods using appropriate utensils with little or no spilling (p. 142)									
1.1 Puts proper amount of food in mouth, chews with mouth closed, swallows before taking another bite									
1.2 Takes in proper amount of liquid and returns cup to surface									
1.3 Eats a variety of food textures									
1.4 Selects and eats a variety of food types									
1.5 Eats with utensils									
2. Prepares and serves food (p. 143)									
2.1 Prepares food for eating									
2.2 Uses knife to spread food									
2.3 Pours liquid into a variety of containers									
2.4 Serves food with utensil									
B. Personal Hygiene									
1. Carries out all toileting functions (p. 145)									
1.1 Uses toilet paper, flushes toilet, washes hands after using toilet									
1.2 Uses toilet									
1.3 Indicates need to use toilet									
2. Washes and grooms self (p. 145)									

	Test period:								
Name: _____	Test date:								
	Examiner:								
	IFSP/IEP	S	N	S	N	S	N	S	N
2.1 Uses tissue to clean nose									
2.2 Brushes teeth									
2.3 Bathes and dries self									
2.4 Brushes or combs hair									
2.5 Washes and dries face									
C. Dressing and Undressing									
1. Unfastens fasteners on garments (p. 147)									
1.1 Unfastens buttons/snaps/Velcro fasteners on garments									
1.2 Unties string-type fastener									
1.3 Unzips zipper									
2. Selects appropriate clothing and dresses self at designated times (p. 147)									
2.1 Puts on long pants									
2.2 Puts on front-opening garment									
2.3 Puts on pullover garment									
2.4 Puts on shoes									
2.5 Puts on underpants, shorts, or skirt									
3. Fastens fasteners on garments (p. 148)									
3.1 Ties string-type fastener									
3.2 Fastens buttons/snaps/Velcro fasteners									
3.3 Threads and zips zipper									

An Area Raw Score can be computed by adding all of the 2 and 1 scores entered in the S column for a specific test period.
To compute the Area Percent Score: divide the Area Raw Score by the Area Raw Score Possible, then multiply by 100.

RESULTS	Test date				
	Area Raw Score				
	Area Raw Score Possible	70	70	70	70
	Area Percent Score				

ADAPTIVE AREA

EXAMINER: _____ DATE: _____

COMMENTS: _____

_____

_____

_____

_____

EXAMINER: _____ DATE: _____

COMMENTS: _____

_____

_____

_____

_____

EXAMINER: _____ DATE: _____

COMMENTS: _____

_____

_____

_____

_____

EXAMINER: _____ DATE: _____

COMMENTS: _____

_____

_____

_____

_____

COGNITIVE AREA

S = Scoring key	N = Notes
2 = Consistently meets criterion	A = Assistance provided
1 = Inconsistently meets criterion	B = Behavior interfered
0 = Does not meet criterion	D = Direct test
	M = Modification/adaptation
	Q = Quality of performance
	R = Report

Name: _____

Test period: ____ ____ ____ ____
Test date: ____ ____ ____ ____
Examiner: ____ ____ ____ ____

	IFSP/ IEP	S	N	S	N	S	N	S	N
A. Concepts									
1. Demonstrates understanding of color, shape, and size concepts (p. 156)									
1.1 Demonstrates understanding of eight different colors									
1.2 Demonstrates understanding of five different shapes									
1.3 Demonstrates understanding of six different size concepts									
2. Demonstrates understanding of qualitative and quantitative concepts (p. 157)									
2.1 Demonstrates understanding of 10 different qualitative concepts									
2.2 Demonstrates understanding of eight different quantitative concepts									
3. Demonstrates understanding of spatial and temporal relations concepts (p. 158)									
3.1 Demonstrates understanding of 12 different spatial relations concepts									
3.2 Demonstrates understanding of seven different temporal relations concepts									
B. Categorizing									
1. Groups objects, people, or events on the basis of specified criteria (p. 160)									
1.1 Groups objects, people, or events on the basis of category									
1.2 Groups objects on the basis of function									
1.3 Groups objects on the basis of physical attribute									
C. Sequencing									
1. Follows directions of three or more related steps that are not routinely given (p. 161)									
1.1 Follows directions of three or more related steps that are routinely given									

Child Observation Data Recording Form II: Cognitive Area

Name:_____

	IFSP/IEP	S	N	S	N	S	N	S	N
Test period:									
Test date:									
Examiner:									
2. Places objects in series according to length or size (p. 161)									
2.1 Fits one ordered set of objects to another									
3. Retells event in sequence (p. 161)									
3.1 Completes sequence of familiar story or event									
D. Recalling Events									
1. Recalls events that occurred on same day, without contextual cues (p. 163)									
1.1 Recalls events that occurred on same day, with contextual cues									
1.2 Recalls events immediately after they occur									
E. Problem Solving									
1. Evaluates solutions to problems (p. 164)									
1.1 Suggests acceptable solutions to problems									
1.2 Identifies means to goal									
2. Makes statements and appropriately answers questions that require reasoning about objects, situations, or people (p. 164)									
2.1 Gives reason for inference									
2.2 Makes prediction about future or hypothetical events									
2.3 Gives possible cause for some event									
F. Play									
1. Engages in cooperative, imaginary play (p. 166)									
1.1 Enacts roles or identities									
1.2 Plans and acts out recognizable event, theme, or storyline									
1.3 Uses imaginary props									
2. Engages in games with rules (p. 167)									
2.1 Maintains participation									
2.2 Conforms to game rules									
G. Premath									
1. Counts at least 20 objects (p. 168)									

Name: _____

	Test period: Test date: Examiner:								
	IFSP/IEP	S	N	S	N	S	N	S	N
1.1 Counts at least 10 objects									
1.2 Counts three objects									
2. Demonstrates understanding of printed numerals (p. 168)									
2.1 Labels printed numerals up to 10									
2.2 Recognizes printed numerals									
H. Phonological Awareness and Emergent Reading									
1. Demonstrates phonological awareness skills (p. 170)									
1.1 Uses rhyming skills									
1.2 Segments sentences and words									
1.3 Blends single sounds and syllables									
1.4 Identifies same and different sounds at the beginning and end of words									
2. Uses letter–sound associations to sound out and write words (p. 171)									
2.1 Writes words using letter sounds									
2.2 Sounds out words									
2.3 Produces correct sounds for letters									
3. Reads words by sight (p. 172)									
3.1 Identifies letter names									

An Area Raw Score can be computed by adding all of the 2 and 1 scores entered in the S column for a specific test period.
To compute the Area Percent Score: divide the Area Raw Score by the Area Raw Score Possible, then multiply by 100.

RESULTS	Test date Area Raw Score Area Raw Score Possible Area Percent Score				
		___	___	___	___
		___	___	___	___
		108	108	108	108
		___	___	___	___

COGNITIVE AREA

EXAMINER: _____ DATE: _____

COMMENTS: _____

_____

_____

_____

_____

EXAMINER: _____ DATE: _____

COMMENTS: _____

_____

_____

_____

_____

EXAMINER: _____ DATE: _____

COMMENTS: _____

_____

_____

_____

_____

EXAMINER: _____ DATE: _____

COMMENTS: _____

_____

_____

_____

_____

SOCIAL-COMMUNICATION AREA

S = Scoring key	N = Notes
2 = Consistently meets criterion	A = Assistance provided
1 = Inconsistently meets criterion	B = Behavior interfered
0 = Does not meet criterion	D = Direct test
	M = Modification/adaptation
	Q = Quality of performance
	R = Report

Name:_____

Test period: ____ ____ ____ ____
Test date: ____ ____ ____ ____
Examiner: ____ ____ ____ ____

	IFSP/IEP	S	N	S	N	S	N	S	N
A. Social-Communicative Interactions									
1. Uses words, phrases, or sentences to inform, direct, ask questions, and express anticipation, imagination, affect, and emotions (p. 177)									
1.1 Uses words, phrases, or sentences to express anticipated outcomes									
1.2 Uses words, phrases, or sentences to describe pretend objects, events, or people									
1.3 Uses words, phrases, or sentences to label own or others' affect/emotions									
1.4 Uses words, phrases, or sentences to describe past events									
1.5 Uses words, phrases, or sentences to make commands to and requests of others									
1.6 Uses words, phrases, or sentences to obtain information									
1.7 Uses words, phrases, or sentences to inform									
2. Uses conversational rules (p. 179)									
2.1 Alternates between speaker/listener role									
2.2 Responds to topic changes initiated by others									
2.3 Asks questions for clarification									
2.4 Responds to contingent questions									
2.5 Initiates context-relevant topics									
2.6 Responds to others' topic initiations									
3. Establishes and varies social-communicative roles (p. 181)									

Child Observation Data Recording Form II: Social-Communication Area

	IFSP/IEP	S	N	S	N	S	N	S	N
Test period:									
Test date:									
Examiner:									
3.1 Varies voice to impart meaning									
3.2 Uses socially appropriate physical orientation									
B. Production of Words, Phrases, and Sentences									
1. Uses verbs (p. 182)									
1.1 Uses auxiliary verbs									
1.2 Uses copula verb "to be"									
1.3 Uses third person singular verb forms									
1.4 Uses irregular past tense verbs									
1.5 Uses regular past tense verbs									
1.6 Uses present progressive "ing"									
2. Uses noun inflections (p. 184)									
2.1 Uses possessive "s"									
2.2 Uses irregular plural nouns									
2.3 Uses regular plural nouns									
3. Asks questions (p. 185)									
3.1 Asks yes/no questions									
3.2 Asks questions with inverted auxiliary									
3.3 Asks "when" questions									
3.4 Asks "why," "who," and "how" questions									
3.5 Asks "what" and "where" questions									
3.6 Asks questions using rising inflections									
4. Uses pronouns (p. 186)									
4.1 Uses subject pronouns									
4.2 Uses object pronouns									

Name: _____

	Test period:								
Name:	Test date:								
	Examiner:								
	IFSP/IEP	S	N	S	N	S	N	S	N
4.3 Uses possessive pronouns									
4.4 Uses indefinite pronouns									
4.5 Uses demonstrative pronouns									
5. Uses descriptive words (p. 188)									
5.1 Uses adjectives									
5.2 Uses adjectives to make comparisons									
5.3 Uses adverbs									
5.4 Uses prepositions									
5.5 Uses conjunctions									
5.6 Uses articles									

An Area Raw Score can be computed by adding all of the 2 and 1 scores entered in the S column for a specific test period.
To compute the Area Percent Score, divide the Area Raw Score by the Area Raw Score Possible, then multiply by 100.

RESULTS	Test date				
	Area Raw Score				
	Area Raw Score Possible	98	98	98	98
	Area Percent Score				

SOCIAL-COMMUNICATION AREA

EXAMINER: _____ DATE: _____

COMMENTS: _____

_____

_____

_____

_____

EXAMINER: _____ DATE: _____

COMMENTS: _____

_____

_____

_____

_____

EXAMINER: _____ DATE: _____

COMMENTS: _____

_____

_____

_____

_____

EXAMINER: _____ DATE: _____

COMMENTS: _____

_____

_____

_____

_____

SOCIAL-COMMUNICATION OBSERVATION FORM (SCOF)[1]

Child's name: ______________________________

Observer/Activity: ______________________________

Others present: ______________________________

Date: ______________ Time (start): __________ Time (stop): __________ Total time: __________

Record child utterances word for word u = unintelligible word (u) = unintelligible phrase	Context	Functions: Initiation	Response to comment	Response to question	Imitation	Unrelated
1.						
2.						
3.						
4.						
5.						
6.						
7.						
8.						
9.						

[1] Users may need to make multiple copies of this form to accommodate an adequate language sample for individual children.

SOCIAL-COMMUNICATION SUMMARY FORM (SCSF)

Strand B: Production of Words, Phrases, and Sentences

Review each utterance on the Social-Communication Observation Form and record the frequency with which specific types of words, word forms, and types of sentences occur by entering tally marks (IIII) in the appropriate spaces below. This information should be used to score all items in Strand B of the Social-Communication Area according to the criterion specified for each individual item. (See Volume 2, Section III.)

1.1	Uses auxiliary verbs (e.g., will, can, do, shall, have)	
1.2	Uses copula verb "to be" (e.g., I am, they are, she is)	
1.3	Uses third person singular verb forms (e.g., "She plays it," "He does not")	
1.4	Uses irregular past tense verbs (e.g., went, ran, made, ate, drank)	
1.5	Uses regular past tense verbs (e.g., walked, talked, jumped)	
1.6	Uses present progressive "ing" (e.g., going, washing, dancing)	
2.1	Uses possessive "s" (e.g., Mom's, Ann's, Sammy's)	
2.2	Uses irregular plural nouns (e.g., mice, leaves, geese, feet)	
2.3	Uses regular plural nouns (e.g., dogs, cups, blocks, dresses)	
3.1	Asks yes/no questions	
3.2	Asks questions with inverted auxiliary (e.g., "Can I have one?")	
3.3	Asks "when" questions	
3.4	Asks "why," "who," and "how" questions	
3.5	Asks "what" and "where" questions	
3.6	Asks questions using rising inflections	
4.1	Uses subject pronouns (e.g., I, she, we, you)	
4.2	Uses object pronouns (e.g., me, her, them, us)	
4.3	Uses possessive pronouns (e.g., my, mine, hers, yours)	
4.4	Uses indefinite pronouns (e.g., none, all)	
4.5	Uses demonstrative pronouns (e.g., this, that, these, those)	
5.1	Uses adjectives (e.g., cold, red, big)	
5.2	Uses adjectives to make comparisons (e.g., "The red one is better")	
5.3	Uses adverbs (e.g., "He's over there," "Let's go fast")	
5.4	Uses prepositions (e.g., in, on, for, at, near, through)	
5.5	Uses conjunctions (e.g., and, so, only, if)	
5.6	Uses articles (e.g., the, a, an)	

SOCIAL AREA

S = Scoring key	N = Notes
2 = Consistently meets criterion	A = Assistance provided
1 = Inconsistently meets criterion	B = Behavior interfered
0 = Does not meet criterion	D = Direct test
	M = Modification/adaptation
	Q = Quality of performance
	R = Report

Name: _____

Test period: _____

Test date: _____

Examiner: _____

	IFSP/IEP	S	N	S	N	S	N	S	N
A. Interaction with Others									
1. Interacts with others as play partners (p. 194)									
1.1 Responds to others in distress or need									
1.2 Establishes and maintains proximity to others									
1.3 Takes turns with others									
1.4 Initiates greetings to others who are familiar									
1.5 Responds to affective initiations from others									
2. Initiates cooperative activity (p. 195)									
2.1 Joins others in cooperative activity									
2.2 Maintains cooperative participation with others									
2.3 Shares or exchanges objects									
3. Resolves conflicts by selecting effective strategy (p. 196)									
3.1 Negotiates to resolve conflicts									
3.2 Uses simple strategies to resolve conflicts									
3.3 Claims and defends possessions									
B. Participation									
1. Initiates and completes age-appropriate activities (p. 198)									
1.1 Responds to request to finish activity									
1.2 Responds to request to begin activity									
2. Watches, listens, and participates during small group activities (p. 198)									

Child Observation Data Recording Form II: Social Area

Name:_____

	IFSP/IEP	S	N	S	N	S	N	S	N
Test period: _____ _____ _____ _____									
Test date: _____ _____ _____ _____									
Examiner: _____ _____ _____ _____									
2.1 Interacts appropriately with materials during small group activities									
2.2 Responds appropriately to directions during small group activities									
2.3 Looks at appropriate object, person, or event during small group activities									
2.4 Remains with group during small group activities									
3. Watches, listens, and participates during large group activities (p. 199)									
3.1 Interacts appropriately with materials during large group activities									
3.2 Responds appropriately to directions during large group activities									
3.3 Looks at appropriate object, person, or event during large group activities									
3.4 Remains with group during large group activities									
C. Interaction with Environment									
1. Meets physical needs in socially appropriate ways (p. 201)									
1.1 Meets physical needs when uncomfortable, sick, hurt, or tired									
1.2 Meets observable physical needs									
1.3 Meets physical needs of hunger and thirst									
2. Follows context-specific rules outside home and classroom (p. 202)									
2.1 Seeks adult permission									
2.2 Follows established rules at home and in classroom									
D. Knowledge of Self and Others									
1. Communicates personal likes and dislikes (p. 203)									
1.1 Initiates preferred activities									
1.2 Selects activities and/or objects									

	IFSP/IEP	S	N	S	N	S	N	S	N
2. Understands how own behaviors, thoughts, and feelings relate to consequences for others (p. 203)									
2.1 Identifies affect/emotions of others									
2.2 Identifies own affect/emotions									
3. Relates identifying information about self and others (p. 204)									
3.1 States address									
3.2 States telephone numbers									
3.3 States birthday									
3.4 Names siblings and gives full name of self									
3.5 States gender of self and others									
3.6 States name and age									

Test period:

Test date:

Examiner:

An Area Raw Score can be computed by adding all of the 2 and 1 scores entered in the S column for a specific test period. To compute the Area Percent Score: divide the Area Raw Score by the Area Raw Score Possible, then multiply by 100.

RESULTS				
Test date				
Area Raw Score				
Area Raw Score Possible	94	94	94	94
Area Percent Score				

SOCIAL AREA

EXAMINER: _____ DATE: _____

COMMENTS: _____

_____

_____

_____

_____

EXAMINER: _____ DATE: _____

COMMENTS: _____

_____

_____

_____

_____

EXAMINER: _____ DATE: _____

COMMENTS: _____

_____

_____

_____

_____

EXAMINER: _____ DATE: _____

COMMENTS: _____

_____

_____

_____

_____

Summary of AEPS Results

For each domain, plot the percent correct for each test period (1–4) to determine if the child's performance is improving over time.

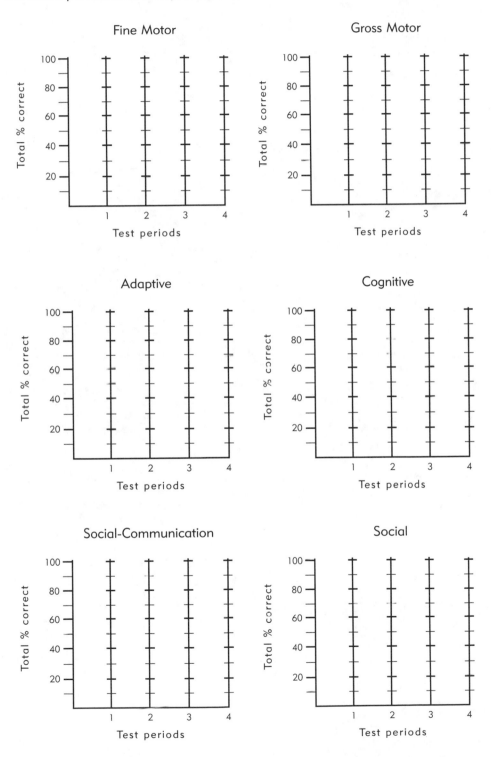

APPENDIX

D

Family Report I
Birth to Three Years

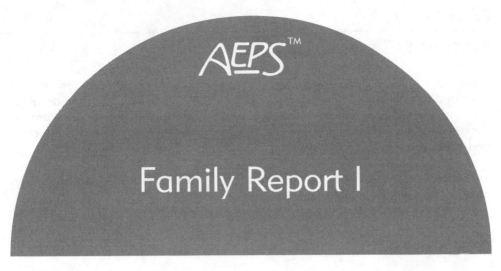

Family Report I

Child's name: _____

Child's date of birth: _____

Today's date: _____

Family's name and address: _____

_____

Name of person completing form: _____

Date of first administration: _____

List child's sibling(s) and provide age(s): _____

_____

_____

Describe your child's strengths: _____

_____

Describe your child's special needs: _____

_____

Completion of the items and questions in this form will assist you and your family members in participating in your child's assessment, goal development, intervention, and evaluation activities. It will also help prepare you to participate in your child's individualized family service plan (IFSP)/individualized education program (IEP) meeting. The Family Report is composed of two sections. Before completing either section, you should decide if you prefer to answer the questions by yourself or with other family members or if you prefer to have assistance from a program staff member. If you have questions or concerns about how to complete either Section 1 or Section 2, ask a member of your team for assistance.

Note: Shaded areas are designed for use by professional staff.

SECTION 1

Directions: To begin, review each item and answer those that are important to your child and family. The information from Section 1 should be helpful in the development of your child's IFSP/IEP and subsequent intervention plans. The form is designed to be used four times per year to permit monitoring changes in your child and changes in family priorities.

In this section, a number of questions are asked about the child's participation in daily, family, and community activities.

Daily Activities

Eating

1. Where, when, and with whom does your child usually eat breakfast, lunch, and dinner?

2. What kinds of food does your child eat?

3. Meals are usually enjoyable because

4. Meals can be difficult because

Date reviewed: _____ Noted changes: _____

_____

Date reviewed: _____ Noted changes: _____

_____

Date reviewed: _____ Noted changes: _____

_____

Sleeping

1. What is your child's bedtime routine (time, activities)?

2. What is your child's nap routine (time, activities)?

3. Naptime/bedtime is usually enjoyable because

4. Naptime/bedtime can be difficult because

Date reviewed: _____ Noted changes: _____
_____

Date reviewed: _____ Noted changes: _____
_____

Date reviewed: _____ Noted changes: _____
_____

Dressing

1. What dressing/undressing skills can your child do independently?

2. How do you help your child get dressed/undressed?

3. Dressing/undressing is usually enjoyable because

4. Dressing/undressing can be difficult because

Date reviewed: _____ Noted changes: _____
_____

Date reviewed: _____ Noted changes: _____
_____

Date reviewed: _____ Noted changes: _____
_____

Bathing/Showering

1. What bathing/showering activities can your child do independently?

2. What kind of help does your child need for bathing/showering?

3. Bathing/showering is usually enjoyable because

4. Bathing/showering can be difficult because

Date reviewed: _____ Noted changes: _____
_____

Date reviewed: _____ Noted changes: _____
_____

Date reviewed: _____ Noted changes: _____
_____

Toileting

1. What is your child's toileting schedule?

2. What type of potty training are you using with your child?

3. Toileting is usually not a problem because

4. Toileting can be difficult because

Date reviewed: _____ Noted changes: _____
_____

Date reviewed: _____ Noted changes: _____
_____

Date reviewed: _____ Noted changes: _____
_____

Playing and Interacting

1. What are your child's favorite objects and toys?

2. What are your child's favorite play activities?

3. Other children usually enjoy playing/interacting with my child because

4. My child's playing/interacting with other children can be difficult because

Date reviewed: _____ Noted changes: _____
_____

Date reviewed: _____ Noted changes: _____
_____

Date reviewed: _____ Noted changes: _____
_____

Communicating with Others

1. How does your child communicate with others?

2. Can others understand your child?

3. My child's speaking and listening are usually not problems because

4. My child's speaking and listening can be difficult because

Date reviewed: _____ Noted changes: _____
_____

Date reviewed: _____ Noted changes: _____
_____

Date reviewed: _____ Noted changes: _____
_____

Family Activities

1. What family activities usually involve your child (e.g., going on family outings, playing games, making crafts)?

2. How does your child participate in family activities?

3. In what other family activities would you like your child to participate?

4. My child's participation in family activities is usually enjoyable because

5. My child's participation in family activities can be difficult because

6. What skills would you like your child to learn to help him or her participate more fully in family activities?

Date reviewed: _____ Noted changes: _____
_____

Date reviewed: _____ Noted changes: _____
_____

Date reviewed: _____ Noted changes: _____
_____

Community Activities

1. In what community activities does your child participate (e.g., attend church, go to parades, participate in community recreation center activities)?

2. How does your child participate in these activities?

3. In what other community activities would you like your child to participate?

4. My child's participation in community activities is usually enjoyable because

5. My child's participation in community activities can be difficult because

6. What skills would you like your child to learn to help him or her participate more fully in community activities?

Date reviewed: _____ Noted changes: _____
_____

Date reviewed: _____ Noted changes: _____
_____

Date reviewed: _____ Noted changes: _____
_____

SECTION 2

Directions: To begin, read the questions that are contained in Section 2. These questions are divided into six developmental areas including Fine Motor, Gross Motor, Adaptive, Cognitive, Social-Communication, and Social. Answers to the questions should produce information that will help the team better understand specific actions and skills that your child does regularly; for example, can your child pull to a standing position or can your child use words? It is important for you to watch your child perform a skill before placing a rating in the box to the right of each question. In some cases, you may have to encourage your child to perform an action. Several questions have lettered sub-items that will help you provide more detailed information on actions or skills that your child performs. At the end of each developmental area, space is provided for you to indicate the actions or skills in that area that you believe are important for your child to learn next. At the end of Section 2, space is provided for you to prioritize the most important actions or skills for your child to learn. This information should help you in the development of your child's IFSP/IEP goals/objectives.

Space is provided at the top of each page in Section 2 to write the date each time that you complete this form. In addition, a box is provided for you to write a "Y" if you feel that your child performs the skill or action described in the question, an "S" if you feel that your child performs the skill or action sometimes to partly, and an "N" if you feel that your child does not yet perform the skill or action. If caregivers are unable to observe an item, then a question mark can be inserted in the box. When to use the "Y," "S," or "N" is described next.

Yes ("Y") is used if your child performs the action or skill described in the question. Also use a "Y" if your child previously was able to do the action or skill described in the question; for example, if the question asks if your child can crawl and now your child can walk, then write a "Y" in the box for this question.

Sometimes ("S") is used if your child does not consistently perform, partially performs, or needs assistance to perform the action or skill described in the question; for example, if your child sometimes takes off his or her coat but usually requires adult help to do so, then write an "S" in the box for this question.

Not Yet ("N") is used if your child does not perform the action or skill described in the question; for example, if your child cannot use a spoon to eat, then write an "N" in the box for this question.

It is important to remember that depending on your child's age and ability, he or she may not perform all of the actions or skills contained in Section 2.

Fine Motor Area

Fine motor skills are those that involve the movement and use of the hands. These skills include grasping, releasing, and using the index finger and thumb.

1. Does your child bring both hands to the middle of the body at the same time? (A1)

2. When playing with toys or objects, does your child bang the toys or objects together at midline when one toy or object is in EACH hand? (A2)

3. Does your child hold a hand-size object, such as a block or a small ball, with either hand using the end of the thumb, the index, and the second finger? The object is held by the fingers and is not resting in the palm. (A3)

4. Does your child pick up pea-size objects such as Cheerios or raisins with either hand using the thumb and index finger without resting the arm or hand on the table? (A4)

5. Does your child stack objects with either hand without knocking them over? Does your child line up objects in a row? For example, your child places a block on top of a block, a can on top of a can, or lines up blocks to make a train. (A5)

6. Does your child use a turning motion with either wrist when playing with objects? For example, your child uses a turning motion with his or her wrist to take a lid off a jar or wind up a toy. (B1)

7. Does your child put together simple toys or objects? For example, your child puts pop beads or Legos together, or puts a lid on a box. (B2)

8. Does your child use the index finger to turn on or off toys or objects? For example, your child uses the index finger to push an elevator button, to dial a telephone, or to push a squeaker button on a busy box. (B3)

9. Does your child hold a picture book front side up and turn the pages one by one? For example, when your child picks up a book, he or she turns it so the pictures are right side up and lifts up a page by the corner to turn it. (B4)

10. If you draw shapes such as squares or crosses, does your child copy the shapes so that they look like yours? (B5)

What fine motor skills do you want your child to learn?

_____

_____

_____

_____

_____

Assessment, Evaluation, and Programming System for Infants and Children (AEPS)™, *Second Edition*, edited by Diane Bricker

Gross Motor Area

Gross motor skills involve moving and getting around in one's surroundings. These skills include rolling, crawling, walking, and riding a wheeled toy.

date

1. Does your child turn his or her head or move arms, legs, and head separately while lying on his or her back? For example, your child waves both arms without kicking, or turns his or her head to the side without waving arms or kicking legs. (A1)

2. Does your child roll over from back to stomach *and* stomach to back, getting both arms out from under the body? (A2)

3. Does your child crawl forward at least 2 feet by alternating arms and legs? For example, your child will move one arm and opposite leg, then the other arm and opposite leg. (A3)

4. Does your child get to a sitting position on the floor from any position (e.g., standing, lying down, hands and knees) without help? (B1)

5. Does your child get into and out of a child-size chair without help? (B2)

6. Without help, does your child *walk* around large toys, furniture, or people without bumping into them? (C1)

7. Does your child bend over at the waist or bend at the knees to reach an object on the floor and then stand back up without sitting down or leaning on something? (C2)

8. Without help, does your child *run* around large toys, furniture, or people without bumping into them? (C3)

9. Does your child walk up and down stairs without help? He or she can hold onto the railing with one hand. (C4)

10. Does your child jump forward with feet together? (D1)

11. Does your child pedal with both feet while steering a tricycle forward at least 5 feet? (D2)

12. Does your child catch and kick balls? (D3)
    NOTE: Place a "Y," "S," or "N" by items a through d:

    ____ a. Does your child catch with two hands? (D3.1)

    ____ b. Does your child kick with one foot without falling? (D3.2)

    ____ c. Does your child throw overhand *or* underhand within 18 inches of a target? (D3.3)

    ____ d. Does your child roll the ball within 18 inches of a target? (D3.4)

13. When playing on outdoor play equipment, does your child climb up and down steps and ladders? (D4)

What gross motor skills do you want your child to learn?

_____

_____

_____

_____

_____

Assessment, Evaluation, and Programming System for Infants and Children (AEPS)™, Second Edition, edited by Diane Bricker

Adaptive Area

Adaptive skills are those that involve being able to care for oneself. These skills include eating, drinking, and undressing.

date

1. Does your child swallow food and liquids without choking or gagging? (A1)

2. Does your child bite off and chew pieces of solid foods such as apples, meat, or hard cookies? (A2)

3. Does your child drink from a cup by bringing the cup to his or her mouth and putting it down without spilling? (A3)

4. Does your child eat with a spoon or fork (i.e., spearing, scooping) without much spilling? (A4)

5. Does your child pour liquid and serve food from one container to another without spilling? For example, he or she pours juice into a cup from a pitcher or spoons applesauce from a jar into a bowl. (A5)

6. Without accidents, does your child go to the toilet on his or her own? (You can help with clothing if needed.) (B1)

7. Without help, does your child wash and dry his or her hands? For example, your child washes with soap, dries hands, and returns the towel to the rack or throws a paper towel away. (You can help to turn the water on and off.) (B2)

8. Does your child brush his or her teeth after you put the toothpaste on the toothbrush? You can help your child to clean his or her teeth well. (B3)

9. Does your child completely take off the following clothes? (You may unfasten the clothes.) (C1)

NOTE: Place a "Y," "S," or "N" by items a through f:

_____ a. Does your child take off a pullover shirt or sweater? (C1.1)

_____ b. Does your child take off a front-fastened coat, jacket, or shirt? (C1.2)

_____ c. Does your child take off long pants? (C1.3)

_____ d. Does your child take off socks? (C1.4)

_____ e. Does your child take off shoes? (C1.5)

_____ f. Does your child take off a hat? (C1.6)

What adaptive skills do you want your child to learn?

_____

_____

_____

_____

_____

Cognitive Area

Cognitive skills are those that involve mental processes and reasoning. These skills include problem solving, counting, recalling, imitating, categorizing, and pre-reading.

1. Does your child pay attention to noises, objects, or contact with objects? (A1)

   NOTE: Place a "Y," "S," or "N" by items a through d:

   ____ a. Does your child look in the direction of sounds or noises? (A1.1)

   ____ b. Does your child look at objects, toys, and/or people? For example, does your child watch a mobile or look at a familiar person? (A1.2)

   ____ c. Does your child respond to touching objects? For example, does your child pull his or her hand away from rough things or stroke a furry stuffed toy? (A1.3)

   ____ d. Does your child react when he or she sees, hears, or touches something? (A1.4)

2. Does your child watch objects, toys, and/or people until they disappear from sight? For example, when you are hiding a toy from your child, he or she looks at the toy until it is out of sight, or stops watching once someone has left the room. (B1)

3. When your child sees you hide an object or toy first in one place and then move the object to another place, does your child immediately go to the second hiding place and find the object? For example, if you first put a cracker under a napkin, and then while your child is watching place the cracker under a cup, does your child first look under the cup for the cracker? (B2)

4. When your child cannot find an object or toy in its regular place, does he or she look in other places to find it? For example, your child looks in other places when a toy is not in the toy box or when a coat is not in the closet. (B3)

5. Does your child turn a crank or pull a string to operate a mechanical toy (e.g., a jack-in-the-box, wind-up radio, See-N-Say toy) if shown how? (C1)

6. When you and your child are playing a game (e.g., Peekaboo, Pat-a-cake), does your child make a gesture to show you he or she wants to keep playing? For example, your child claps both hands to keep playing Pat-a-cake. (C2)

7. If you did a gesture that was new to your child, could he or she copy the gesture? For example, when you pat your head, your child pats his or her head. (D1)

8. If you say a word that is *new* to your child, does he or she try to say what you said? (D2)

9. Does your child find some way to hold objects or toys that he or she is already playing with when you give him or her another one? For example, your child holds several objects in one hand while putting some objects in his or her lap, between both legs, or in a container or pocket when handed another toy. (E1)

10. Does your child use something to get an object or toy that is out of reach? For example, he or she uses a stool to reach the cookie jar, or uses a stick to get a ball that rolled under the couch. (E2)

11. When playing with large push toys such as a doll carriage, cart, or riding toy, can your child move the toy *around* objects such as furniture or toys that are in the room? For example, he or she pushes a cart around the couch. (E3)

12. Does your child try different ways to solve a problem? For example, when your child wants something from a container that is hard to open, he or she bangs the container on the floor and asks for your help. (E4)

Assessment, Evaluation, and Programming System for Infants and Children (AEPS)™, Second Edition, edited by Diane Bricker
© 2002 Paul H. Brookes Publishing Co., Inc. All rights reserved.

13. Does your child pretend to use objects when the objects are not present? For example, he or she holds one hand to the ear and pretends to be talking on the telephone, pretends to eat food from an empty bowl, or goes to outer space in a pretend rocket. (F1)

14. Does your child put three or more similar objects in a group by category (e.g., foods, clothing, animals)? For example, your child puts all stuffed animals on the bed, dishes and utensils on the table, and clothes in the drawer. (G1)

15. Does your child give or place one object for each of two or more people or objects? For example, the child gives one cookie to each family member, or puts one spoon next to each bowl on the table. (G2)

16. Does your child recognize signs and symbols of familiar things in the home or neighborhood (e.g., labels of favorite foods, such as soup or macaroni and cheese; favorite restaurants or stores, such as *McDonald's* or *Toys 'R Us*; favorite book titles, such as *Cat in the Hat*; familiar signs, such as STOP or a street name)? (G3)

17. Does your child show interest in story books? (G4)

NOTE: Place a "Y," "S," or "N" by items a through c:

_____a. Does your child tell you a story from the pictures in the story book? (G4.1)

_____ b. Does your child talk with you about the pictures in the story book? (G4.2)

_____ c. Does your child sit and listen as an entire story is read? (G4.3)

18. Does your child understand and say opposite words? (G5) Circle the words that your child knows:

big/little	hot/cold	wet/dry	black/white	short/tall
up/down	fast/slow	top/bottom	in/out	full/empty
stop/go	light/dark	day/night	on/off	

19. Does your child repeat simple nursery rhymes? (G6)

What cognitive skills do you want your child to learn?

_____

_____

_____

_____

_____

Social-Communication Area[1]

Social-communication skills are those that involve communicating with others. These skills include listening, speaking, and understanding.

date

1. Does your child turn to look at someone who is talking nearby? For example, when playing near you, your child looks at you when you talk. (A1)

2. Does your child turn and look in the same direction that you are looking? For example, when playing together, you turn and look out the window and your child also turns and looks out the window. (A2)

3. Does your child make at least two vocal interactions with others by babbling? For example, you say, "Hi, baby," and your child says, "ba-ba." You then say, "What?" and your child says, "ba-ba-ba." (A3)

4. Does your child get your attention and then point to an object, person, or event? For example, he or she pulls on your arm and then points to a ball, or looks at you and then looks at a cat. (B1)

5. Does your child use *at least* 10 consistent words or sounds that resemble words? For example, your child sees a dog and says, "gog," or says, "ju" when asking for juice. (B2)

6. Without help, does your child find *at least* 20 familiar objects or people after you have named them? The people or objects should not be right in front of your child, but they should be familiar and easy to find. For example, you say, "Where's Spot?"and the child goes to the window and points to the doghouse. (C1)

7. Does your child carry out two-step directions with objects that are out of sight or reach? For example, when your child's doll is not in the same room, you tell the child to "Go get your doll and put it on the chair." Your child gets the doll and puts it on the chair. (C2)

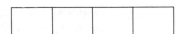

---

[1] Some caregivers may require the assistance of a communication specialist to complete the Social Communication Area.

8. Does your child use different kinds of words? (D1)
   NOTE: Place a "Y," "S," or "N" by items a through e:

   _____ a. Does your child use at least five words that describe objects (e.g., *red, big, hot*)? For example, your child sees a red ball and says, "red," or looks at the stove and says "hot." (D1.1)

   _____ b. Does your child use at least five action words (e.g., *go, want, run, eat, sit*)? For example, your child hands you a box and says, "open," or walks to the door and says, "go." (D1.2)

   _____ c. Does your child use at least two pronouns (e.g., *me, my, it, I, he, you*)? For example, your child looks in a mirror and says, "me," or takes a toy and says, "mine." (D1.3)

   _____ d. Does your child use at least 15 words to correctly label things he or she sees? For example, your child looks at a cat and says, "kitty," or points to a ball and says, "ball." (D1.4)

   _____ e. Does your child use at least three proper names (e.g., *Mommy, Daddy, Anita, Spot*)? For example, your child looks at his or her mother and says, "Mama." (D1.5)

9. Does your child use *two words together?* (D2)
   NOTE: Place a "Y," "S," or "N" by items a through f:

   _____ a. Does your child use two words to talk about people, actions, and objects? For example, your child says, "Mama go" (person and action), "Roll ball" (action and object), and "Daddy truck" (person and object). (D2.1)

   _____ b. Does your child use two words to talk about who has an object or who owns an object? For example, the child points to a car and says, "Mama's car," or takes a book from a friend and says, "My book." (D2.2)

   _____ c. Does your child use two words to talk about *where* things or people are? For example, the child points to his or her mother and says, "Mama there," or holds up a cup and says, "In cup." (D2.3)

   _____ d. Does your child use two words to describe people, events, or objects? For example, your child points to a pan and says, "Pan hot," or picks up a ball and says, "Red ball." (D2.4)

   _____ e. Does your child use two words to tell you when he or she wants more of something or when he or she wants something to happen again? For example, your child holds up a cup and says, "More juice," or when being pushed in a swing, your child says, "Go again." (D2.5)

_____ f. Does your child use two words to tell you when he or she does not want something, has not done something, or that something is gone? For example, your child finishes some juice and says, "All gone," or gives a wind-up toy to an adult and says, "Not go." (D2.6)

10. Does your child use *three words together?* (D3)

NOTE: Place a "Y," "S," or "N" by items a through d:

_____ a. Does your child use negative words (e.g., *no, not, don't, can't*) with two or more other words? For example, your child says, "No do that," or "Not baby's ball." (D3.1)

_____ b. Does your child use three words to ask questions using "Wh-" words (e.g., *what, who, where*) or a rising voice? For example, your child asks, "Where my coat? "or "We get lunch?" (D3.2)

_____ c. Does your child use three words to tell you where to place an object or where to find an object? For example, your child says, "Put baby in," or "Roll ball here." (D3.3)

_____ d. Does your child use three words to tell you about a person, an action, and an object? For example, your child says, "He throw ball," "Baby drink bottle," or "Mama drive car." (D3.4)

What social-communication skills do you want your child to learn?

_____

_____

_____

_____

_____

Assessment, Evaluation, and Programming System for Infants and Children (AEPS)™, Second Edition, edited by Diane Bricker
© 2002 Paul H. Brookes Publishing Co., Inc. All rights reserved.

Social Area

Social skills are those that involve interactions and participation with others as well as taking care of bodily needs. These skills include showing affection, playing with others, choosing activities, sharing toys, or finding a jacket when cold.

date

1. Does your child react appropriately to familiar adults' behaviors, such as smiling at them, giving a hug when asked, or looking sad or crying when corrected? (A1)

2. Does your child *start* and continue playing with you or other familiar adults? For example, your child starts a game like Pat-a-cake by clapping hands. You then say, "Pat-a-cake"; your child claps hands again, and you say, "Pat-a-cake." (A2)

3. Does your child *start* and continue communication with you or another familiar adult by gesturing, vocalizing, signing, or talking? For example, when your child says "Ba," you ask, "Do you want your ball?" Your child points to the ball and says, "Ba,"and you say, "Here's your ball." (A3)

4. Is your child able to take care of needs like a runny nose, dirty hands, minor injuries, and wet or soiled clothing? For example, if your child's clothes are wet, he or she asks you for help or tries to take off the wet clothing. If your child gets a cut, he or she comes to you for help. (B1)

5. When you let your child know it is time for a usual event such as bathing, dressing, eating, or toileting, does he or she do at least two things to get ready for the event without being asked? For example, when you turn on the bath water or say, "Let's take your bath," your child goes to the tub, begins taking off his or her clothes, and gets the tub toys. (B2)

6. Does your child *start* and continue playing with other children? For example, your child starts playing cars by rolling a car to a friend, the friend rolls the car back, and your child rolls the car back to the friend. (C1)

7. Does your child *start* and continue communication with other children by gesturing, vocalizing, signing, or talking? For example, your child gestures to a friend to play cars, and the friend says, "Okay." Your child then rolls the car and says, "Zoom," and the friend says, "Zoom, zoom." (C2)

What social skills do you want your child to learn?

_____

_____

_____

_____

_____

Intervention Priorities

Please list the most important intervention priorities for your child. _____(date)

1. _____

2. _____

3. _____

4. _____

Please list the most important intervention priorities for your child. _____(date)

1. _____

2. _____

3. _____

4. _____

Please list the most important intervention priorities for your child. _____(date)

1. _____

2. _____

3. _____

4. _____

Please list the most important intervention priorities for your child. _____(date)

1. _____

2. _____

3. _____

4. _____

APPENDIX
D

Family Report II
Three to Six Years

Family Report II

Child's name: _____

Child's date of birth: _____

Today's date: _____

Family's name and address: _____

_____

Name of person completing form: _____

Date of first administration: _____

List child's sibling(s) and provide age(s): _____

_____

_____

Describe your child's strengths: _____

_____

Describe your child's special needs: _____

_____

Completion of the items and questions in this form will assist you and your family members in participating in your child's assessment, goal development, intervention, and evaluation activities. It will also help prepare you to participate in your child's individualized family service plan (IFSP)/individualized education program (IEP) meeting. The Family Report is composed of two sections. Before completing either section, you should decide if you prefer to answer the questions by yourself or with other family members or if you prefer to have assistance from a program staff member. If you have questions or concerns about how to complete either Section 1 or Section 2, ask a member of your team for assistance.

Note: Shaded areas are designed for use by professional staff.

SECTION 1

Directions: To begin, review each item and answer those that are important to your child and family. The information from Section 1 should be helpful in the development of your child's IFSP/IEP and subsequent intervention plans. The form is designed to be used four times per year to permit monitoring changes in your child and changes in family priorities.

In this section, a number of questions are asked about the child's participation in daily, family, and community activities.

Daily Activities

Eating

1. Where, when, and with whom does your child usually eat breakfast, lunch, and dinner?

2. What kinds of food does your child eat?

3. Meals are usually enjoyable because

4. Meals can be difficult because

Date reviewed: _____ Noted changes: _____
_____

Date reviewed: _____ Noted changes: _____
_____

Date reviewed: _____ Noted changes: _____
_____

Sleeping

1. What is your child's bedtime routine (time, activities)?

2. What is your child's nap routine (time, activities)?

3. Naptime/bedtime is usually enjoyable because

4. Naptime/bedtime can be difficult because

Date reviewed: _____ Noted changes: _____
_____

Date reviewed: _____ Noted changes: _____
_____

Date reviewed: _____ Noted changes: _____
_____

Dressing

1. What dressing/undressing skills can your child do?

2. How do you help your child get dressed/undressed?

3. Dressing/undressing is usually enjoyable because

4. Dressing/undressing can be difficult because

Date reviewed: _____ Noted changes: _____
_____

Date reviewed: _____ Noted changes: _____
_____

Date reviewed: _____ Noted changes: _____
_____

Bathing/Showering

1. What bathing/showering activities can your child do independently?

2. What kind of help does your child need for bathing/showering?

3. Bathing/showering is usually enjoyable because

4. Bathing/showering can be difficult because

Date reviewed: _____ Noted changes: _____
_____

Date reviewed: _____ Noted changes: _____
_____

Date reviewed: _____ Noted changes: _____
_____

Toileting

1. What is your child's toileting schedule?

2. What type of potty training are you using with your child?

3. Toileting is usually not a problem because

4. Toileting can be difficult because

Date reviewed: _____ Noted changes: _____
_____

Date reviewed: _____ Noted changes: _____
_____

Date reviewed: _____ Noted changes: _____
_____

Playing and Interacting

1. What are your child's favorite objects and toys?

2. What are your child's favorite play activities?

3. Other children usually enjoy playing/interacting with my child because

4. My child's playing/interacting with other children can be difficult because

Date reviewed: _____ Noted changes: _____
_____

Date reviewed: _____ Noted changes: _____
_____

Date reviewed: _____ Noted changes: _____
_____

Communicating with Others

1. How does your child communicate with others?

2. Can others understand your child?

3. My child's speaking and listening are usually not problems because

4. My child's speaking and listening can be difficult because

Date reviewed: _____ Noted changes: _____
_____

Date reviewed: _____ Noted changes: _____
_____

Date reviewed: _____ Noted changes: _____
_____

Family Activities

1. What family activities usually involve your child (e.g., going on family outings, playing games, making crafts)?

2. How does your child participate in family activities?

3. In what other family activities would you like your child to participate?

4. My child's participation in family activities is usually enjoyable because

5. My child's participation in family activities can be difficult because

6. What skills would you like your child to learn to help him or her participate more fully in family activities?

Date reviewed: _____ Noted changes: _____

_____

Date reviewed: _____ Noted changes: _____

_____

Date reviewed: _____ Noted changes: _____

_____

Community Activities

1. In what community activities does your child participate (e.g., attend church, go to parades, participate in community recreation center activities)?

2. How does your child participate in these activities?

3. In what other community activities would you like your child to participate?

4. My child's participation in community activities is usually enjoyable because

5. My child's participation in community activities can be difficult because

6. What skills would you like your child to learn to help him or her participate more fully in community activities?

Date reviewed: _____ Noted changes: _____
_____

Date reviewed: _____ Noted changes: _____
_____

Date reviewed: _____ Noted changes: _____
_____

SECTION 2

Directions: To begin, read the questions that are contained in Section 2. These questions are divided into six developmental areas including Fine Motor, Gross Motor, Adaptive, Cognitive, Social-Communication, and Social. Answers to the questions should produce information that will help the team better understand specific actions and skills that your child does regularly; for example, can your child walk up and down stairs or can your child use words? It is important for you to watch your child perform a skill before placing a rating in the box to the right of each question. In some cases, you may have to encourage your child to perform an action. Several questions have lettered sub-items that will help you provide more detailed information on actions or skills that your child performs. At the end of each developmental area, space is provided for you to indicate the actions or skills in that area that you believe are important for your child to learn next. At the end of Section 2, space is provided for you to prioritize the most important actions or skills for your child to learn. This information should help you in the development of your child's IFSP/IEP goals/objectives.

Space is provided at the top of each page in Section 2 to write the date each time you complete this form. In addition, a box is provided for you to write a "Y" if you feel that your child performs the skill or action described in the question, an "S" if you feel that your child performs the skill or action sometimes to partly, and an "N" if you feel that your child does not yet perform the skill or action. If caregivers are unable to observe an item, then a question mark can be inserted in the box. When to use the "Y," "S," or "N" is described next.

Yes ("Y") is used if your child performs the action or skill described in the question. Also use a "Y" if your child previously was able to do the action or skill described in the question; for example, if the question asks if your child can say words and now your child uses sentences, then write a "Y" in the box for this question.

Sometimes ("S") is used if your child does not consistently perform, partially performs, or needs assistance to perform the action or skill described in the question; for example, if your child sometimes takes off his or her coat but usually requires adult help to do so, then write an "S" in the box for this question.

Not Yet ("N") is used if your child does not perform the action or skill described in the question; for example, if your child does not use words to describe past events, then write an "N" in the box for this question.

It is important to remember that depending on your child's age and ability, he or she may not perform all of the actions or skills contained in Section 2.

Fine Motor Area

Fine motor skills are those that involve the use of the hands. These skills include handling objects, using scissors and writing implements, drawing shapes, writing letters, and printing the child's first name.

date

1. Does your child use two hands to touch, play, or move small objects, with each hand being used separately? For example, string small beads or button small buttons. (A1)

2. Does your child use scissors to cut out shapes such as circles and ovals by cutting close to the line? (A2)

3. Does your child grasp and use a pencil or crayon using only three fingers? (B1)

4. Does your child draw or print shapes or figures that resemble letters? (B2)

5. Without help, does your child print his or her own first name? The letters must be in the correct order but can be upside down or backward. (B3)

What fine motor skills do you want your child to learn?

_____

_____

_____

_____

_____

Family Report II

Gross Motor Area

Gross motor skills involve moving and getting around in one's surroundings. These skills include running, walking, jumping, playing with balls, skipping, and riding a bicycle.

date

1. Does your child *run* around large toys, furniture, and people without bumping into them? (A1)

2. Does your child walk up and down stairs, putting one foot on each stair, without holding onto a handrail or wall? (A2)

3. Does your child jump forward with feet together using arms to go forward? (B1)

4. Does your child catch and kick balls? (B2)
   NOTE: Place a "Y," "S," or "N" by items a through d:

   _____ a. Does your child bounce a large ball at least twice in a row? (B2.1)

   _____ b. Does your child catch a ball thrown from 6 to 10 feet, using both hands? (B2.2)

   _____ c. Does your child kick a ball placed in front of him or her, without falling? (B2.3)

   _____ d. Does your child throw a ball forward with one hand, using an overhand throw? (B2.4)

5. Does your child skip at least 15 feet? (B3)

6. Does your child ride and steer a two-wheel bicycle without training wheels at least 20 feet? (B4)

What gross motor skills do you want your child to learn?

Adaptive Area

Adaptive skills are those that involve being able to care for oneself. These skills include eating, drinking, preparing and serving food, using the toilet independently, taking care of personal care needs, dressing, and undressing.

1. Does your child eat and drink appropriately? (A1)
   NOTE: Place a "Y," "S," or "N" by items a through e:

   ____ a. Does your child put a proper amount of food in his or her mouth, chew with mouth closed, and swallow the food before taking another bite? (A1.1)

   ____ b. Does your child drink from a cup and return the cup to the table without spilling? (A1.2)

   ____ c. Does your child eat and drink foods of different textures? For example, does your child eat soft foods such as bananas, drink liquids such as milk, and eat hard foods such as raw vegetables? (A1.3)

   ____ d. Does your child choose to eat different kinds of food, such as dairy, meat, and fruit? (A1.4)

   ____ e. Does your child eat and drink many kinds of foods using forks, spoons, and other utensils with little or no spilling? (A1.5)

2. Does your child help prepare and serve food? (A2)
   NOTE: Place a "Y," "S," or "N" by items a through d:

   ____ a. Does your child remove peels and wrappers before eating food? For example, your child peels a banana and removes a candy wrapper. (A2.1)

   ____ b. Does your child use a knife to spread soft foods such as cream cheese or peanut butter onto bread or crackers? (A2.2)

   ____ c. Does your child pour liquid from one container into another, such as juice into a cup? (A2.3)

   ____ d. Does your child serve food from one container to another with a fork or spoon? For example, your child spoons applesauce from a jar into a bowl. (A2.4)

3. Does your child use the toilet without help? For example, your child walks to toilet, adjusts clothing, uses toilet paper, flushes toilet, pulls up clothing, washes hands, and stays dry/unsoiled between trips. (B1)

4. Does your child take care of personal care needs? (B2) NOTE: Place a "Y," "S," or "N" by items a through e:

     _____ a. Does your child use a tissue to blow or wipe nose? (B2.1)

     _____ b. Does your child brush his or her own teeth? For example, your child puts toothpaste on brush, brushes teeth, and rinses mouth. (B2.2)

     _____ c. Does your child take off clothes, get into tub or shower, use soap to clean body, get a towel, dry off body, and put the towel back on the rack? (B2.3)

     _____ d. Does your child brush and comb his or her own hair? (B2.4)

     _____ e. Does your child wash and dry his or her face? For example, your child turns water on and off, uses soap, dries with a towel, and puts towel on the rack or throws paper towel away. (B2.5)

5. Does your child *unfasten* buttons and *unzip* zippers? (C1)

6. Does your child choose, without help, the right clothes to wear for the time of day and weather conditions, and dress self only with a few reminders? For example, your child puts on pajamas at bedtime and puts on coat to go outside. (C2) NOTE: Place a "Y," "S," or "N" by items a through e:

     _____ a. Does your child put long pants over both feet and pull them up to the waist? (C2.1)

     _____ b. Does your child put on front-opening clothes (e.g., blouse, shirt, coat)? (C2.2)

     _____ c. Does your child put on pullover clothes (e.g., T-shirt, dress, sweater)? (C2.3)

     _____ d. Does your child put shoes on both feet? (C2.4)

     _____ e. Does your child put on underpants, shorts, or skirts? (C2.5)

7. Does your child fasten buttons/snaps/Velcro fasteners when dressing? (C3)

What adaptive skills do you want your child to learn?

_____

_____

_____

_____

_____

Cognitive Area

Cognitive skills are those that involve mental processes and reasoning. These skills include using color, shape, and size words; quality and quantity words; spatial and temporal words; carrying out directions; retelling events or stories; problem solving; pretend play; playing games with rules; and early literacy.

1. Does your child use color, shape, and size words correctly? (A1) NOTE: Place a "Y," "S," or "N" by items a through c:

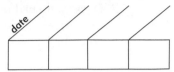

_____ a. Does your child use at least eight color words? Circle the words that your child uses correctly; for example, your child says, "I have a green ball" while holding a green ball. (A1.1)

red	blue	orange	pink	yellow	black
purple	gray	green	white	brown	

_____ b. Does your child use at least five shape words? Circle the words that your child uses correctly; for example, your child says, "That's a square," when pointing to a box. (A1.2).

circle	triangle	diamond
square	rectangle	star

_____ c. Does your child use at least six size words? Circle the words that your child uses correctly. (A1.3)

big	thick	small	skinny	chubby
tall	thin	short	tiny	itsy bitsy
little	fat	large	gigantic	long

2. Does your child use quality and quantity words correctly? (A2) NOTE: Place a "Y," "S," or "N" by items a and b:

_____ a. Does your child use at least 10 quality words? Circle the words that your child uses correctly; for example, your child says, "The banana is soft." (A2.1)

hot	hard	light	cold	different	clean
soft	same	loud	sour	quiet	dirty
good	rough	heavy	wet	slow	
bad	smooth	dry	sweet	fast	

_____ b. Does your child use at least eight quantity words? Circle the words that your child uses correctly; for example, your child says, "My cup is empty," after drinking all of the milk. (A2.2)

all	many	none	full
less	empty	lots	some
few	each	more	any

Family Report II

3. Does your child use spatial position and time words correctly? (A3) NOTE: Place a "Y," "S," or "N" by items a and b:

____ a. Does your child use at least 12 words to describe the position of objects or people? Circle the words that your child uses correctly; for example, your child says, "Sit beside me." (A3.1)

into	back	front	behind	under
here	middle	last	in back of	bottom
beside	down	up	in front of	on
next to	between	there	first	

____ b. Does your child use at least seven time words? Circle the words that your child uses correctly; for example, your child says, "Yesterday, I went to school." (A3.2)

yesterday	early	before	if–then	today
later	after	tomorrow	last	first

4. Does your child put things into groups on his or her own? For example, when cleaning the bedroom, your child puts all of the cars on the shelf, all of the airplanes in the toy box, and all of the clothes in the closet. (B1)

5. Does your child carry out three-step directions that you would NOT usually give? For example, your child follows your directions to go to the bathroom, get a toothbrush, and put it in the bedroom. (C1)

6. Does your child put three objects in order according to length or size? For example, you give your child three blocks and your child lines them up on a shelf with the smallest first and the largest last. (C2)

7. Does your child retell an event or story that involves a beginning, middle, and end? For example, you ask your child how he or she made a picture, and your child says, "First we got paper, then we put glue on it, and then we stuck beans on it." (C3)

8. Does your child tell you about something that happened at least 30 minutes earlier on the same day? For example, you ask your child what he or she had for lunch and your child tells you. (D1)

9. Does your child tell you why a solution to a problem would or would not work? For example, your child stands on a chair to reach a book on the shelf and says, "This chair is too small. I can't reach." (E1)

10. Can your child give answers to questions that require thinking? (E2) NOTE: Place a "Y," "S," or "N" by items a through c:

_____ a. Does your child give a reason for something? For example, your child says, "She is sad," and you ask, "How do you know that the girl is sad?" Your child answers, "She is crying." (E2.1)

_____ b. Does your child make a prediction? For example, when you are reading an unfamiliar story you pause and ask your child, "What do you think will happen?" Your child tells a possible event. (E2.2)

_____ c. Does your child determine a possible cause? For example, your child tells a possible cause in response to your question, "Why do you think she is crying?" by saying, "Because she fell down." (E2.3)

11. Does your child pretend play with other children? (F1) NOTE: Place a "Y," "S," or "N" by items a through c:

_____ a. Does your child pretend to be someone else and tell other children who they can pretend to be? For example, your child says, "I'll be the bus driver, and you be the kid." (F1.1)

_____ b. Does your child act out a pretend story or event? For example, your child says he or she is going fishing and then pretends to catch some fish and cook them. (F1.2)

_____ c. Does your child use pretend objects or motions to play? For example, your child pretends to brush hair without a brush. (F1.3)

12. Does your child play games following rules? (F2)

13. Does your child count at least 20 objects? (G1)

14. Does your child recognize and label correctly printed numbers from 1 to 10? For example, when numerals are seen in books, on cards, or on road signs, your child correctly identifies the numbers. (G2)

15. Does your child understand that words are made of different sounds that are said or written in order? (H1) NOTE: Place a "Y," "S," or "N" by items a through d:

_____ a. Does your child try to make rhymes? For example," My name is MIKE, I have a BIKE" or "What's in the POT and is it HOT?" (H1.1)

_____ b. Does your child understand that words are made up of individual sounds and that words are put together to make sentences? For example, if asked, can your child say the sounds in a word separately (e.g., C-A-T), and repeat separately the words in a sentence (e.g., I-want-it)? (H1.2)

_____ c. Does your child put several syllables or sounds into words after hearing you say the word? For example, "telephone," "macaroni," "patio," "bubble bath." (H1.3)

_____ d. Does your child recognize spoken or printed words with both same and different beginning and ending sounds? For example, CAR and CAKE, and BEG and DOG (same and different beginning sounds), and MAMA and LLAMA, and TOP and TOY (same and different ending sounds). (H1.4)

16. Does your child correctly associate spoken sounds with written letters or words? (H2)
NOTE: Place a "Y," "S," or "N" by items a through c:

_____ a. Does your child correctly say the sound of the letters he or she writes in simple words? For example, the child might write his dog's name by saying each sound as it is written (e.g., "S-P-O-T"). (H2.1)

_____ b. Does your child sound out simple words in print by combining the letter sounds? For example, the child looks at a store sign and says, "T-O-Y-S, toys." (H2.2)

_____ c. Does your child know the sounds for about half of the letters of the alphabet? For example, when looking at a book, he or she points to the letter B and makes the correct sound. (H2.3)

17. Does your child read at least three common words? (H3) List the words that your child can read:

_____

_____

_____

_____

What cognitive skills do you want your child to learn?

_____

_____

_____

_____

_____

Social-Communication Area[2]

Social-communication skills are those that involve communicating with others. These skills include understanding conversational rules and use of grammar.

1. Does your child use words, phrases, and sentences to express feelings, needs, and questions, and to provide information? (A1) NOTE: Place a "Y," "S," or "N" by items a through g:

   ____ a. Does your child talk about the future? For example, your child predicts the ending of a story or says, "I'm going swimming tomorrow." (A1.1)

   ____ b. Does your child talk about pretend objects, events, or people? For example, your child says, "This is my magic spaceship and I'm going to drive it to the moon." (A1.2)

   ____ c. Does your child talk about how he or she feels? For example, your child says, "I am happy when I play with my puppy." (A1.3)

   ____ d. Does your child talk about the past? For example, your child says, "I fell down yesterday," or "I had soup at school today." (A1.4)

   ____ e. Does your child tell other people what to do? For example, your child says, "Give me the red block." (A1.5)

   ____ f. Does your child ask questions to gain information? For example, when you are cooking, your child says, "What are you making?" (A1.6)

   ____ g. Does your child talk about what he or she sees, hears, or does? For example, your child says, "I saw a cat today," or "I'm going outside to play." (A1.7)

2. Does your child carry on a conversation appropriately with others? (A2) NOTE: Place a "Y," "S," or "N" by items a through f:

   ____ a. Does your child take turns being the speaker and the listener when talking to others? (A2.1)

   ____ b. Does your child change the subject when you do? For example, your child says, "I want to play outside some more," and you say, "We need to go inside now and fix a snack." Your child responds by changing the subject and saying, "What are we going to eat?" (A2.2)

   ____ c. Does your child ask questions during conversations if he or she needs more information? (A2.3)

---

[2] Some caregivers may require the assistance of a communication specialist to complete the Social-Communication Area.

_____ d. Does your child answer questions about things he or she sees, hears, says, or does? For example, your child says, "I want that," and you ask, "What do you want?" Your child says, "I want the red truck." (A2.4)

_____ e. Does your child talk about things that are relevant to the situation or to the person he or she is talking to? For example, your child sees you cutting carrots and asks for one. (A2.5)

_____ f. Does your child respond to things you talk about? For example, you say, "You look nice," and your child says, "I have on my new sweater." (A2.6)

3. Does your child vary the way he or she talks to match his or her needs? (A3) NOTE: Place a "Y," "S," or "N" by items a and b:

_____ a. Does your child change his or her voice through a variety of techniques to provide greater meaning? For example, your child may speak words slowly, with small pauses between words to convey seriousness, or speak through clenched teeth to tell you the need for the bathroom is great. (A3.1)

_____ b. Does your child change position to face the person to whom he or she is speaking? (A3.2)

4. Does your child use a variety of verbs (action words)? (B1) NOTE: Place a "Y," "S," or "N" by items a through f:

_____ a. Does your child use verbs, such as _is, will, have?_ For example, "She _is_ running," "He _will_ go with us," "The girls _have_ the toys." (B1.1)

_____ b. Does your child use _am, is, are,_ and _was?_ (B1.2)

_____ c. Does your child use _he_ and _she_ when talking _about_ another person? For example, your child says, "She plays, he doesn't." (B1.3)

_____ d. Does your child use past tense verbs such as _came, ran, fell, did, told, went,_ and _sat?_ (B1.4)

_____ e. Does your child use past tense verbs such as _walked, washed, played,_ and _helped?_ (B1.5)

_____ f. Does your child use "ing" verbs such as _washing, going,_ and _eating?_ (B1.6)

5. Does your child use words to express possession and more than one of something? (B2) NOTE: Place a "Y," "S," or "N" by items a through c:

_____ a. Does your child use possessive "s" (a word followed by an apostrophe and "s" to show something belongs to someone)? For example, your child says, "Mom's hat," or "Ann's shoes." (B2.1)

_____ b. Does your child use irregular plural nouns such as *men, mice,* and *children*? (B2.2)

_____ c. Does your child use regular plural nouns such as *dogs, houses, boats,* and *blocks*? (B2.3)

6. Does your child use different types of words to ask questions? (B3) NOTE: Place a "Y," "S," or "N" by items a through f:

_____ a. Does your child ask questions with "yes" or "no" as the answer? (B3.1)

_____ b. Does your child ask questions such as, "Can I go?" or "Is he hiding?" (not "I go?" or "He hiding?") (B3.2)

_____ c. Does your child ask questions that begin with the word "when"? (B3.3)

_____ d. Does your child ask questions that begin with the words "why," "who," and "how"? (B3.4)

_____ e. Does your child ask questions that begin with the words "what" and "where?" (B3.5)

_____ f. Does your child ask questions by a rise in pitch at the end of a sentence? For example, your child asks, "I go?" (B3.6)

7. Does your child use a variety of pronouns? (B4)
NOTE: Place a "Y," "S," or "N" by items a through e:

_____ a. Does your child use *I, she, he, they,* and *we*? For example, your child says, "He went home" or "I did it." (B4.1)

_____ b. Does your child use *you, me, him, her, us, them,* and *it* as the object in phrases and sentences? For example, your child says, "John hurt me." (B4.2)

_____ c. Does your child use *my, your, her, its, our, their, mine, yours, hers, ours,* and *theirs* to show possession? For example, your child says, "Those are her shoes." (B4.3)

_____ d. Does your child use pronouns such as *some, any, none, every, anything, something, nothing, all, lots, many,* and *more*? For example, your child says, "He doesn't have any" or "I have some." (B4.4)

_____ e. Does your child use pronouns such as *this, that, these,* and *those* to point out objects? For example, your child says, "I want those." (B4.5)

8. Does your child use a variety of words to describe?

(B5) NOTE: Place a "Y," "S," or "N" by items a through f:

_____ a. Does your child use words to describe things? For example, your child says, "Throw the *big* ball," or "I want the *red* pepper." (B5.1)

_____ b. Does your child use words to talk about how things are different from one another? For example, your child says, "I have the *biggest* bowl of ice cream," "My car is *best*," or "She is the *strongest*." (B5.2)

_____ c. Does your child use words to describe actions? For example, your child says, "He runs *fast*" or "She eats *slowly*." (B5.3)

_____ d. Does your child use words to describe position such as *in, on, out, up, down, under, by, of,* and *for*? For example, your child says, "My books are *on* the bookshelf." (B5.4)

_____ e. Does your child use words that connect other words such as *and, but, because, if,* and *or*? For example, your child says, "We could play *or* take a nap." (B5.5)

_____ f. Does your child use words such as *the, an,* and *a*? For example, your child says, "I want *an* apple," or "Where's *the* ball?" (B5.6)

What social-communication skills do you want your child to learn?

_____

_____

_____

_____

_____

Social Area

Social skills are those that involve interactions and participation with others as well as meeting bodily needs. These skills include playing with others, managing conflict, taking part in group activities, following rules, showing preferences, identifying emotions, and knowing personal information.

date

1. Does your child play with other children? (A1)

2. Does your child begin activities and encourage friends to join in? For example, your child says to friends, "Come on, let's build a house" and then gives them jobs to do. (A2)

3. Does your child find ways to stop conflicts? (A3)
   NOTE: Place a "Y," "S," or "N" by items a through c:

   _____ a. Does your child try to find a solution to disagreements with playmates? For example, when your child is not getting along with a friend, your child says, "I'll play with the ball first, and then it's your turn." (A3.1)

   _____ b. Does your child tell an adult when he or she is having trouble with a friend? (A3.2)

   _____ c. Does your child claim a toy that belongs to him or her by taking the toy back or by saying, "That's mine!" (A3.3)

4. Does your child begin playing with toys and finish the activity without being told? For example, your child gets out a puzzle, puts it together, and puts it away. (B1)

5. Does your child take part in a *small* group activity with adult supervision? (B2)

6. Does your child take part in a *large* group activity with adult supervision? (B3)

7. Can your child meet his or her physical needs? (C1) NOTE: Place a "Y," "S," or "N" by items a through c:

   _____ a. Does your child ask for help when uncomfortable, sick, hurt, or tired? (C1.1)

   _____ b. Does your child take care of his or her own physical needs? For example, your child washes his or her dirty hands or takes off wet clothes. (C1.2)

   _____ c. Does your child ask for or get food or drink when hungry or thirsty? (C1.3)

8. Does your child follow rules in places outside of his or her home or school? For example, your child follows rules to stay seated during a bus ride or follows directions to not touch food in the grocery store. (C2)

9. Does your child tell you what he or she likes and does not like? For example, your child says, "I love chocolate cake," or "I don't like to play football." (D1)

10. Does your child understand how his or her behavior affects others? For example, after pushing another child, your child says, "I'm sorry," or your child chooses to play with a child who is alone. (D2)
NOTE: Place a "Y," "S," or "N" by items a and b:

_____ a. Does your child correctly identify the emotions of others when they are hurt, sad, angry, or happy? (D2.1)

_____ b. Does your child correctly identify his or her own emotions when he or she is hurt, sad, angry, or happy? (D2.2)

11. Does your child know personal information about self and others? (D3) NOTE: Place a "Y," "S," or "N" by items a through f:

_____ a. Does your child know own address, including number, street, and town? (D3.1)

_____ b. Does your child know own telephone number? (D3.2)

_____ c. Does your child know own birthday, including the month and the day? (D3.3)

_____ d. Does your child know brother's and sister's first names *and* own first and last name? (D3.4)

_____ e. Does your child know whether he or she and others are boys or girls? (D3.5)

_____ f. Does your child know own first name and age? (D3.6)

What social skills do you want your child to learn?

_____

_____

_____

_____

_____

Intervention Priorities

Please list the most important intervention priorities for your child. _____(date)

1. _____

2. _____

3. _____

4. _____

Please list the most important intervention priorities for your child. _____(date)

1. _____

2. _____

3. _____

4. _____

Please list the most important intervention priorities for your child. _____(date)

1. _____

2. _____

3. _____

4. _____

Please list the most important intervention priorities for your child. _____(date)

1. _____

2. _____

3. _____

4. _____

Assessment, Evaluation, and Programming System for Infants and Children (AEPS)™, *Second Edition*, edited by Diane Bricker
© 2002 Paul H. Brookes Publishing Co.

APPENDIX
E

Child Progress Record I

Birth to Three Years

Child Progress Record I

Child's name: _____

Child's date of birth: _____

Today's date: _____

Family's name and address: _____

_____

Name of person completing form: _____

Initial assessment date: _____   Follow-up dates: _____

List child's sibling(s) and provide age(s): _____

_____

Assessment team: _____

_____

_____

_____

The Child Progress Record is organized like the AEPS Test. Six areas (Fine Motor, Gross Motor, Adaptive, Cognitive, Social-Communication, and Social) are organized into strands, which are then divided into goals and associated objectives. On the Child Progress Record, the objectives are illustrated in a series of arrows moving left to right, from easiest to most difficult, and culminating in an oval representing the goal. In this way, the Child Progress Record provides a visual display of current abilities, intervention targets, and child progress.

Directions: The Child Progress Record can be used in conjunction with the AEPS Test. Shade and date goals and objectives for which the child has met criteria. Use an asterisk to indicate those goals and objectives selected as individualized family service plan (IFSP)/individualized education program (IEP) targets. As the child achieves each of the goals and objectives, shade and date each arrow and oval following the direction of the arrows. This process provides a visual display of child progress over time.

Assessment, Evaluation, and Programming System for Infants and Children (AEPS)™, Second Edition, edited by Diane Bricker
©2002 Paul H. Brookes Publishing Co., Inc. All rights reserved.

FINE MOTOR AREA

Strand A: Reach, Grasp, and Release

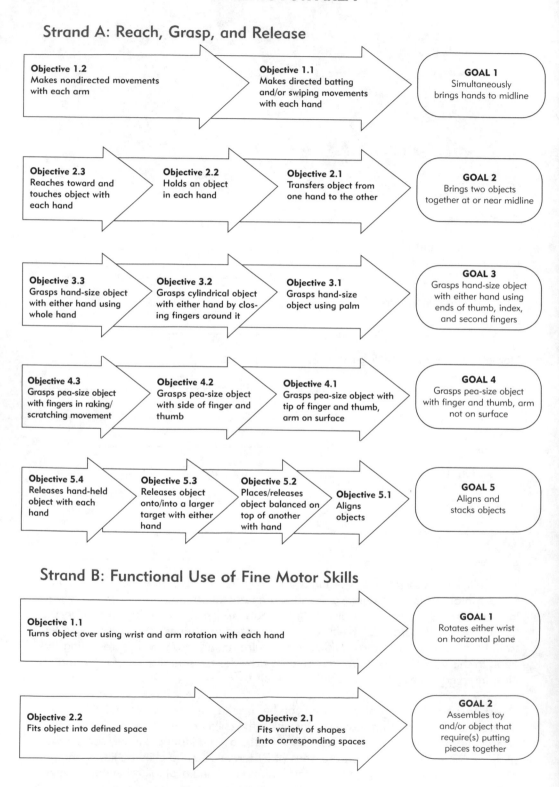

Objective 1.2
Makes nondirected movements with each arm

Objective 1.1
Makes directed batting and/or swiping movements with each hand

GOAL 1
Simultaneously brings hands to midline

Objective 2.3
Reaches toward and touches object with each hand

Objective 2.2
Holds an object in each hand

Objective 2.1
Transfers object from one hand to the other

GOAL 2
Brings two objects together at or near midline

Objective 3.3
Grasps hand-size object with either hand using whole hand

Objective 3.2
Grasps cylindrical object with either hand by closing fingers around it

Objective 3.1
Grasps hand-size object using palm

GOAL 3
Grasps hand-size object with either hand using ends of thumb, index, and second fingers

Objective 4.3
Grasps pea-size object with fingers in raking/scratching movement

Objective 4.2
Grasps pea-size object with side of finger and thumb

Objective 4.1
Grasps pea-size object with tip of finger and thumb, arm on surface

GOAL 4
Grasps pea-size object with finger and thumb, arm not on surface

Objective 5.4
Releases hand-held object with each hand

Objective 5.3
Releases object onto/into a larger target with either hand

Objective 5.2
Places/releases object balanced on top of another with hand

Objective 5.1
Aligns objects

GOAL 5
Aligns and stacks objects

Strand B: Functional Use of Fine Motor Skills

Objective 1.1
Turns object over using wrist and arm rotation with each hand

GOAL 1
Rotates either wrist on horizontal plane

Objective 2.2
Fits object into defined space

Objective 2.1
Fits variety of shapes into corresponding spaces

GOAL 2
Assembles toy and/or object that require(s) putting pieces together

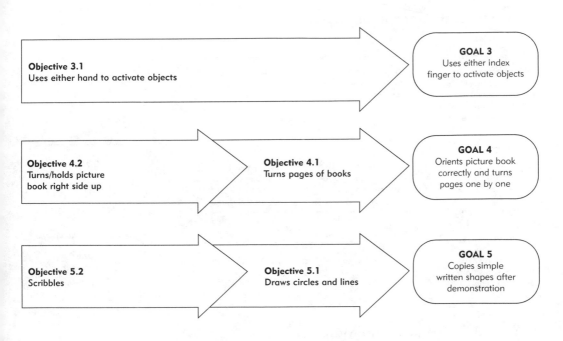

Objective 3.1
Uses either hand to activate objects

GOAL 3
Uses either index finger to activate objects

Objective 4.2
Turns/holds picture book right side up

Objective 4.1
Turns pages of books

GOAL 4
Orients picture book correctly and turns pages one by one

Objective 5.2
Scribbles

Objective 5.1
Draws circles and lines

GOAL 5
Copies simple written shapes after demonstration

GROSS MOTOR AREA

Strand A: Movement and Locomotion in Supine and Prone Position

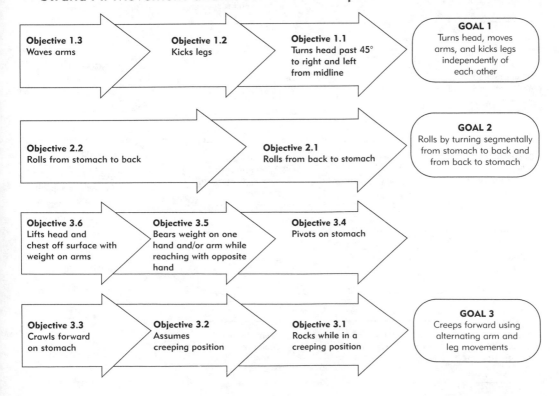

Objective 1.3
Waves arms

Objective 1.2
Kicks legs

Objective 1.1
Turns head past 45° to right and left from midline

GOAL 1
Turns head, moves arms, and kicks legs independently of each other

Objective 2.2
Rolls from stomach to back

Objective 2.1
Rolls from back to stomach

GOAL 2
Rolls by turning segmentally from stomach to back and from back to stomach

Objective 3.6
Lifts head and chest off surface with weight on arms

Objective 3.5
Bears weight on one hand and/or arm while reaching with opposite hand

Objective 3.4
Pivots on stomach

Objective 3.3
Crawls forward on stomach

Objective 3.2
Assumes creeping position

Objective 3.1
Rocks while in a creeping position

GOAL 3
Creeps forward using alternating arm and leg movements

Strand B: Balance in Sitting

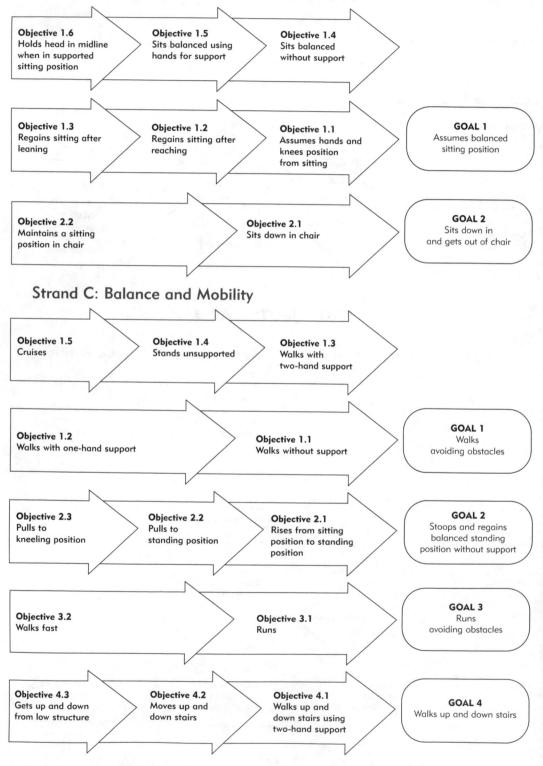

Objective 1.6
Holds head in midline when in supported sitting position

Objective 1.5
Sits balanced using hands for support

Objective 1.4
Sits balanced without support

Objective 1.3
Regains sitting after leaning

Objective 1.2
Regains sitting after reaching

Objective 1.1
Assumes hands and knees position from sitting

GOAL 1
Assumes balanced sitting position

Objective 2.2
Maintains a sitting position in chair

Objective 2.1
Sits down in chair

GOAL 2
Sits down in and gets out of chair

Strand C: Balance and Mobility

Objective 1.5
Cruises

Objective 1.4
Stands unsupported

Objective 1.3
Walks with two-hand support

Objective 1.2
Walks with one-hand support

Objective 1.1
Walks without support

GOAL 1
Walks avoiding obstacles

Objective 2.3
Pulls to kneeling position

Objective 2.2
Pulls to standing position

Objective 2.1
Rises from sitting position to standing position

GOAL 2
Stoops and regains balanced standing position without support

Objective 3.2
Walks fast

Objective 3.1
Runs

GOAL 3
Runs avoiding obstacles

Objective 4.3
Gets up and down from low structure

Objective 4.2
Moves up and down stairs

Objective 4.1
Walks up and down stairs using two-hand support

GOAL 4
Walks up and down stairs

Strand D: Play Skills

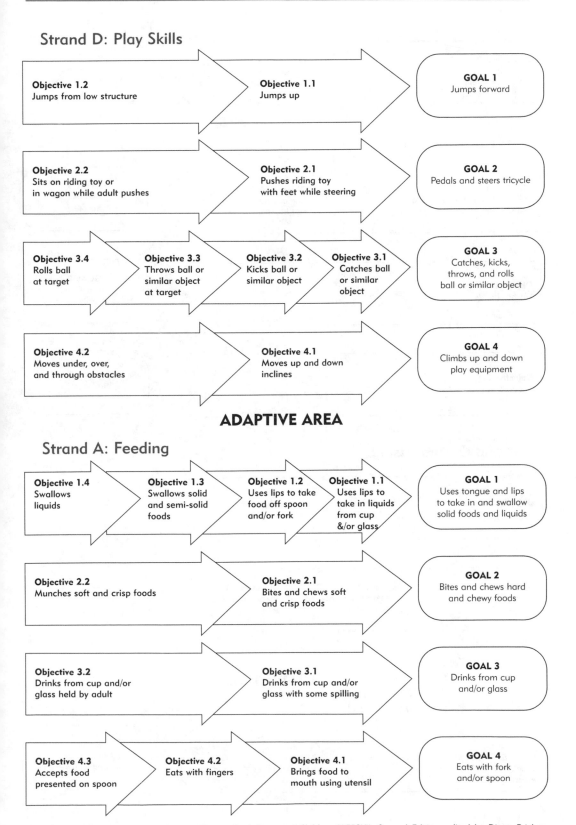

Objective 1.2 Jumps from low structure	Objective 1.1 Jumps up	**GOAL 1** Jumps forward

Objective 2.2 Sits on riding toy or in wagon while adult pushes	Objective 2.1 Pushes riding toy with feet while steering	**GOAL 2** Pedals and steers tricycle

Objective 3.4 Rolls ball at target	Objective 3.3 Throws ball or similar object at target	Objective 3.2 Kicks ball or similar object	Objective 3.1 Catches ball or similar object	**GOAL 3** Catches, kicks, throws, and rolls ball or similar object

Objective 4.2 Moves under, over, and through obstacles	Objective 4.1 Moves up and down inclines	**GOAL 4** Climbs up and down play equipment

ADAPTIVE AREA

Strand A: Feeding

Objective 1.4 Swallows liquids	Objective 1.3 Swallows solid and semi-solid foods	Objective 1.2 Uses lips to take food off spoon and/or fork	Objective 1.1 Uses lips to take in liquids from cup &/or glass	**GOAL 1** Uses tongue and lips to take in and swallow solid foods and liquids

Objective 2.2 Munches soft and crisp foods	Objective 2.1 Bites and chews soft and crisp foods	**GOAL 2** Bites and chews hard and chewy foods

Objective 3.2 Drinks from cup and/or glass held by adult	Objective 3.1 Drinks from cup and/or glass with some spilling	**GOAL 3** Drinks from cup and/or glass

Objective 4.3 Accepts food presented on spoon	Objective 4.2 Eats with fingers	Objective 4.1 Brings food to mouth using utensil	**GOAL 4** Eats with fork and/or spoon

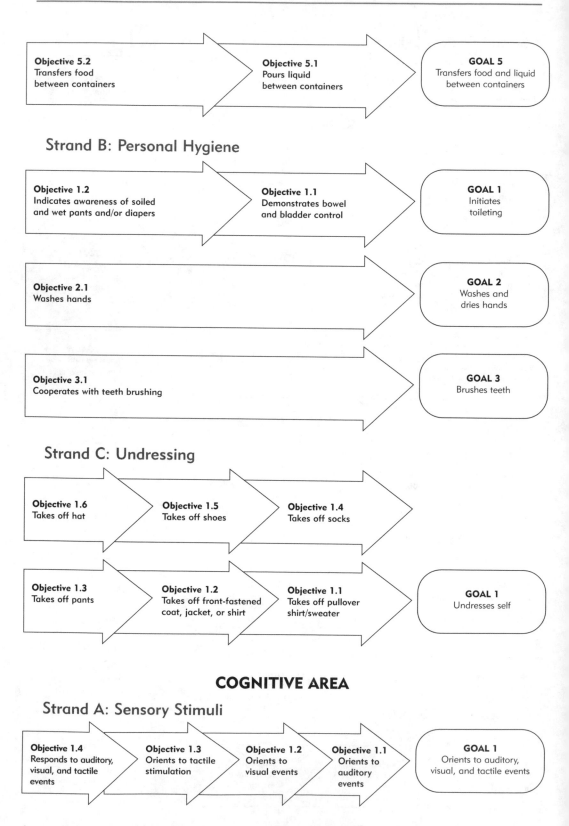

Objective 5.2
Transfers food
between containers

Objective 5.1
Pours liquid
between containers

GOAL 5
Transfers food and liquid
between containers

Strand B: Personal Hygiene

Objective 1.2
Indicates awareness of soiled
and wet pants and/or diapers

Objective 1.1
Demonstrates bowel
and bladder control

GOAL 1
Initiates
toileting

Objective 2.1
Washes hands

GOAL 2
Washes and
dries hands

Objective 3.1
Cooperates with teeth brushing

GOAL 3
Brushes teeth

Strand C: Undressing

Objective 1.6
Takes off hat

Objective 1.5
Takes off shoes

Objective 1.4
Takes off socks

Objective 1.3
Takes off pants

Objective 1.2
Takes off front-fastened
coat, jacket, or shirt

Objective 1.1
Takes off pullover
shirt/sweater

GOAL 1
Undresses self

COGNITIVE AREA

Strand A: Sensory Stimuli

Objective 1.4
Responds to auditory,
visual, and tactile
events

Objective 1.3
Orients to tactile
stimulation

Objective 1.2
Orients to
visual events

Objective 1.1
Orients to
auditory
events

GOAL 1
Orients to auditory,
visual, and tactile events

Strand B: Object Permanence

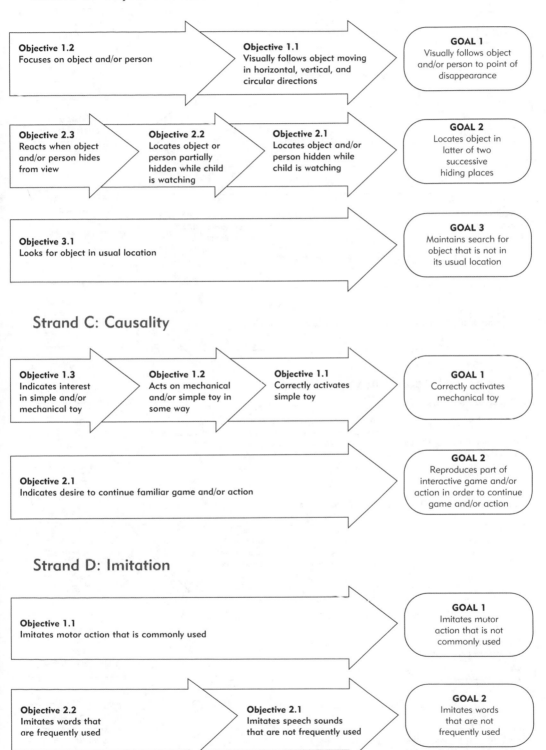

Objective 1.2
Focuses on object and/or person

Objective 1.1
Visually follows object moving in horizontal, vertical, and circular directions

GOAL 1
Visually follows object and/or person to point of disappearance

Objective 2.3
Reacts when object and/or person hides from view

Objective 2.2
Locates object or person partially hidden while child is watching

Objective 2.1
Locates object and/or person hidden while child is watching

GOAL 2
Locates object in latter of two successive hiding places

Objective 3.1
Looks for object in usual location

GOAL 3
Maintains search for object that is not in its usual location

Strand C: Causality

Objective 1.3
Indicates interest in simple and/or mechanical toy

Objective 1.2
Acts on mechanical and/or simple toy in some way

Objective 1.1
Correctly activates simple toy

GOAL 1
Correctly activates mechanical toy

Objective 2.1
Indicates desire to continue familiar game and/or action

GOAL 2
Reproduces part of interactive game and/or action in order to continue game and/or action

Strand D: Imitation

Objective 1.1
Imitates motor action that is commonly used

GOAL 1
Imitates motor action that is not commonly used

Objective 2.2
Imitates words that are frequently used

Objective 2.1
Imitates speech sounds that are not frequently used

GOAL 2
Imitates words that are not frequently used

Child Progress Record I

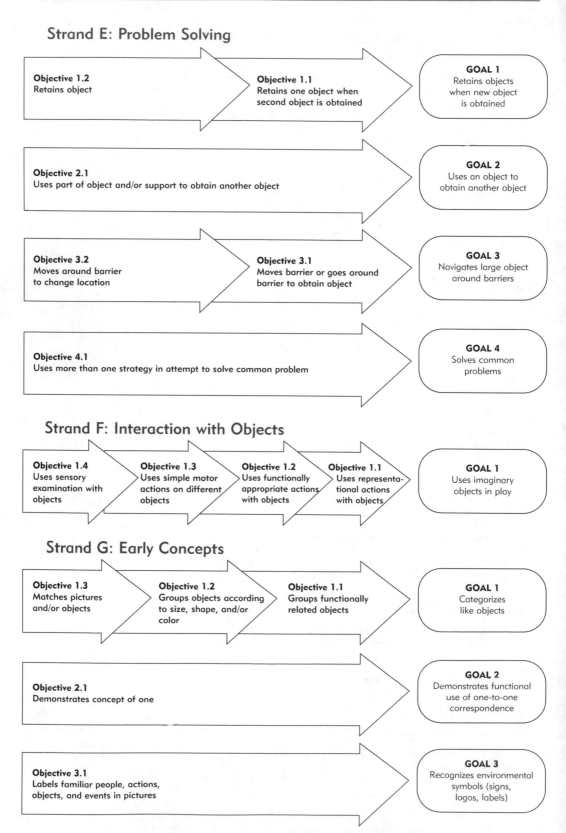

Strand E: Problem Solving

Objective 1.2
Retains object

Objective 1.1
Retains one object when second object is obtained

GOAL 1
Retains objects when new object is obtained

Objective 2.1
Uses part of object and/or support to obtain another object

GOAL 2
Uses an object to obtain another object

Objective 3.2
Moves around barrier to change location

Objective 3.1
Moves barrier or goes around barrier to obtain object

GOAL 3
Navigates large object around barriers

Objective 4.1
Uses more than one strategy in attempt to solve common problem

GOAL 4
Solves common problems

Strand F: Interaction with Objects

Objective 1.4
Uses sensory examination with objects

Objective 1.3
Uses simple motor actions on different objects

Objective 1.2
Uses functionally appropriate actions with objects

Objective 1.1
Uses representational actions with objects

GOAL 1
Uses imaginary objects in play

Strand G: Early Concepts

Objective 1.3
Matches pictures and/or objects

Objective 1.2
Groups objects according to size, shape, and/or color

Objective 1.1
Groups functionally related objects

GOAL 1
Categorizes like objects

Objective 2.1
Demonstrates concept of one

GOAL 2
Demonstrates functional use of one-to-one correspondence

Objective 3.1
Labels familiar people, actions, objects, and events in pictures

GOAL 3
Recognizes environmental symbols (signs, logos, labels)

Assessment, Evaluation, and Programming System for Infants and Children (AEPS)™, Second Edition, edited by Diane Bricker
© 2002 Paul H. Brookes Publishing Co., Inc. All rights reserved.

Objective 4.3
Sits and attends to entire story during shared reading time

Objective 4.2
Makes comments and asks questions while looking at picture books

Objective 4.1
Orally fills in or completes familiar text while looking at picture books

GOAL 4
Demonstrates functional use of reading materials

Objective 5.2
Demonstrates use of at least two pairs of common opposite concepts

Objective 5.1
Demonstrates use of at least four pairs of common opposite concepts

GOAL 5
Demonstrates use of common opposite concepts

Objective 6.2
Says nursery rhymes along with familiar adult

Objective 6.1
Fills in rhyming words in familiar rhymes

GOAL 6
Repeats simple nursery rhymes

SOCIAL-COMMUNICATION AREA

Strand A: Prelinguistic Communicative Interactions

Objective 1.2
Turns and looks toward noise-producing object

Objective 1.1
Turns and looks toward object and person speaking

GOAL 1
Turns and looks toward person speaking

Objective 2.2
Looks toward an object

Objective 2.1
Follows person's pointing gesture to establish joint attention

GOAL 2
Follows person's gaze to establish joint attention

Objective 3.1
Engages in vocal exchanges by cooing

GOAL 3
Engages in vocal exchanges by babbling

Strand B: Transition to Words

Objective 1.4
Uses gestures or vocalizations to protest or reject objects or people

Objective 1.3
Gestures and/or vocalizes to greet others

Objective 1.2
Points to an object, person, and/or event

Objective 1.1
Responds with a vocalization and gesture to questions

GOAL 1
Gains person's attention and refers to an object, person, and/or event

Objective 2.4
Vocalizes open syllables

Objective 2.3
Vocalizes to express affective states

Objective 2.2
Uses nonspecific consonant–vowel combinations and/or jargon

Objective 2.1
Uses consistent consonant–vowel combinations

GOAL 2
Uses consistent word approximations

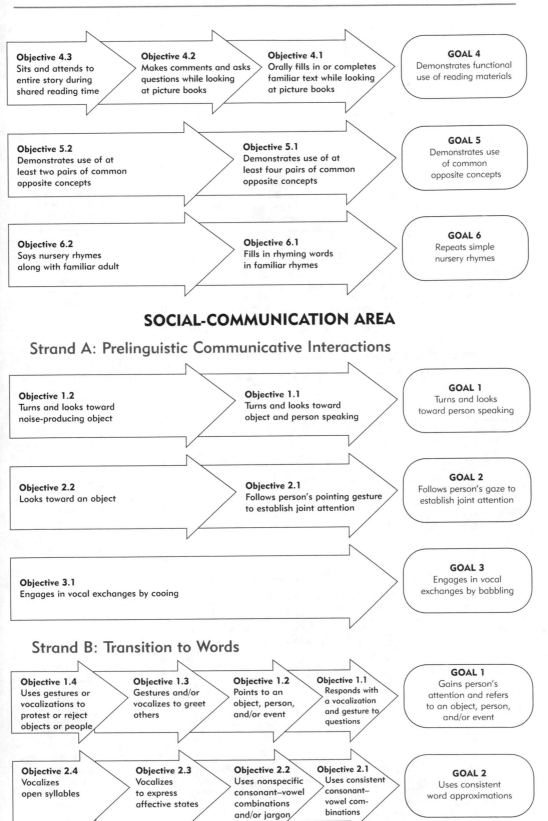

Strand C: Comprehension of Words and Sentences

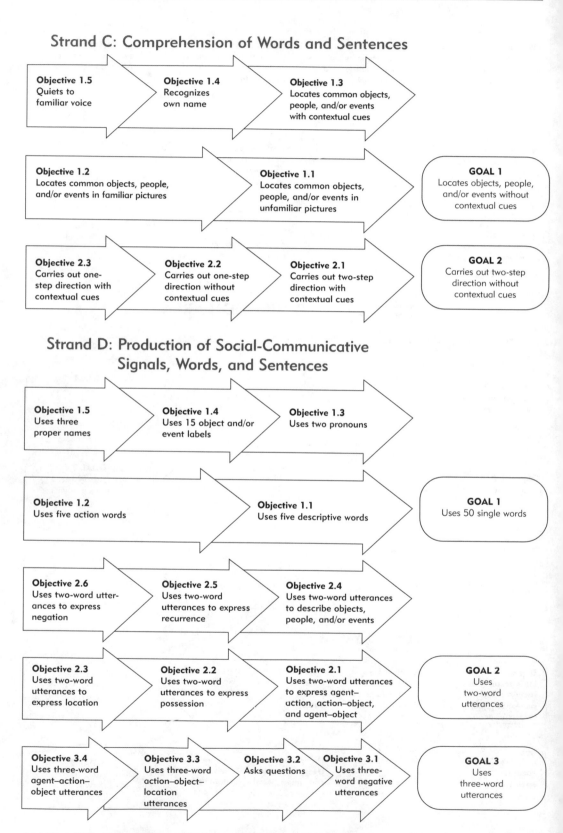

Objective 1.5
Quiets to familiar voice

Objective 1.4
Recognizes own name

Objective 1.3
Locates common objects, people, and/or events with contextual cues

Objective 1.2
Locates common objects, people, and/or events in familiar pictures

Objective 1.1
Locates common objects, people, and/or events in unfamiliar pictures

GOAL 1
Locates objects, people, and/or events without contextual cues

Objective 2.3
Carries out one-step direction with contextual cues

Objective 2.2
Carries out one-step direction without contextual cues

Objective 2.1
Carries out two-step direction with contextual cues

GOAL 2
Carries out two-step direction without contextual cues

Strand D: Production of Social-Communicative Signals, Words, and Sentences

Objective 1.5
Uses three proper names

Objective 1.4
Uses 15 object and/or event labels

Objective 1.3
Uses two pronouns

Objective 1.2
Uses five action words

Objective 1.1
Uses five descriptive words

GOAL 1
Uses 50 single words

Objective 2.6
Uses two-word utterances to express negation

Objective 2.5
Uses two-word utterances to express recurrence

Objective 2.4
Uses two-word utterances to describe objects, people, and/or events

Objective 2.3
Uses two-word utterances to express location

Objective 2.2
Uses two-word utterances to express possession

Objective 2.1
Uses two-word utterances to express agent–action, action–object, and agent–object

GOAL 2
Uses two-word utterances

Objective 3.4
Uses three-word agent–action–object utterances

Objective 3.3
Uses three-word action–object–location utterances

Objective 3.2
Asks questions

Objective 3.1
Uses three-word negative utterances

GOAL 3
Uses three-word utterances

SOCIAL AREA

Strand A: Interaction with Familiar Adults

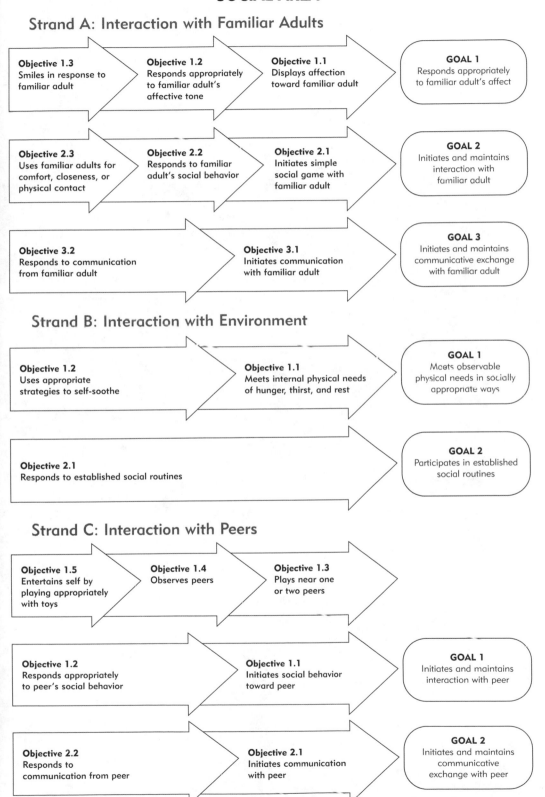

Objective 1.3
Smiles in response to familiar adult

Objective 1.2
Responds appropriately to familiar adult's affective tone

Objective 1.1
Displays affection toward familiar adult

GOAL 1
Responds appropriately to familiar adult's affect

Objective 2.3
Uses familiar adults for comfort, closeness, or physical contact

Objective 2.2
Responds to familiar adult's social behavior

Objective 2.1
Initiates simple social game with familiar adult

GOAL 2
Initiates and maintains interaction with familiar adult

Objective 3.2
Responds to communication from familiar adult

Objective 3.1
Initiates communication with familiar adult

GOAL 3
Initiates and maintains communicative exchange with familiar adult

Strand B: Interaction with Environment

Objective 1.2
Uses appropriate strategies to self-soothe

Objective 1.1
Meets internal physical needs of hunger, thirst, and rest

GOAL 1
Meets observable physical needs in socially appropriate ways

Objective 2.1
Responds to established social routines

GOAL 2
Participates in established social routines

Strand C: Interaction with Peers

Objective 1.5
Entertains self by playing appropriately with toys

Objective 1.4
Observes peers

Objective 1.3
Plays near one or two peers

Objective 1.2
Responds appropriately to peer's social behavior

Objective 1.1
Initiates social behavior toward peer

GOAL 1
Initiates and maintains interaction with peer

Objective 2.2
Responds to communication from peer

Objective 2.1
Initiates communication with peer

GOAL 2
Initiates and maintains communicative exchange with peer

APPENDIX

E

Child Progress Record II

Three to Six Years

Child Progress Record II

Child's name: _____

Child's date of birth: _____

Today's date: _____

Family's name and address: _____

_____

Name of person completing form: _____

Initial assessment date: _____ Follow-up dates: _____

List child's sibling(s) and provide age(s): _____

_____

Assessment team: _____

_____

_____

_____

Designed to assist caregivers and interventionists in monitoring child change, the Child Progress Record is organized like the AEPS Test. Six areas (Fine Motor, Gross Motor, Adaptive, Cognitive, Social-Communication, and Social) are organized into strands, which are then divided into goals and associated objectives. On the Child Progress Record, the objectives are illustrated in a series of arrows moving left to right, from easiest to most difficult, and culminating in an oval representing the goal. In this way, the Child Progress Record provides a visual display of current abilities, intervention targets, and child progress.

Directions: The Child Progress Record can be used in conjunction with the AEPS Test. Shade and date goals and objectives for which the child has met criteria. Use an asterisk to indicate those goals and objectives selected as individualized family service plan (IFSP)/individualized education program (IEP) targets. As the child achieves each of the goals and objectives, shade and date each arrow and oval following the direction of the arrows. This process provides a visual display of child progress over time.

Assessment, Evaluation, and Programming System for Infants and Children (AEPS)™, Second Edition, edited by Diane Bricker

FINE MOTOR AREA

Strand A: Bilateral Motor Coordination

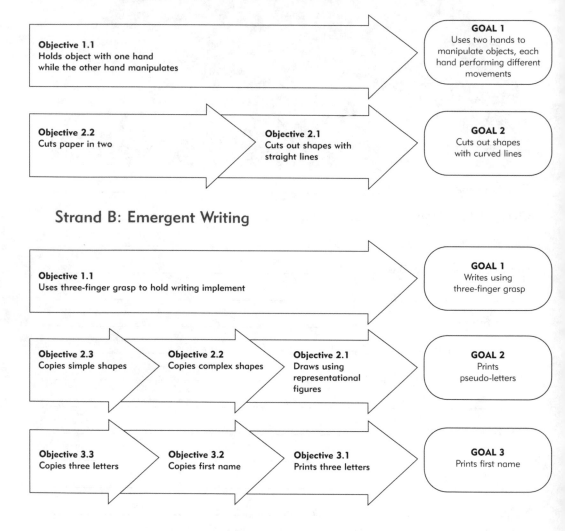

Objective 1.1
Holds object with one hand while the other hand manipulates

GOAL 1
Uses two hands to manipulate objects, each hand performing different movements

Objective 2.2
Cuts paper in two

Objective 2.1
Cuts out shapes with straight lines

GOAL 2
Cuts out shapes with curved lines

Strand B: Emergent Writing

Objective 1.1
Uses three-finger grasp to hold writing implement

GOAL 1
Writes using three-finger grasp

Objective 2.3
Copies simple shapes

Objective 2.2
Copies complex shapes

Objective 2.1
Draws using representational figures

GOAL 2
Prints pseudo-letters

Objective 3.3
Copies three letters

Objective 3.2
Copies first name

Objective 3.1
Prints three letters

GOAL 3
Prints first name

GROSS MOTOR AREA

Strand A: Balance and Mobility

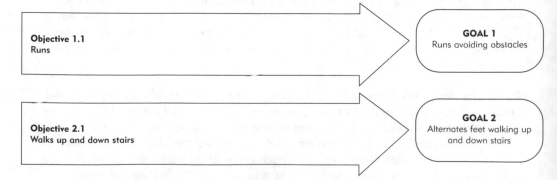

Objective 1.1
Runs

GOAL 1
Runs avoiding obstacles

Objective 2.1
Walks up and down stairs

GOAL 2
Alternates feet walking up and down stairs

Assessment, Evaluation, and Programming System for Infants and Children (AEPS)™, Second Edition, edited by Diane Bricker
© 2002 Paul H. Brookes Publishing Co., Inc. All rights reserved.

Strand B: Play Skills

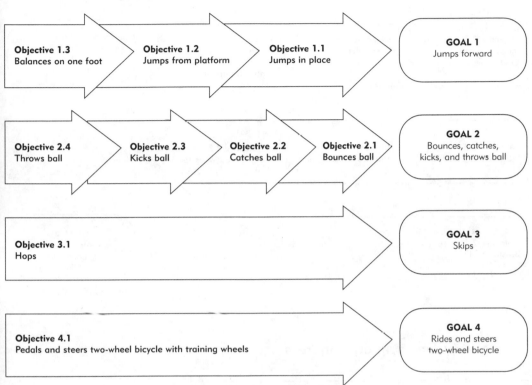

Objective 1.3
Balances on one foot

Objective 1.2
Jumps from platform

Objective 1.1
Jumps in place

GOAL 1
Jumps forward

Objective 2.4
Throws ball

Objective 2.3
Kicks ball

Objective 2.2
Catches ball

Objective 2.1
Bounces ball

GOAL 2
Bounces, catches,
kicks, and throws ball

Objective 3.1
Hops

GOAL 3
Skips

Objective 4.1
Pedals and steers two-wheel bicycle with training wheels

GOAL 4
Rides and steers
two-wheel bicycle

ADAPTIVE AREA

Strand A: Mealtime

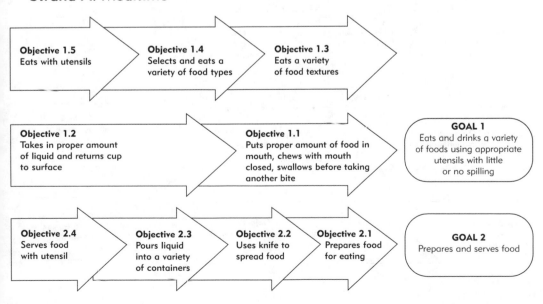

Objective 1.5
Eats with utensils

Objective 1.4
Selects and eats a
variety of food types

Objective 1.3
Eats a variety
of food textures

Objective 1.2
Takes in proper amount
of liquid and returns cup
to surface

Objective 1.1
Puts proper amount of food in
mouth, chews with mouth
closed, swallows before taking
another bite

GOAL 1
Eats and drinks a variety
of foods using appropriate
utensils with little
or no spilling

Objective 2.4
Serves food
with utensil

Objective 2.3
Pours liquid
into a variety
of containers

Objective 2.2
Uses knife to
spread food

Objective 2.1
Prepares food
for eating

GOAL 2
Prepares and serves food

Strand B: Personal Hygiene

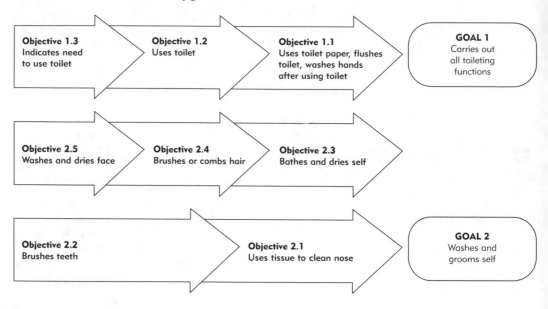

Objective 1.3
Indicates need to use toilet

Objective 1.2
Uses toilet

Objective 1.1
Uses toilet paper, flushes toilet, washes hands after using toilet

GOAL 1
Carries out all toileting functions

Objective 2.5
Washes and dries face

Objective 2.4
Brushes or combs hair

Objective 2.3
Bathes and dries self

Objective 2.2
Brushes teeth

Objective 2.1
Uses tissue to clean nose

GOAL 2
Washes and grooms self

Strand C: Dressing and Undressing

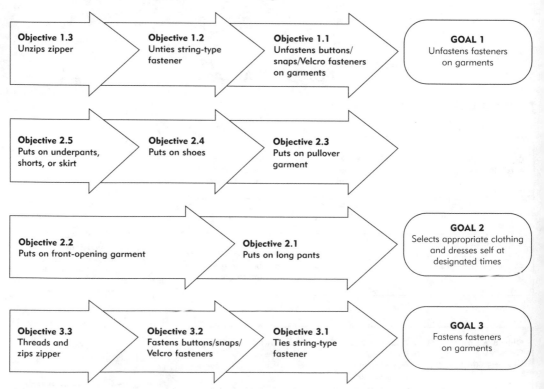

Objective 1.3
Unzips zipper

Objective 1.2
Unties string-type fastener

Objective 1.1
Unfastens buttons/ snaps/Velcro fasteners on garments

GOAL 1
Unfastens fasteners on garments

Objective 2.5
Puts on underpants, shorts, or skirt

Objective 2.4
Puts on shoes

Objective 2.3
Puts on pullover garment

Objective 2.2
Puts on front-opening garment

Objective 2.1
Puts on long pants

GOAL 2
Selects appropriate clothing and dresses self at designated times

Objective 3.3
Threads and zips zipper

Objective 3.2
Fastens buttons/snaps/ Velcro fasteners

Objective 3.1
Ties string-type fastener

GOAL 3
Fastens fasteners on garments

COGNITIVE AREA

Strand A: Concepts

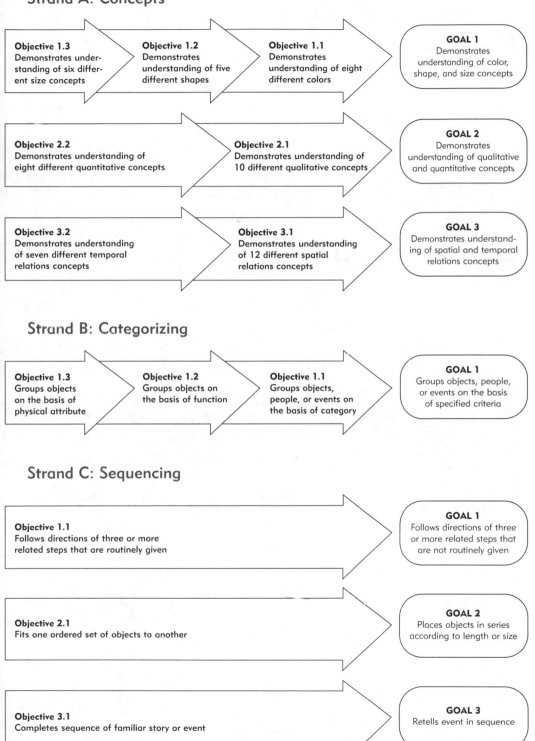

Objective 1.3 Demonstrates understanding of six different size concepts → **Objective 1.2** Demonstrates understanding of five different shapes → **Objective 1.1** Demonstrates understanding of eight different colors → **GOAL 1** Demonstrates understanding of color, shape, and size concepts

Objective 2.2 Demonstrates understanding of eight different quantitative concepts → **Objective 2.1** Demonstrates understanding of 10 different qualitative concepts → **GOAL 2** Demonstrates understanding of qualitative and quantitative concepts

Objective 3.2 Demonstrates understanding of seven different temporal relations concepts → **Objective 3.1** Demonstrates understanding of 12 different spatial relations concepts → **GOAL 3** Demonstrates understanding of spatial and temporal relations concepts

Strand B: Categorizing

Objective 1.3 Groups objects on the basis of physical attribute → **Objective 1.2** Groups objects on the basis of function → **Objective 1.1** Groups objects, people, or events on the basis of category → **GOAL 1** Groups objects, people, or events on the basis of specified criteria

Strand C: Sequencing

Objective 1.1 Follows directions of three or more related steps that are routinely given → **GOAL 1** Follows directions of three or more related steps that are not routinely given

Objective 2.1 Fits one ordered set of objects to another → **GOAL 2** Places objects in series according to length or size

Objective 3.1 Completes sequence of familiar story or event → **GOAL 3** Retells event in sequence

Child Progress Record II

Strand D: Recalling Events

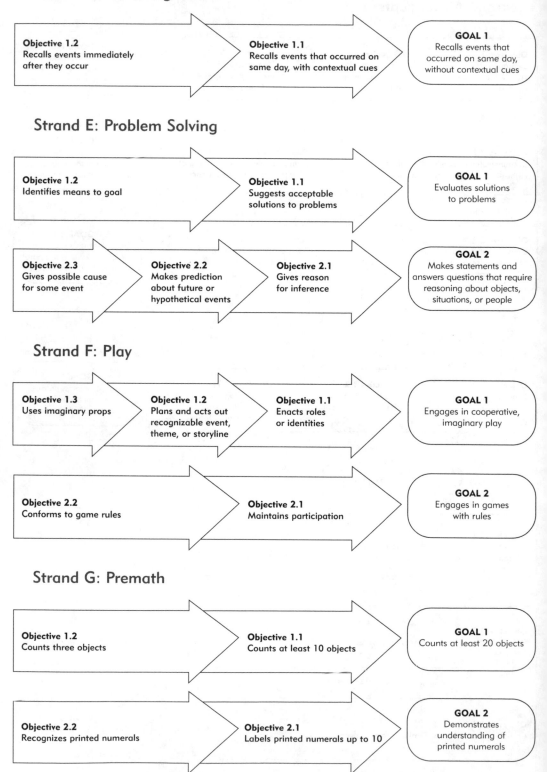

Objective 1.2
Recalls events immediately after they occur

Objective 1.1
Recalls events that occurred on same day, with contextual cues

GOAL 1
Recalls events that occurred on same day, without contextual cues

Strand E: Problem Solving

Objective 1.2
Identifies means to goal

Objective 1.1
Suggests acceptable solutions to problems

GOAL 1
Evaluates solutions to problems

Objective 2.3
Gives possible cause for some event

Objective 2.2
Makes prediction about future or hypothetical events

Objective 2.1
Gives reason for inference

GOAL 2
Makes statements and answers questions that require reasoning about objects, situations, or people

Strand F: Play

Objective 1.3
Uses imaginary props

Objective 1.2
Plans and acts out recognizable event, theme, or storyline

Objective 1.1
Enacts roles or identities

GOAL 1
Engages in cooperative, imaginary play

Objective 2.2
Conforms to game rules

Objective 2.1
Maintains participation

GOAL 2
Engages in games with rules

Strand G: Premath

Objective 1.2
Counts three objects

Objective 1.1
Counts at least 10 objects

GOAL 1
Counts at least 20 objects

Objective 2.2
Recognizes printed numerals

Objective 2.1
Labels printed numerals up to 10

GOAL 2
Demonstrates understanding of printed numerals

Strand H: Phonological Awareness and Emergent Reading

Objective 1.4
Identifies same and different sounds at the beginning and end of words

Objective 1.3
Blends single sounds and syllables

Objective 1.2
Segments sentences and words

Objective 1.1
Uses rhyming skills

GOAL 1
Demonstrates phonological awareness skills

Objective 2.3
Produces correct sounds for letters

Objective 2.2
Sounds out words

Objective 2.1
Writes words using letter sounds

GOAL 2
Uses letter–sound associations to sound out and write words

Objective 3.1
Identifies letter names

GOAL 3
Reads words by sight

SOCIAL-COMMUNICATION AREA

Strand A: Social-Communicative Interactions

Objective 1.7
Uses words, phrases, or sentences to inform

Objective 1.6
Uses words, phrases, or sentences to obtain information

Objective 1.5
Uses words, phrases, or sentences to command and request

Objective 1.4
Uses words, phrases, or sentences to describe past events

Objective 1.3
Uses words, phrases, or sentences to label own or others' affect/emotions

Objective 1.2
Uses words, phrases, or sentences to describe pretend objects, events, or people

Objective 1.1
Uses words, phrases, or sentences to express anticipated outcomes

GOAL 1
Uses words, phrases, or sentences to inform, direct, ask questions, and express anticipation, imagination, affect, and emotions

Objective 2.6
Responds to others' topic initiations

Objective 2.5
Initiates context-relevant topics

Objective 2.4
Responds to contingent questions

Objective 2.3
Asks questions for clarification

Objective 2.2
Responds to topic changes initiated by others

Objective 2.1
Alternates between speaker/listener role

GOAL 2
Uses conversational rules

Objective 3.2
Uses socially appropriate physical orientation

Objective 3.1
Varies voice to impart meaning

GOAL 3
Establishes and varies social-communicative roles

Assessment, Evaluation, and Programming System for Infants and Children (AEPS)™, Second Edition, edited by Diane Bricker
© 2002 Paul H. Brookes Publishing Co., Inc. All rights reserved.

Strand B: Production of Words, Phrases, and Sentences

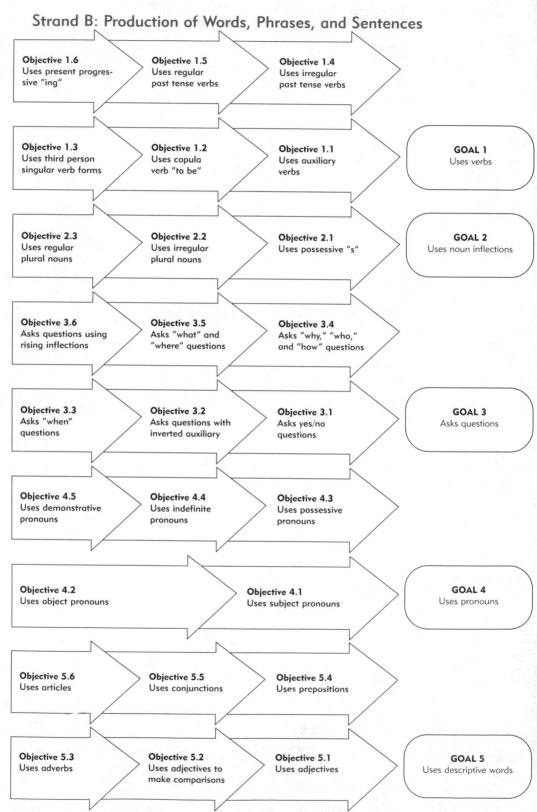

Objective 1.6
Uses present progressive "ing"

Objective 1.5
Uses regular past tense verbs

Objective 1.4
Uses irregular past tense verbs

Objective 1.3
Uses third person singular verb forms

Objective 1.2
Uses copula verb "to be"

Objective 1.1
Uses auxiliary verbs

GOAL 1
Uses verbs

Objective 2.3
Uses regular plural nouns

Objective 2.2
Uses irregular plural nouns

Objective 2.1
Uses possessive "s"

GOAL 2
Uses noun inflections

Objective 3.6
Asks questions using rising inflections

Objective 3.5
Asks "what" and "where" questions

Objective 3.4
Asks "why," "who," and "how" questions

Objective 3.3
Asks "when" questions

Objective 3.2
Asks questions with inverted auxiliary

Objective 3.1
Asks yes/no questions

GOAL 3
Asks questions

Objective 4.5
Uses demonstrative pronouns

Objective 4.4
Uses indefinite pronouns

Objective 4.3
Uses possessive pronouns

Objective 4.2
Uses object pronouns

Objective 4.1
Uses subject pronouns

GOAL 4
Uses pronouns

Objective 5.6
Uses articles

Objective 5.5
Uses conjunctions

Objective 5.4
Uses prepositions

Objective 5.3
Uses adverbs

Objective 5.2
Uses adjectives to make comparisons

Objective 5.1
Uses adjectives

GOAL 5
Uses descriptive words

SOCIAL AREA

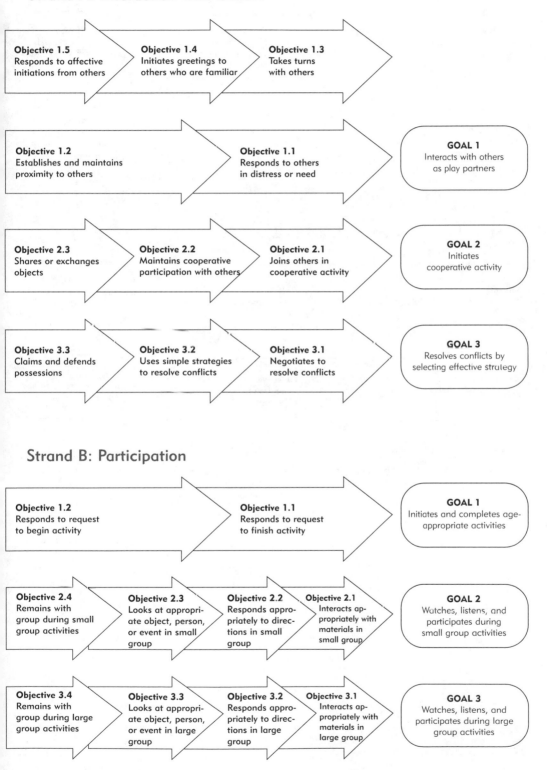

Strand A: Interaction with Others

Objective 1.5
Responds to affective initiations from others

Objective 1.4
Initiates greetings to others who are familiar

Objective 1.3
Takes turns with others

Objective 1.2
Establishes and maintains proximity to others

Objective 1.1
Responds to others in distress or need

GOAL 1
Interacts with others as play partners

Objective 2.3
Shares or exchanges objects

Objective 2.2
Maintains cooperative participation with others

Objective 2.1
Joins others in cooperative activity

GOAL 2
Initiates cooperative activity

Objective 3.3
Claims and defends possessions

Objective 3.2
Uses simple strategies to resolve conflicts

Objective 3.1
Negotiates to resolve conflicts

GOAL 3
Resolves conflicts by selecting effective strategy

Strand B: Participation

Objective 1.2
Responds to request to begin activity

Objective 1.1
Responds to request to finish activity

GOAL 1
Initiates and completes age-appropriate activities

Objective 2.4
Remains with group during small group activities

Objective 2.3
Looks at appropriate object, person, or event in small group

Objective 2.2
Responds appropriately to directions in small group

Objective 2.1
Interacts appropriately with materials in small group

GOAL 2
Watches, listens, and participates during small group activities

Objective 3.4
Remains with group during large group activities

Objective 3.3
Looks at appropriate object, person, or event in large group

Objective 3.2
Responds appropriately to directions in large group

Objective 3.1
Interacts appropriately with materials in large group

GOAL 3
Watches, listens, and participates during large group activities

Child Progress Record II

Strand C: Interaction with Environment

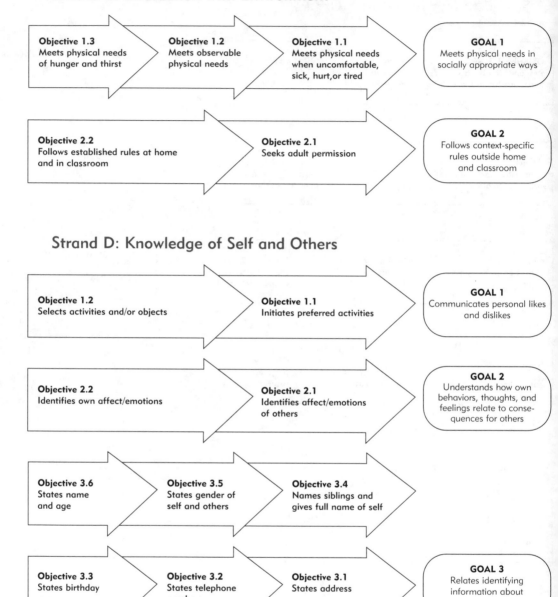

Objective 1.3
Meets physical needs of hunger and thirst

Objective 1.2
Meets observable physical needs

Objective 1.1
Meets physical needs when uncomfortable, sick, hurt, or tired

GOAL 1
Meets physical needs in socially appropriate ways

Objective 2.2
Follows established rules at home and in classroom

Objective 2.1
Seeks adult permission

GOAL 2
Follows context-specific rules outside home and classroom

Strand D: Knowledge of Self and Others

Objective 1.2
Selects activities and/or objects

Objective 1.1
Initiates preferred activities

GOAL 1
Communicates personal likes and dislikes

Objective 2.2
Identifies own affect/emotions

Objective 2.1
Identifies affect/emotions of others

GOAL 2
Understands how own behaviors, thoughts, and feelings relate to consequences for others

Objective 3.6
States name and age

Objective 3.5
States gender of self and others

Objective 3.4
Names siblings and gives full name of self

Objective 3.3
States birthday

Objective 3.2
States telephone numbers

Objective 3.1
States address

GOAL 3
Relates identifying information about self and others

Assessment, Evaluation, and Programming System for Infants and Children (AEPS)™, Second Edition, edited by Diane Bricker
© 2002 Paul H. Brookes Publishing Co., Inc. All rights reserved.

APPENDIX

F

Corroborating Eligibility Decisions

The AEPS Test is a curriculum-based measure designed to yield a comprehensive and detailed picture of children's behavioral repertoires. The primary purposes of the AEPS Test are to 1) determine a child's present level of functioning across six developmental areas, 2) provide content for formulating goals and objectives for individualized family service plans (IFSPs)/individualized education programs (IEPs), 3) guide subsequent individualized intervention activities, and 4) monitor child progress toward selected intervention targets over time. These purposes dictate that the AEPS Test items be selected based on their educational and treatment relevancy rather than for their ability to discriminate between children on the basis of global developmental status. In addition, items should be targeted as children's goals or objectives because they address the next developmental step or skill in a teaching sequence, not because they are typically acquired at a particular chronological age. For these reasons, assigning age norms to AEPS items is *not* appropriate. Nevertheless, the need for authentic, family-guided, and psychometrically sound assessments to assist in determining eligibility for services remains a need in the field. Thus, requests are often made to use AEPS Test results to corroborate findings from standardized, norm-referenced tests. These requests are most often inspired by state regulations that require early intervention/early childhood special education (EI/ECSE) diagnostic evaluation teams to use at least two sources of information to establish a child's eligibility for services. In many states, results from an individual developmental test such as the *Bayley Scales of Infant Development* (Bayley, 1993) or the *Battelle Developmental Inventory* (Newborg, Stock, & Wnek, 1988) must be supported or corroborated by data from at least one additional valid source that documents the child's delay or problem.

Feedback from EI/ECSE personnel suggests that using results from the AEPS Test as the corroborating second source would be advantageous for three reasons. First, using AEPS Test results expands both the depth and breadth of developmental information on children. Second, using AEPS Test results would engender significant time savings because evaluation teams would not have to administer a second standardized measure. Third, information generated by the AEPS Test permits the development of quality IFSP/IEP goals/objectives (e.g., Pretti-Frontczak & Bricker, 2000). These persuasive reasons provided a strong impetus for finding a strategy that would permit use of AEPS Test outcomes to serve as a secondary source for establishing eligibility but to do so without assigning age norms to individual test items. To meet this need, a middle ground solution was developed. This solution entailed collecting data that were translated into cutoff scores that can be used to corroborate findings from standardized, norm-referenced measures. For many programs, AEPS Test cutoff scores may serve as the second source for substantiating a child's eligibility for services.

It is important to note that the AEPS Test cutoff scores are *not* related to test indices such as percent delay or standard scores. Cutoff scores should *not*

Paul Yovanoff was instrumental in conducting the Item Response Theory analyses reported in this appendix.

be used to calculate standard scores or to determine percent of delay but rather to corroborate or substantiate eligibility decisions made from standardized, norm-referenced measures. The next two sections of this appendix describe how the AEPS cutoff scores were obtained and how cutoff scores can be used to corroborate findings from standardized, norm-referenced measures.

DEVELOPMENT OF CUTOFF SCORES FOR THE AEPS TEST: BIRTH TO THREE YEARS AND THREE TO SIX YEARS

Establishing AEPS Test cutoff scores to corroborate eligibility decisions required the following steps: 1) collection of AEPS Test performance and age data for a group of typically developing children and a group of children already determined eligible who were receiving EI/ECSE services; 2) completion of Item Response Theory (IRT) analyses of the AEPS Test: Birth to Three Years and Three to Six Years; and 3) creation of tables that show the established cutoff score by age interval for the AEPS Test: Birth to Three Years and Three to Six Years.

Study Sample and Data Collection Procedures

Date of birth and AEPS Test performance data (i.e., completed AEPS Child Observation Data Recording Forms) were collected on two groups of children. The first group was composed of 603 typically developing children who ranged in age from 1 to 72 months. *Typically developing* was defined as the child having no history or no current evidence of a developmental delay or disability. AEPS Test performance data were also collected on a second group of 258 children who were currently receiving services under the Individuals with Disabilities Education (IDEA) Act Amendments of 1997, PL 105-17, for a diagnosed disability. For the disability group, the chronological ages also ranged from 1 to 72 months.

Data were collected using the first edition of the AEPS (Bricker, 1993; Bricker & Pretti-Frontczak, 1996) and the current edition of the AEPS. As discussed in the Introduction to Volume 1, the changes in the content of the test from the first to the second edition were minimal; thus, the rationale for combining the data from the first and second editions. The combining of data from the first and second editions received further support from the IRT analysis that did not find significant variations between test editions with respect to item characteristics.

The study sample was obtained by contacting community-based programs that offered educational or child care services to a range of young children. The Child Observation Data Recording Forms were completed on this sample of 861 children by the staffs of EI/ECSE and child care programs located in Oregon, Washington, Wisconsin, Kentucky, Ohio, and Florida. Training background and experience levels of staff differed across and within programs; however, the majority of staff completing the AEPS Test protocols had received some training on how to use the AEPS. Completed Child Observation Data

Table F1.   The distribution of study sample by child's eligibility status

Test level	Typical	Eligible
Birth to Three Years	307	129
Three to Six Years	296	129
Total	603	258

Recording Forms were identified by identification numbers assigned to each child. In addition, each test protocol noted the child's birth date and status (i.e., typical or eligible). Table F1 shows the distribution of the study sample by child status and AEPS level used to conduct the IRT analyses.

When using AEPS Test results to corroborate eligibility decisions, only a sum of goals scored with a 2 were used to compare with cutoff scores (i.e., goals scored 1 and scores for objectives are not included). AEPS Test protocols for all children were reviewed and the number of goals receiving a score of 2 were added to obtain a Total Goal Score for each child.[1] Once protocols were scored, a computer file was constructed that contained the following information for each child: identification number, birth date, status (i.e., typical or eligible), and Total Goal Score.

Data Analyses To Establish Cutoff Scores

Procedures for establishing AEPS Test cutoff scores to corroborate eligibility decisions relied on IRT modeling. IRT identifies psychometric properties of the AEPS Test (or any test) that are essential to understanding measurement error at specific levels of performance. A hallmark of IRT is the assessment of *conditional* measurement error (i.e., conditional on the ability level; Kolen, Zeng, & Hanson, 1996; Lord, 1980). All psychological measurements have errors, and similar to all tests, the AEPS functions better at some performance levels than others. For instance, the AEPS for Three to Six Years has less measurement error when a child scores a 2 on 12 to 38 goals than when a child has extreme scores (e.g., low performance [six or fewer goals are correct] and high performance [44 or more goals are correct]). Conditional measurement error is attributable to the specific objectives that compose the test. Note, as discussed next, the number of goals achieved is translated into age because it is assumed (and tested) that goals achieved are linearly correlated with age.

A one-parameter IRT model was used to estimate age specific cutoff scores. Several important measurement assumptions underlie the IRT model used to estimate the AEPS cutoff scores.

- The AEPS Test scored across goals (i.e., 64 for Birth to Three Years and 54 for Three to Six Years) provides a unitary Total Goal Score (i.e., one dominant latent trait which governs the observed scores).

---

[1]For example, if a child received a 2 on 30 goals, then his or her Total Goal Score would be 60 (i.e., 30 × 2 = 60).

- For the typical sample, Total Goal Score is assumed to increase as a direct function of age—that is, older children score higher (i.e., receive more scores of 2) than younger children. This substantiates the need for age-appropriate cutoff scores (not to be confused with age norms).

- Children with disabilities perform lower (i.e., receive fewer scores of 2 on goals) than typical children. At all age levels, children with disabilities receive significantly lower total goal scores than typical children of the same age level.

- Implicit in using the AEPS Test to discriminate "typical" from "eligible" children is the assumption that the test functions identically for both groups. This is the assumption of unbiased measurement.

IRT analyses were conducted separately for the AEPS Test: Birth to Three Years and Three to Six Years. For each analysis, the following steps occurred.

1. *Goal scoring:* Each AEPS Test goal was scored dichotomously. A goal was scored 2 (i.e., the child met the criterion independently and consistently) if, and only if, all objectives associated with the goal were fully achieved. Otherwise, the goal was scored 0 (i.e., the child did not meet the criterion). This rigorous goal scoring ensured a score of 2 only if the goal had been fully achieved. Scoring each goal provides a total score that correlates with age 0.87 for Birth to Three Years and 0.58 for Three to Six Years.

2. *Test dimensionality:* The test dimensionality and measurement error for the analysis was based on the typical sample (N = 307 for Birth to Three Years and N = 296 for Three to Six Years). The IRT item fit statistics are used as a test of dimensionality. The fit statistics were acceptable and confirmed the unidimensionality assumption. In addition, the IRT analysis estimates the standard error of measurement at each ability level.

3. *Differential item functioning:* The two samples (i.e., typical and eligible) were compared for item/test bias with a test of differential item functioning (Holland & Wainer, 1993). Ideally, the item difficulty (IRT calibrations) for the two groups should not be statistically different. A test is essentially a test of measurement bias. The AEPS Test for Birth to Three Years and Three to Six Years is unbiased and can be used to discriminate performance for the two target populations (i.e., typical and eligible).

4. *Collapse sample into age brackets:* The sample for both AEPS age levels and for typical and eligible groups were divided into 6-month age brackets (e.g., birth–6, 7–12, 13–18).

5. *Compute average level of performance:* The average level of performance (i.e., Total Goal Score) was computed for the typical sample for Birth to Three Years and Three to Six Years.

6. *Determine standard error of measurement:* The standard error of measurement was computed for each of the 6-month age brackets for Birth to Three Years and Three to Six Years and for typical samples.

7. *Compute confidence bounds:* Using the standard error of measurement for the average performance at each 6-month age bracket, the lower confidence bounds at 99% were calculated. The lower confidence bounds effectively provide the cutoff scores, with 99% confidence. These cutoff scores identify children who are "probably" not performing typically for their chronological age and are approximately 2.33 standard deviations below the average performance of typical children.

8. *Compute cross-classification tables:* Using cutoff scores generated at Step 7, the error rate in the sample (i.e., typical and eligible), sensitivity, specificity, false positive, false negative, percent agreement, underidentification, and overidentification were calculated. Of particular interest are the specificity and sensitivity (Fleiss, 1981). *Specificity* is the ability of the cutoff score to identify typical children accurately. *Sensitivity* refers to the ability of the cutoff score to identify only children who are eligible for services. The AEPS Test is designed to be sensitive to nontypical behavior, and the goal scoring described previously is very restrictive, thus making it likely that the cutoff scores will be extremely sensitive (e.g., will accurately identify children who are not performing typically). The cutoff scores, however, may also result in overidentification (e.g., children who are typically developing may be classified as meeting eligibility guidelines). The overidentification should not pose a problem because AEPS Test results should only be used to corroborate eligibility of children already deemed eligible by a standardized, norm-referenced test.

RECOMMENDED CUTOFF SCORES AND CLASSIFICATION TABLES

Using the procedures outlined previously, a table containing the cutoff scores for the 6-month age intervals was created for the Birth to Three and Three to Six levels of the AEPS. In addition, the sensitivity, specificity, and other parameters were calculated for each age interval.

Table F2 presents the recommended cutoff scores for Birth to Three Years and Three to Six Years. To properly use this table, the AEPS Test administrator must do the following:

- Determine the child's chronological age using the procedure specified later in this appendix.

- Review the entire Child Observation Data Recording Form and note each of the goals that received a score of 2 (i.e., met criterion independently and consistently).

- Add all 2s for a Total Goal Score. The Total Goal Score can then be compared to the scores contained in Table F2 using the child's chronological age. The cutoff scores should be used only if a complete AEPS Test has been administered to the child.

Table F2. Cutoff scores for the 99% confidence band at 6-month age intervals for the AEPS Test: Birth to Three Years and Three to Six Years

Level	Age intervals (months)	Cutoff score
Birth to Three Years	1–6	12
	7–12	32
	13–18	60
	19–24	88
	25–30	98
	31–36	106
Three to Six Years	37–42	34
	43–48	38
	49–54	46
	55–60	56
	61–66	58
	67–72	80

Note: This information also appears in the "How to Use the AEPS Test Cutoff Scores" section. Only use the AEPS cutoff scores if a complete AEPS Test has been administered.

Once the cutoff scores were obtained for each 6-month age bracket, the next step was to determine if these scores accurately identified children as being eligible for services. Using the cutoff scores contained in Table F2, classification tables addressing the sensitivity, specificity, false positive, false negative, percent agreement, underidentified, and overidentified for each 6-month interval for Birth to Three Years and Three to Six Years were calculated. Twelve cross-classification tables were created and are contained in Figure F.1.

The findings presented in the cross-classification tables suggest that the cutoff scores are highly accurate in identifying children eligible for services (i.e., sensitivity). This is an important finding and suggests the AEPS Test results may work well to corroborate the eligibility findings of standardized, norm-referenced tests. The specificity findings suggest the AEPS Test may make more errors by overidentifying children who are typically developing as eligible. The overidentification should not be a problem for most programs because the AEPS Test should only be used to corroborate findings of standardized tests that have *already* found children to be eligible for services.

HOW TO USE THE AEPS TEST
CUTOFF SCORES TO CORROBORATE ELIGIBILITY

Using the AEPS Test scores to corroborate standardized test findings for determining child eligibility is a straightforward and simple process. The process involves computing a Total Goal Score that can be compared with a cutoff score for a particular chronological age. A three-step process should be followed to use AEPS cutoff scores to corroborate eligibility.

1–6 months

	Eligibility status		
	Typical	Eligible	Total

Status determined by AEPS cutoff scores		Typical	Eligible	Total
	Typical	40	2	42
	Eligible	15	7	22
	Total	55	9	64

Sensitivity	Specificity	False positive	False negative	Percent agreement	Under-identified	Over-identified
77.8%	72.7%	27.3%	22.2%	78.8%	3.1%	23.4%

7–12 months

Status determined by AEPS cutoff scores		Eligibility status		
		Typical	Eligible	Total
	Typical	56	2	58
	Eligible	24	16	40
	Total	80	18	98

Sensitivity	Specificity	False positive	False negative	Percent agreement	Under-identified	Over-identified
88.9%	70%	30%	11.1%	73.4%	2%	24.5%

13–18 months

Status determined by AEPS cutoff scores		Eligibility status		
		Typical	Eligible	Total
	Typical	54	3	57
	Eligible	13	16	29
	Total	67	19	86

Sensitivity	Specificity	False positive	False negative	Percent agreement	Under-identified	Over-identified
84.2%	80.6%	19.4%	15.8%	81.4%	3.5%	15.1%

19–24 months

Status determined by AEPS cutoff scores		Eligibility status		
		Typical	Eligible	Total
	Typical	40	1	41
	Eligible	8	14	22
	Total	48	15	63

Sensitivity	Specificity	False positive	False negative	Percent agreement	Under-identified	Over-identified
93.3%	83.3%	16.7%	6.7%	85.7%	1.6%	12.7%

Figure F.1. Cross-classification of agreement between eligibility status and status determined by AEPS cutoff score by 6-month age intervals at the 99% confidence interval.

25–30 Months

		Eligibility status		
		Typical	Eligible	Total
Status determined by AEPS cutoff scores	Typical	30	2	32
	Eligible	9	26	35
	Total	39	28	67

Sensitivity	Specificity	False positive	False negative	Percent agreement	Under-identified	Over-identified
92.9%	76.9%	23.1%	7.1%	83.6%	3%	13.4%

31–36 months

		Eligibility status		
		Typical	Eligible	Total
Status determined by AEPS cutoff scores	Typical	15	2	17
	Eligible	3	38	41
	Total	18	40	58

Sensitivity	Specificity	False positive	False negative	Percent agreement	Under-identified	Over-identified
95%	83.3%	16.7%	5%	91.4%	3.4%	5.2%

37–42 months

		Eligibility status		
		Typical	Eligible	Total
Status determined by AEPS cutoff scores	Typical	29	1	30
	Eligible	12	16	28
	Total	41	17	58

Sensitivity	Specificity	False positive	False negative	Percent agreement	Under-identified	Over-identified
94.1%	70.7%	29.3%	5.9%	77.6%	1.7%	20.7%

43–48 months

		Eligibility status		
		Typical	Eligible	Total
Status determined by AEPS cutoff scores	Typical	29	1	30
	Eligible	37	2	39
scores	Total	53	29	82

Sensitivity	Specificity	False positive	False negative	Percent agreement	Under-identified	Over-identified
93.1%	69.8%	30.2%	6.9%	78%	2.4%	19.5%

(continued)

49–54 months

		Eligibility status		
		Typical	Eligible	Total
Status determined by AEPS cutoff scores	Typical	41	2	43
	Eligible	18	29	47
	Total	59	31	90

Sensitivity	Specificity	False positive	False negative	Percent agreement	Under-identified	Over-identified
93.5%	69.5%	30.5%	6.5%	77.8%	3.1%	20%

55–60 months

		Eligibility status		
		Typical	Eligible	Total
Status determined by AEPS cutoff scores	Typical	50	0	50
	Eligible	15	21	36
	Total	59	31	90

Sensitivity	Specificity	False positive	False negative	Percent agreement	Under-identified	Over-identified
100%	76.9%	23.1%	0%	82.5%	0%	17.4%

61–66 months

		Eligibility status		
		Typical	Eligible	Total
Status determined by AEPS cutoff scores	Typical	37	3	40
	Eligible	14	15	29
	Total	51	18	69

Sensitivity	Specificity	False positive	False negative	Percent agreement	Under-identified	Over-identified
83.3%	72.5%	27.5%	16.7%	75.3%	4.3%	27.5%

67–72 months

		Eligibility status		
		Typical	Eligible	Total
Status determined by AEPS cutoff scores	Typical	24	3	27
	Eligible	3	10	13
	Total	27	13	40

Sensitivity	Specificity	False positive	False negative	Percent agreement	Under-identified	Over-identified
76.9 %	88.9 %	11.1 %	23.1 %	85 %	7.5 %	7.5 %

Step 1: Determine Child's Chronological Age

The child's chronological age should be determined by subtracting the date of birth from the date of test and converting to months. For example, if a child was born in January 2001, and today's date is April 2002, then he would be 15 months old (e.g., he was 12 months old in January 2001, plus 3 months until April 2002 = 15 months), and, therefore, his Total Goal Score should be compared with the 13–18 month age interval cutoff score. If another child was born in March 1998, and today's date is April 2002, then she would be 47 months old (e.g., she will be 48 months old in May 2002, minus 1 month = 47 months), and, therefore, her Total Goal Score should be compared with the 43–48 age interval cutoff score. If a child's age falls at an interval boundary point (e.g., if the child is almost 14 months old and, therefore, at the lower end of the interval of 13 months), then the day of the child's birth should be considered. For example, if the child's birth date is January 10, 2001, and today's date is February 1, 2002, then he could be included with the 13–18 month group because he is more than 12½ months old. If the child's age has been adjusted for prematurity on the standardized test, then a similar adjustment should be made for the AEPS Test.

Step 2: Calculate the Child's Total Goal Score

After administering the AEPS Test, the number of goals that received a score of 2 should be summed across developmental areas. For example, if a child received a score of 2 on 24 goals across developmental areas, then the child's Total Goal Score would be 48. Goal scores other than 2 (e.g., 1) and scores on objectives should be ignored when calculating the Total Goal Score. Scores on objectives and scores less than 2 on goals are useful for programmatic decisions but are not used to corroborate eligibility.

Step 3: Compare the Child's Total Goal Score with the Cutoff Scores

Once a Total Goal Score is calculated, the examiner is ready to use the chart to compare the child's Total Goal Score with the cutoff scores. The examiner must first locate the age bracket that corresponds to the child's chronological age in order to locate the child's cutoff score. If the child's Total Goal Score is less than the cutoff score, then the child is likely eligible for services. If the child's Total Goal Score is greater than the cutoff score, then the child may not be eligible for services.

This chart can be used for determining if children's Total Goal Scores on the AEPS Test corroborate eligibility decisions. The scores contained in this chart should only be used if a complete AEPS Test has been administered to the child, permitting the calculation of a Total Goal Score composed of all six areas.

Chart of the AEPS Total Goal Scores for corroborating eligibility

Level	Age in months	Eligibility may be corroborated if the child's Total Goal Score falls at or below:
Birth to Three Years	1–6	12
	7–12	32
	13–18	60
	19–24	88
	25–30	98
	31–36	106
Three to Six Years	37–42	34
	43–48	38
	49–54	46
	55–60	56
	61–66	58
	67–72	80

Note: The scores contained in this chart should only be used if a complete AEPS Test has been administered, permitting the calculation of a Total Goal Score composed of all six areas.

EXAMPLES FOR USING AEPS CUTOFF SCORES

BIANCA

Upon referral, the diagnostic team administered the *Bayley Scales of Infant Development* (Bayley, 1993) to 2-year-old Bianca. The findings indicated that Bianca had significant delays in the cognitive and language areas, producing a mental age score significantly below 24 months. Local program and state regulations require that at least two assessment sources be used to determine a child's eligibility for services. The team then administered the AEPS Test: Birth to Three Years to Bianca. Following completion of the AEPS Test, the goals on which she received a score of 2 were tallied and her age in months determined. Bianca received a 2 on 22 goals, giving her a Total Goal Score of 44, and she was 24 months of age. The Total Goal Score was then compared with the cutoff scores contained in the chart for her chronological age. For the 19- to 24-month age bracket, the cutoff score for the 99% confidence band is 88. Bianca's performance (i.e., Total Goal Score of 44) is well below the cutoff, supporting findings from the *Bayley Scales of Infant Development* that she is eligible for intervention services.

DANIEL

Daniel (5 years, 1 month) was referred for services because of a speech delay. State law required administration of two measures, at least one of which is standardized, in areas of concern. Because communication was the only area of concern, the assessment team decided to use two standardized speech and language measures to determine eligibility. The team's decision to use two standardized measures and not the AEPS was appropriate. To use AEPS cutoff scores, the child's abilities on goals across all six areas must be assessed. Because Daniel seems to be functioning within age expectations for all areas except communication, an AEPS Total Goal Score will not likely reflect a delay. The team decided to administer the AEPS Social-Communication area after eligibility was determined to identify appropriate goals and objectives for Daniel's IEP and plan intervention.

LATOYA

LaToyu (3 years, 11 months) attends a Head Start program. She was referred for early childhood special education assessment because her developmental functioning was generally below her peers and for unusual behaviors suggesting a possible diagnosis of autism. The assessment team administered the *Battelle Developmental Inventory* (Newborg, Stock, & Wnek, 1988) and the AEPS. LaToya's *Battelle Developmental Inventory* standard score indicated that she was eligible for services. State law mandates a second measure to establish eligibility, and the team hoped LaToya's AEPS Total Goal Score would provide that corroboration. LaToya achieved a score of 2 on 12 goals across six areas of the AEPS that gave her a Total Goal Score of 24. The AEPS cutoff score for her age bracket (43–48 months) is 38. Because LaToya's Total Goal Score is less than the cutoff score, the AEPS Test results corroborate the eligibility findings of the *Batelle Developmental Inventory*.

IMPORTANT CAUTIONS

As we have noted previously, the AEPS Test is not a standardized, norm-referenced test, and, therefore, it should *not* be used as a substitute for such tests. For reasons noted, AEPS Test results may be used as a second source to supplement or corroborate the findings of standardized tests but not used to substitute for them. When AEPS Test results do not support the findings of a norm-referenced, standardized test, we strongly recommend the administration of a third tool and/or extensive observation of the child by a professional.

It is also important to note that the cutoff scores located in Table F2 are *not* age equivalencies. The AEPS Test cutoff scores should only be used as a secondary source for corroboration of eligibility decisions and should not be used to assign age or developmental levels. The primary purpose of the AEPS is to assist professional teams and caregivers in the development of IFSPs/IEPs, intervention content, and to monitor child progress toward intervention targets over time.

REFERENCES

Fleiss, J.L. (1981). *Statistical methods for rates and proportions* (2nd ed.). New York: John Wiley & Sons.

Holland, P.W., & Wainer, H. (Eds.). (1993). *Differential item functioning.* Mahwah, NJ: Lawrence Erlbaum Associates.

Lord, F.M. (1980). *Applications of item response theory to practical testing problems.* Mahwah, NJ: Lawrence Erlbaum Associates.

Kolen, M.J., Zeng, L., & Hanson, B.A. (1996). Conditional standard errors of measurement for scale scores using IRT. *Journal of Educational Measurement, 33,* 129–140.

INDEX

Page references followed by *f, t,* or *n* indicate figures, tables, or notes, respectively.

Order Form

Set Savings!

____ **Complete AEPS™, SECOND EDITION** | Administration Guide,
Test: Birth to Three Years and Three to Six Years, Curriculum for
Birth to Three Years, and Curriculum for Three to Six Years
$205.00 • Stock #5613

____ **AEPS™ Birth to Three Set** |
Administration Guide, Test, Curriculum for Birth to Three Years
$150.00 • Stock #6024

____ **AEPS™ Three to Six Set** |
Administration Guide, Test, Curriculum for Three to Six Years
$150.00 • Stock #6032

AEPS™ Components

____ **AEPS™ Administration Guide**
$55.00 • 336 pages • 7 x 10 • spiral-bound • ISBN 1-55766-562-1

____ **AEPS™ Test: Birth to Three Years and Three to Six Years**
$70.00 • 304 pages • 7 x 10 • spiral-bound • ISBN 1-55766-563-X

____ **AEPS™ Curriculum for Birth to Three Years**
$65.00 • 512 pages • 7 x 10 • spiral-bound • ISBN 1-55766-564-8

____ **AEPS™ Curriculum for Three to Six Years**
$65.00 • 352 pages • 7 x 10 • spiral-bound • ISBN 1-55766-565-6

____ **AEPS™ Forms CD-ROM** | Stock #6350 • $249.95 • printable forms • 8 1/2 x 11 • PC and Mac compatable

____ **AEPS™ Child Observation Data Recording Form I** (Birth to Three Years)
$25.00 • package of 10 • 28 pages • 7 x 10 • saddle-stitched • ISBN 1-55766-583-4

____ **AEPS™ Child Observation Data Recording Form II** (Three to Six Years)
$25.00 • package of 10 • 24 pages • 7 x 10 • saddle-stitched • ISBN 1-55766-584-2

____ **AEPS™ Child Progress Record I** (Birth to Three Years)
$20.00 • package of 30 • 6 pages • 7 x 10 • gatefold • ISBN 1-55766-586-9

____ **AEPS™ Child Progress Record II** (Three to Six Years)
$20.00 • package of 30 • 6 pages • 7 x 10 • gatefold • ISBN 1-55766-587-7

____ **AEPS™ Family Report I** (Birth to Three Years)
$25.00 • package of 10 • 28 pages • 7 x 10 • saddle-stitched • ISBN 1-55766-588-5

____ **AEPS™ Family Report II** (Three to Six Years)
$28.00 • package of 10 • 24 pages • 7 x 10 • saddle-stitched • ISBN 1-55766-589-3

(Opened packages of AEPS™ forms are nonreturnable.)

Purchase the CD-ROM
with any **AEPS™** set and
save 20% on the CD-ROM!

Credit Card #: _____ Exp. Date: _____

Signature (required with credit card use): _____

Name: _____ Daytime phone: _____

Street Address: _____ ❏ residential   ❏ commercial
Complete street address required.

City/State/ZIP: _____ Country: _____

E-mail Address: _____
❏ Yes! I want to receive special web site discount offers! My e-mail address will not be shared with any other party.

Photocopy this form and mail it to **Brookes Publishing Co.**, P.O. Box 10624, Baltimore, MD 21285-0624, U.S.A.;
FAX 410-337-8539; call 1-800-638-3775 (8 A.M.—5 P.M. ET) or 410-337-9580 (outside the U.S. and Canada);
or order online at **www.brookespublishing.com**

Shipping rates for orders within the
continental U.S. sent via UPS Ground delivery*
If your product total (before tax) is:
$0.00 to $49.99, add $5.00
$50.00 to $399.99, add 10% of product total
$400.00 and over, add 8% of product total
*For other shipping options and rates,
call 1-800-638-3775 (in the U.S. and Canada)
and 410-337-9580 (worldwide).

Policies and prices subject to change
without notice. Prices may be higher
outside the U.S.
You may return books within 30 days
for a full credit of the product price.
Refunds will be issued for prepaid
orders. Items must be returned in
resalable condition.

Product Total $_____
Shipping Rate (see chart) $_____
Maryland Orders add 5%
sales tax (to product total only) $_____

Grand Total U.S.$_____
Your source code is **BA 7.**